To the Love of My Life for Fifty-Plus Years
Who Woulda Thunk?

www.mascotbooks.com

Kentucky Barracuda: Parker Hardin French

For more information, please contact:
Mascot Books
620 Herndon Parkway, Suite 320
Herndon, VA 20170
info@mascotbooks.com

Library of Congress Control Number: 2018904435

CPSIA Code: PROPM0718A
ISBN-13: 978-1-68401-791-1

Printed in the United States

KENTUCKY BARRACUDA

Parker Hardin French
(1826-1878)

The Notorious Scoundrel and
Delightful Rogue of Antebellum
& Civil War America

JOE GOODBODY

TABLE OF CONTENTS

PREFACE

I learned about Parker Hardin French in 2012. My brother Steve and I were working on our family genealogy and researching our great-grandfather Francis (Frank) Alexander Goodbody (1828-1906). We only knew he had been part of the California Gold Rush in 1850, had a tough time getting across the continent and had been moderately successful in the California gold fields. Steve found a reference to Frank's involvement in French's Express Passenger Train, did some initial exploration, and then continued with other research. He had not retired yet; I was retired and had plenty of time. After seeing the Wikipedia article on Parker Hardin French, I was fascinated with the man and the story—our great-grandfather had been scammed! How did our great-grandfather—whose family viewed as a smart, skeptical, and a very tough guy—get swindled? Casual interest changed to intrigue and then to a five-year compulsive drive as I hit the web, gathered references, researched digitized records and newspapers, and visited historical archives and government record centers. Great-grandfather, I found, was not alone in being conned; he was in great company with foreign leaders, business tycoons, prominent politicians, frontier toughs and army officers. And, some of Parker French's capers and antics were downright funny.

The few published accounts on Parker French had elements of truth, but they also told conflated stories and twisted what really happened. In some cases, the treatment was completely fanciful. Multiple journals and diaries gave great accounts of the California Gold Rush and French's Express Passenger Train, but there was no integrated story of the expedition. The rest of his life was very poorly documented. Historians either used the flawed accounts or peppered their narratives with small entries or summaries of isolated events. He was seen as a generally inconsequential character, albeit interesting, somewhat humorous and perhaps quixotic. As I researched I found that his story was much more significant to history and provides an interesting perspective on antebellum and civil war Americana. While I proudly called myself a history buff before this research, I started questioning that characterization as I discovered elements of American history of which I was completely unaware. When asking other well-read acquaintances and even history professionals, I found that my ignorance was not atypical.

My thanks go out to a lot of people who helped me through this experience. First and foremost, my wife Carol was a jewel. Humored when peeking into a very messy "war room," she was very supportive and understanding when I turned into a sun-deprived mole, absorbed and preoccupied. A great reviewer, Carol offered wonderful perceptions and recommendations and helped me improve. Brother Steve was always a supportive cheerleader who contributed much of the research and critical insights. Family, friends, and neighbors were polite and patient as they listened to my latest Parker French anecdotes, and sometimes even chuckled moderately. John Stack gave great comments and recommendations; his granddaughter McKenzie introduced me to my publisher. As a group (and way too many for individual acknowledgment), archivists, records staffs, and librarians were magnificent: helpful, professional, and friendly. Especially obliging were the folks at Chinn library in Prince William County Virginia, principally Judith Corea of the Interlibrary Loan Office. Of special note and last but not least, is the entire staff of Mascot Publishing who have been outstanding, particularly: CEO Naren Aryal; Services and Acquisitions Editor Ben Simpson; Project Manager and Senior Production Editor Daniel Wheatley; Copyeditor Lorna Partington Walsh; and Marketing Representative Jessica Holloway, who introduced and sponsored my project.

THE BARRACUDA

Barracuda: con man, crook, hustler, swindler, clip artist, fraud, scam artist. Or put more simply and directly: Parker Hardin French. The first known use of "con man" was in 1849, when the New York press labeled small-time swindler Samuel Thompson as a "confidence man." He got suckers to part with their pocket money or watches as an expression of their confidence and then betrayed them. French was not small-time; he got his gulls to part with much more than watches. An opportunist not averse to milking small amounts from his marks, he also engaged in elaborate, bold, and ambitious exploits. Some of those efforts may have begun as legitimate endeavors, but they inevitably resulted in double-crossed partners, betrayed allies, and swindled creditors.

Few history students might recognize the name Parker Hardin French; he is not now considered of historical significance. But his capers, both grand schemes and small efforts, provide history lovers a unique view of a pivotal and formative period in the nation's development. From 1850 to 1862, French was well known to political leaders, the press, and casual newspaper readers alike. They became exasperated with his exploits, captivated by his audacity and nervy cheek, or humored by his latest escapade. He was judged an incorrigible scoundrel, labeled a chronic megalomaniac, or peddled as a misunderstood victim of his enemies. Some believed him a hero. Some just thought him insane. The writing style and content of some contemporaneous newspaper articles bring to mind a supermarket tabloid-esque character; they present an "everyman" appeal, a popular attraction to and captivation with French's ambitious and imaginative adventures and schemes—he was a "delightful rogue." Curiously, there were no apparent questions about his military rank. His self-appointment to "captain" and then self-promotion to "colonel" were generally accepted. Such was the wide interest in him, even advertisements for products and services used his name in playful, sometimes sarcastic jest. Copy-cat con artists replicated some of his more publicized and questionable adventures.

Michael Baldridge, who would be a close subordinate of Parker Hardin French, wrote:

> *"Reviewing his career, I could not help contrasting what he was with what he might have been, if his ability, energy and perseverance had been directed in the proper channel. In any case, it is fair to presume, he has seen many times when he could speak from his own experience and say emphatically, 'The way of the transgressor is hard.'"* [1]

Parker French Portrait, *Frank Leslie's Illustrated Newspaper,* January 12, 1856. Reproduction held by Library of Congress of a wood engraving by S.F. Baker from a Matthew Brady ambrotype.

"He was rather below medium height and weight: his compact build suggests more than average physical power, while his physiognomy indicated great executive ability. He had an eye that could read his man at a glance, was fluent in conversation, affable in manner and seemed to combine all the qualities a gentleman should possess."[2]

Any historical treatment of Parker Hardin French's life has heavily relied on two accounts: *Strange Eventful History of Parker H. French*, by Edward (Ned) McGowan and edited by Kenneth M. Johnson; and *Reminiscences of a Ranger: Or, Early Times in Southern California*, by Horace Bell. Ned McGowan knew French in California in 1854-1855 when they were political allies. McGowan had interviewed French, likely heard others tell stories about his background, and summarized his life in two newspaper articles in 1879. McGowan's work is an interesting narrative with elements of truth, but it conflates multiple stories and twists reality. The account by Horace Bell is almost completely fanciful. Kenneth Johnson, who edited Ned McGowan's work and reviewed Bell's reminiscences, should have had an easy time trying to establish which version, as he wrote, had "the lesser amount of misinformation."

The complete and true account of the life of Parker Hardin French is much more complex, compelling, and colorful.

After his mother died when he was six, Parker Hardin French was taken in by a rich and influential uncle who raised him like a son. With all the accoutrements of an elite Kentucky family, he became well-read, imaginative, and adventurous. Catching wanderlust, he ran away and fought in the British navy, later returning as a prodigal son to his uncle, who continued to give him every advantage: a first-class education, introductions to the socially and politically powerful, and a fast track start on life. Sent to Alton, Illinois to live with the family of a renowned judge, French attended a prestigious college, married the judge's daughter, and joined one of the most influential families in America. He was a golden boy; a young man with an apparently wonderful and prosperous future. And, he had become an astute and shrewd adherent of Machiavelli.

His upbringing, preparation, intelligence, energy, and ambition could have led to a very successful, respectable life. His resume, leaving out unpleasant adjectives, presents an extremely adventurous and successful serial entrepreneur always seeking the next opportunity. Almost everything Parker French attempted, however, had some characteristic of a simple fraud, complex swindle, sham, or embezzlement. Persuasive, confident, and tough, he counted on quick wits, charisma, and a disarming manner. When challenged, he was able to use his magnetic personality and gift of gab to maneuver himself out of precarious, sometimes life-threatening, situations. When all else failed, he resorted to intimidation and threats of blackmail, extortion, or lawsuits. Although not apparent in official records or period newspapers, he likely took advantage of close family ties that facilitated political or business connections, and that perhaps provided a get-out-of-jail card. He had a remarkable capability to convince even the most experienced and successful people of the greatness and profitability of his deals. The normally skeptical seemed curiously vulnerable to his schemes and deceptions. His targets were common citizens and the influential alike. Trusting marks included exuberant investors, innocent travelers, frontier toughs, business tycoons, prominent politicians, and US army officers. Even seemingly innocent forays into legitimate business ventures concluded with someone being duped.

The rapidity of movement and breadth of his adventures is almost mind-numbing. When he was just 22 years old, he was a commission merchant and, a year later, built the first ocean going ship on the upper Mississippi. Before he was 30, he was a gold rush expedition leader; implicated in an irregular invasion of Cuba; jailed bandit and then military hero in Mexico; lawyer, district attorney, legislator, journalist, and political enforcer in California; part of an American cabal which governed Nicaragua; and, appointed but rejected Nicaraguan ambassador to the United States. He didn't slow down in his 30s: he was a real estate developer; lawyer; journalist; part of a conspiracy to invade Mexico; suspected seditionist agitator and Confederate agent; jailed as a political prisoner; lawyer, and purveyor for Union troops. But first and foremost, he was a con man, a barracuda.

When Colonel Parker Hardin French died in 1878, his death went generally unnoticed. Newspapers had reported the death of French before—at least five separate times. He had been twice killed in gunfights, twice executed in Mexico—once by a firing squad, once by hanging—and once killed in Nicaragua. Acquaintances thought he might have drunk himself to death. For a while, there was a lapse of interesting press reports, so many just presumed that he was already dead and were surprised when he was not. Some pondered his many misadventures and wondered how he escaped retribution from a hangman, a firing squad, or an irate victim.

The New York Times had previously published a summary of his life and wrote:

"The mutability of human things has been a theme on which essayists have written and preachers dilated. But never has it been more fully illustrated then by the changes in the life and fortunes of Colonel Parker H. French. Many telegraphic dispatches appeared in the columns of the New

York papers, giving news of our hero's acts and condition. Reports, strong and for some time undoubted, of his murder... were printed in every paper and believed throughout the Union. The whirl of events, and rush of other items had almost pushed Captain French out of men's memories and newspaper columns when we received the news that he had clung to life with more than feline tenacity...When the Colonel has really died for the last time, what a field will the novelist find in his romantic career for their cultivation. How stupid, in comparison to him, will the heroes of past romances seem!"

The novelist would probably fail in fictionalizing the life of Parker Hardin French, this cat-like character. The story would likely not be credible.

"'Tis strange, —but true; for truth is always strange; Stranger than fiction; if it could be told."

Lord Byron, *Don Juan* (1833).[3]

"Some stories have to be written because no one would believe the absurdity of it all."

Shannon L. Alder

And, as Paul Harvey would have said: "Stay tuned for the rest of the story."

2

EARLY LIFE: A GOOD KENTUCKY BOY

Ned McGowan wrote that Parker Hardin French was orphaned in Kentucky and adopted by neighbor Judge Edwards. He later married the judge's daughter. In effect, French married his foster sister. McGowan's version probably conflated a few different stories that Parker French told about his youth, and the account likely got distorted with time. Hampered by lack of access to genealogical records and unassisted by the digital age, historians have accepted the McGowan version of French's early life. But the real story is much different.

In an article about a particularly disreputable period of Parker French's life, the *Louisville Courier* gave a glowing appraisal of his promise as a youth. It had been

"but a few short years since we knew French as a lad, whose reputation was without blemish or reproach, and whose daily walk was such as not only to win the confidence and esteem of his employer, but of the entire community in which he then resided."

The rest of the article can be summarized as: "He was such a good boy, what happened to him?"

Parker Hardin French was born on April 2, 1826, in Mason County, Kentucky. French himself would give various years of birth depending, perhaps, on whim, plan, complacency, or mistake. His parents

were Hiram Duncan French (ca. 1795-1872) and
Margaret Calhoun Hardin (1802-1832). They had
married on April 16, 1821, in Washington County,
Kentucky. Hiram was from a farming family that
had relocated from Virginia to Kentucky in the early
1790s.

Margaret, the daughter of Martin L. Hardin, was
the progeny of a highly cultured, prominent, and
powerful Kentucky family full of military heroes,
lawyers, judges, and politicians. For the first several
years, the young Parker French lived on what was
probably a struggling farm, with older sister Juliet
Catherine (1822-1905), and younger sister Mary Jane
(1830-1913). In 1832, sister Arzelia (1832-1924) was
born, possibly precipitating the death of Parker's
mother in October. In December 1835, Hiram was
remarried to Frances Henderson (1813-1901). At the
time, Hiram may have been disabled, since census
records would later show that he was mute or deaf.[4]

At some point after his mother died, but
certainly by 1836, the young Parker's life changed
dramatically. His maternal uncle and namesake,
Judge Parker Calhoun Hardin (1800-1876), took in
the young boy. Parker Hardin was an established
lawyer in Adair County and had practiced in the
county seat of Columbia since 1822. He would serve
two terms in the State Senate and be elected twice
as county judge. Hardin treated the boy like a son,
namesake that he was, and fostered his development,
education, and lifelong connections. Judge Hardin
provided French the best education available to
affluent antebellum Kentuckians. Hardin enrolled
French in Robertson's Academy in Columbia; he was
on the student roster as a ten-year-old in 1836. There
he studied with the some of the sons of Kentucky
elite, with whom he would cross paths again. Notable
students would become both state and national

politicians, judges, lawyers, and military leaders.
French was likely particularly close to students from
the Monroe family, descendants of the founding
father, and a boy named Samuel Bell Maxey. Both
surnames would be prominent in French's future: he
would use them as aliases.[5]

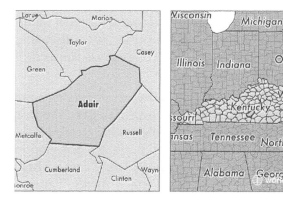

Location of Adair County Kentucky. *World Atlas Map.*

Growing up under the tutelage of his uncle and
boosted by access to an extensive and valuable
private library, Parker was recognized as a
remarkably intelligent, interesting, and charismatic
youngster with a real gift for fluent and entertaining
discussion. He visited courthouse square in Columbia
to seek out prominent citizens, including politicians
such as the future governor Thomas Bramlette, who
conversed for hours with the magnetic and charming
lad. French described reading about foreign and
exotic lands and expressed an ambition to travel. As
the boy acquired and practiced what would become
a life-long command of language, Judge Hardin and
other lawyers likely provided an early education in the
law, rhetoric, and logic. His education at Robertson's
Academy, as well as his self-education, inevitably led
to what the local paper described as a "disposition to

roam." Parker Hardin French caught wanderlust.[6]

When French was about thirteen years old, he stole away from the Hardin household and traveled down the Mississippi to New Orleans. There, McGowan wrote, "he shipped as a cabin boy on an English Man-of-War." Since there is no record of a British warship visiting New Orleans at that time, it was more likely that he gained passage or worked as a crew member on one of the considerable number of trading ships that plied the waters between New Orleans and London or Liverpool.

Antebellum New Orleans was the transfer point for American products being shipped all over the world, including Great Britain. On flatboats, keelboats, and steamboats, products flowed along the Mississippi and its tributaries. From the Midwest came wheat, corn, lard, pork, furs and hides, whiskey, hemp, and lead. From the South came cotton, sugar, molasses, and tobacco. These products were offloaded and stored in warehouses of commission merchants or transferred directly to ships heading to Great Britain.

Upon reaching England, Parker French would have made his way to the historic naval base at Portsmouth, the home of the British Navy. He was going to sail in the service of Queen Victoria against the Chinese Qing Dynasty and fight in the First Anglo-Chinese War, known popularly as the first Opium War. The causes and aims of the war still stir academic and international debate. Some see the war as an ideological conflict: British commitments to free trade and progress clashed with traditional Confucian notions and a bias against international commerce. Others assert that the British rationalized a "just war" moral justification to protect a profitable (and, to the Chinese, illegal) trade in opium. The British Empire's addiction to silk, ceramics, and tea had created what could have been a disastrous deficit in balance of payments; opium was a commodity that could help balance the books.

By early 1840, almost all the ships making war on the Chinese were already in the Far East or well on the way. The only ship preparing to sail and requiring a large number of "boys" was *HMS Blenheim.* There is no evidence substantiating that French was part of the crew on the *Blenheim.* But given the timeline of French, as well as the location and sailing schedules of other British ships, the *Blenheim* was the most likely option.[7]

HMS Blenheim was an old Vengeur-class sailing "Ship Of The Line," launched in 1813. It was over 1,740 tons, carried 74 guns, and had a crew of 625, including 53 boys.

As a cabin boy, and at the bottom of the naval hierarchy, French would have been assigned as the servant of an officer. He would have taken care of the officer's personal quarters, gear, and uniforms while accommodating his every wish. On the voyage, French would have trained hard with the other boys, likely to exhaustion, as he "learned the ropes," helping to handle the hawsers and lines, scrambling in the rigging, and setting the sails. On the bottom rung of the ship's company, one of his additional duties would have been taking care of the live animals on board, cleaning out the pig sties and chicken coops. His most dangerous job, however, would have been as a "powder monkey" during battles with the Chinese.

Warships needed to store gunpowder in magazines deep below decks for protection from fire or explosion.

The gunpowder, along with water and other supplies, needed to be quickly moved to sustain the gun crews. Small, strong, agile teenagers were perfect for swiftly moving the gunpowder through the confined space between decks and up ladders to the gun crews. French would have participated in drill after drill, training with the crew for battle action.

Along with the dangers of combat, cabin boys routinely risked harsh discipline. Instant punishment in the form of on-the-spot caning could be inflicted by any officer for even minor offenses, slackness, or carelessness. Six strokes to the hands or the buttocks were authorized. It was common to save the hands and treat the posterior, so the boy could better climb the rigging. For more serious offenses, discipline was administered by more formal and ceremonial floggings conducted with the approval of the ship's captain.

The *Blenheim* was towed out of Portsmouth harbor on February 1, 1840, and was soon on its way for the five-month voyage to China. She worked southerly through the Atlantic, crossed the equator on March 10, sailed around the Cape of Good Hope, and made port for resupply on May 15 at Simon's Town, South Africa. The town is now a suburb of Cape Town on the eastern shore of the peninsula. It was a long-time center of British naval power, which dominated the south Atlantic and the Indian oceans. Today, Simon's Town is the home of the South African Navy.

She transited the Indian Ocean, resupplied in Singapore, and was engaged in operations at Chusan (Zhoushan) by July 5. After reaching the Chinese coast, the *Blenheim* was initially assigned as part of a fleet blockading the Canton River. For the rest of the war, the ship ranged along the coast of China, as part of a force capturing port cities, subduing the Chinese military and forcing the Qing Dynasty to capitulate and come to the negotiating table. The only reported casualty was Captain Humphrey Senhouse, who died of fever. The action continued until August 1842, when the Treaty of Nanking marked the end of the war.

The Chinese were required to open new trade ports, compensate British citizens for debts, and pay war reparations to the British government. The biggest and longest-lived concession was the perpetual cession of Hong Kong to the British Empire as a crown colony. In March of 1843, the *Blenheim* returned to Portsmouth, quickly taken out of commission, and scheduled to be modernized. French had served his commitment and was homesick; he left the British Navy and immediately departed for home.[8,9,10,11]

Of course, the whole story of the Opium War, told by French and narrated by Ned McGowan, may have been a fantastic fiction, an exaggeration of a much more mundane voyage. What is known from newspaper reports in Kentucky is that the young boy did run away from home and that he did travel the world. A later exploit involved a colleague named Robert Trimm, who reported that he had served with French on board a merchant ship. Perhaps both were true.[12]

Back in Kentucky, the lad astonished his family and citizens of Columbia with his adventurous tales of sailing, war, and exotic places. He also came back matured beyond his years, self-assured and able to win the confidence and esteem of all he encountered. With a substantial amount of money in his pocket, he moved to Louisville, where some extended family lived, and started engaging in business. In early dealings in Louisville, he was described as a young man whose character and reputation were not questioned, and he was already pursuing "mercantile interests."[13,14]

It appears at this time that uncle Parker Calhoun Hardin helped the career and prospects of French. Hardin doubtless wanted his namesake to follow in his footsteps, finish his schooling, study the law, and be admitted to the bar. He looked for a prominent man to help further his nephew's education and development. The Hardin family was well positioned within the Kentucky legal and political community and had been influential in shaping the course of early Kentucky. Uncle Parker was a sitting Kentucky state senator during 1840-1848 and was the chairman of the Judiciary Committee. Friends and acquaintances would help young gentlemen of prominence and would certainly be happy to help the Hardin family. Cousins were expected to help cousins; that was part of the extended family tradition. Parker Hardin had read law under his uncle, Benjamin Hardin, who was regarded by some as one of the greatest legal minds in the country and who had served as a congressional representative and Kentucky secretary of state. Benjamin in turn had studied under Cousin Martin Davis Hardin. Martin had likewise been an influential politician as a state representative, United States senator, and Kentucky secretary of state. The early contact with family, friends, and acquaintances, as well as with legal and political colleagues, must have influenced young Parker French. Such connections would improve his prospects as he maneuvered through the insider's web of political, business, and social elites and the halls of power. Even if these direct connections were not fruitful in and of themselves, the traditions of the time would have demanded courteous introductions to others.

Parker Hardin's son, Charles Alfred (1836-1897), effectively French's younger "brother," would marry Jane Magoffin, the niece of Civil War-era Kentucky governor, Beriah Magoffin. French's cousin, Lucinda Barbour Hardin (1809-1805), would have a son, General (CSA) Benjamin Hardin Helm (1831-1863). Helm was Abraham Lincoln's brother-in-law by marriage to Mary Todd's sister, Emilie.[15]

For Parker French, perhaps his uncle's most important connections were with another prominent Kentucky family, the Edwards. The Edwards family was originally from Montgomery County, Maryland, where patriarch Benjamin had been an officer in the Revolutionary War, a member of the Maryland legislature that ratified the Constitution, and then a member of congress. The Edwards family moved to Kentucky before 1800 and established themselves in farming, law, and politics.

Members of both the Hardin and Edwards families traveled all over the state to represent their clients. Every lawyer of note must have known Benjamin's son, Ninian, who had been a judge at general court, circuit court, and court of appeals. Ninian culminated his Kentucky legal career as the Chief Justice of the state. In 1809, President Madison appointed Ninian the first territorial governor of Illinois. He later won state election as one of the first United States senators and as the third governor. The close ties between the families was demonstrated when Ninian Edwards appointed Martin Hardin, Parker French's cousin, to be the clerk for the Court of Appeals.

Ninian's younger brother, Cyrus, had also practiced law in Kentucky and moved his family to Illinois in 1830. There he became an acclaimed member of the Illinois bar and an astute politician. He served in the legislature with Abraham Lincoln, narrowly lost two bids for the United States senate, and twice lost gubernatorial elections. Cyrus was now a judge and one of the most distinguished citizens of the city of Alton in Madison County.

By 1843, Parker French was on his way to Alton, Illinois to live with Judge Cyrus Edwards and his family. There he would continue his education, likely read law under the judge's tutelage, and marry his daughter. He would also forge tight relationships with the extended Edwards family and establish linkages with legal, business, and political leaders reaching to the nation's capital.

3

ALTON, ILLINOIS: INTO A YOUNG MAN

Parker Hardin French arrived in Alton, Illinois no later than 1844, when he was about eighteen years old. With a population of a little over 3,000, Alton was the center of commerce and largest city in the southwestern part of Illinois.[16]

"French was received ... with open arms by the Edwards family, whom he delighted and astonished with the tale of his stirring adventures ... and charmed, won and married one of the daughters of Judge Edwards. Like the fair Desdemona, she 'loved him for the dangers he had passed.'"[17]

Established near the confluence of the Illinois, Missouri, and Mississippi rivers, the city in Madison County was advantageously located as a steamboat port and as a hub of commerce for the area's agricultural output. During the 1830s, Alton grew rapidly, rivaling Chicago and the state capital of Springfield. Newly arrived businessmen established factories, mills, stores, and services. River trade was brisk as commission and wholesale merchants forged business relations with St. Louis, New Orleans, and other river port cities. Alton men owned several steamboats and were active in regional and international trade. The community fabric was strengthened with the arrival of educated professionals and men of distinction: lawyers, physicians, educators, and ministers. The social scene was robust with lodges, societies, churches, and charitable groups. Alton was flourishing, and prospects were bright.

Then, the "Panic of 1837" financial crisis struck with a major recession to follow. Banks reduced credit to farmers and suspended specie payments in gold and silver to the commission merchants, forwarders, and steamship operators. Mississippi River commerce and steamboat traffic plummeted, and railway construction and other infrastructure projects failed. Unemployment was common, salaries and wages tumbled, and property values collapsed.[18]

Exacerbated by the buckled economy, the social structure was torn apart due to the escalating national dispute between adherents of slavery and abolition. Many of the elite citizens, including the Edwards family, had migrated from the south to Alton but retained southern plantations, where they continued to own slaves. In Illinois, they had become adept in retention of their slaves through a de facto slavery system of long-term indentures, apprenticeships, rental contracts, and state enforcement statutes. On the other hand, much of the new immigration was from the north, which included strident advocates of abolition. Alton became ground zero for a violent cultural clash.[19]

The city was an important way-station on the Underground Railroad. Escaped slaves from Missouri and farther south along the Mississippi, would cross into the free state of Illinois and shelter in Alton. From there, abolitionists would help them move to safer places in the north. Concurrently, some pro-slavery townspeople would act as informants and actively help Missouri slave catchers, who often raided the town and returned the fugitive slaves to their owners.

Alton was a tinderbox waiting for a spark. The tension was such that the established politicians in the Illinois House of Representatives, heavily Southern, weighed in. Early in 1837, they adopted a resolution that "the right of property in slaves is sacred" and that they highly disapproved of the formation of abolition societies.[20]

Reverend Elijah P. Lovejoy was a Presbyterian minister and abolitionist journalist who had been run out of St. Louis after several of his printing presses had been destroyed. In 1837, Lovejoy set up shop in Alton to publish the abolitionist paper *Alton Observer*. Again, some of his printing presses were destroyed by mob action. Community leaders, including Parker French's future sponsor, Cyrus Edwards, tried to forge a compromise to quell any further violence. They proposed that Lovejoy and his family stop publishing and leave Alton; in return, they would be faced with no further injury. Rejecting the "compromise," Lovejoy said he would continue to exercise his right of free speech.

Image courtesy of the Missouri History Museum

The pro-slavery riot of November 7, 1837, in Alton, Illinois, and the death of Reverend E.P. Lovejoy. From a woodcut made in 1838. Held by the Missouri History Museum, Photograph and Prints collections.

The tinderbox had its tinder and awaited a spark; Lovejoy had just a couple of days to live. He had stored a new press in an Alton waterfront warehouse. A pro-slavery mob attacked the warehouse, while Lovejoy and supporters tried to defend themselves and their property. During the melee, Lovejoy was fatally shot; his press was destroyed and dumped in the river.

The news had predictable results. His murder became a symbol of both intersectional tensions and the national conflict over slavery. Some papers, both northern and southern, blamed Lovejoy. The *Alexandria Gazette* of November 30, 1837, posited that "all reasonable people must acknowledge his obstinacy, fool-hardiness and contempt of public opinion. Abolitionism will never raise seed from the blood of such martyrs as Mr. Lovejoy, however freely it may be poured on the ground."

The murder shocked both abolitionists and advocates of the First Amendment. Lovejoy was considered a martyr to the cause and would be later described as the first casualty of the Civil War. Others started recognizing that real freedoms of press and expression could not coexist with the slavery culture.

The riot and murder were terrible, but the following judicial proceedings further roiled the nation. Both the Lovejoy defenders and the rioters were indicted, though no one was convicted. Many saw the judicial failure as an endorsement of crime and violence as well as an attack on religious liberty and free expression. The riotous assailants, murderers, and opponents of the First Amendment were indicted but found not guilty at trial. The Lovejoy men who were defending private property and freedom of speech were also blamed and indicted. Although they were also found not guilty, the indictment itself was seen as a travesty of justice. Alton was branded by many as a law-breaking community that endorsed crime and violence while failing to support religious liberty, property, and free expression.

The combination of financial crisis, pro-slavery riot, murder, acquittal, and national stigma was devastating. The reputation of Alton plummeted, and families lost faith in the future prosperity, safety, and social stability of the town. Many left for greener pastures, and the exodus took many of the best and brightest. Immigration virtually ceased. In 1837, the prospects for the town were no longer bright.[21,22]

When Parker French arrived in Alton in the mid-1840s, Alton was just starting to recover from the economic turmoil and the devastating social strife. The Edwards family, which French joined, was on the top rung of local society, and French would benefit by access to the associated schooling, legal training, business opportunities, and social contacts.

French studied law under Judge Cyrus Edwards and perhaps other lawyers in the area. There is some circumstantial evidence that he may have studied under the wing of Joseph Gillespie, who himself had trained under Cyrus Edwards. Gillespie was a friend of Abe Lincoln; the pair had famously jumped out of a window to stop a quorum in the Illinois House of Representatives. Although there is no record of French being admitted to the bar, he would later claim status as an attorney and was quite competent when he concentrated on that profession. He attended, but apparently did not graduate from, Shurtleff College in Alton.

Besides being a crucial part of the city's social fabric, the school served as the leading institution of higher education in Southwestern Illinois. For more than a century, its graduates became productive citizens of Alton, Madison County, the St. Louis region, and the wider world. Attendees included many members of the extended Edwards family, as well as future husbands of the Edwards girls. French would later encounter Shurtleff alumni, such as his good friend Hugh Murray, Chief Justice of the California Supreme Court and his brother, Charles, a local Alton politician. Fellow student and future Presbyterian minister Addison Madeira would be the private secretary to General Ulysses Grant in the Civil War.[23]

The large Edwards family included four beautiful young daughters: Matilda, Isabella, Lucretia, and Ellen. French would spend hours with the sisters and regale them with his adventures, likely both real and fictional. The girls were wonderful conversationalists as well. Already well-cultured and probably well-read, they had been educated at Monticello Seminary. The seminary provided girls a liberal arts curriculum with an additional concentration on social graces such as conversation, hosting, dancing, and letter writing. French would continue to develop the charm, charisma, and ingratiating manner he would later use to so much effect. Especially smitten was the young teen Lucretia, who would become French's wife. As Ned McGowan wrote, "She grew to love him like the fair Desdemona who fell for Othello." Lucretia's sisters, along with their husbands, would play prominently in his life.[24,25]

Matilda had already made history in 1840 when she was in Springfield visiting her cousin Ninian Wirt Edwards, son of the first territorial governor. A former state attorney general, Ninian was then sitting in the Illinois House of Representatives along with political ally and friend Abraham Lincoln. Ninian's wife was Elizabeth Todd, Mary Todd's sister. Like many other pretty Illinois girls, Matilda saw an invitation to the capital as a much sought-after honor. The visit gave her the chance to attend the many parties and to socialize with the large numbers of bachelors. Matilda was known as a very intelligent, beautiful, graceful, and fascinating girl; she was also somewhat of an enchanting and flirtatious tease. Mary Todd, who was then engaged to Abraham Lincoln, was also a visitor in the house; she and Matilda were reported as the center of swarms of bachelors who hovered around them. When Lincoln famously broke off his engagement with Mary, Matilda may have been the cause. Whatever Matilda really had to do with the temporary breakup, Lincoln fell for the beautiful, vivacious, and flirtatious young woman. Some observers said Matilda just tended to lead men on and had no serious intentions with the future president. She herself commented to Elizabeth Edwards that Lincoln had paid no attention to her and never even paid her a compliment; Lincoln was too shy to approach her. Reunited and betrothed again, Abe and Mary were married in Ninian and Elizabeth's home in November of 1842. Matilda was courted by the best of Springfield society; other beaus included Lincoln's best friend, Joshua Speed, as well as political rival-to-be Stephen Douglas. Matilda reportedly received some twenty-two proposals before marrying Newton Deming Strong, a prominent and politically connected lawyer. Newton's brother William, of Berks County, Pennsylvania, would become a congressional representative, sit on the Pennsylvania Supreme Court, and be appointed an Associate Justice of the United States Supreme Court.[26]

The Edwards family had other connections that reached across the country to the nation's capital. Lucretia's namesake, Aunt Lucretia Edwards, had married Duff Green, labeled and chronicled by author Stephen Belko as the "Whig of the West." Green had been a powerful congressman and senator, as well as a diplomat in Great Britain, France, Texas and Mexico. But perhaps his most influential role was as a newspaper owner and member of President Jackson's famed "Kitchen Cabinet." A strident advocate of states' rights, expansionism, manifest destiny, and secession, he was an ardent friend of John C. Calhoun, the seventh vice president of the United States. During the Civil War, Green would become an advisor to Confederate President Jefferson Davis on financial and industrial matters. Green would have a substantial impact on French, schooling him on the power of the press, assisting him with various exploits, and easing access to the corridors of power in Washington D.C. Duff and his wife Lucretia had a daughter, Maria, who would marry Andrew Pickens Calhoun, son of the vice president.[27,28]

So, to recap, we have interesting family connections. Parker French will marry Lucretia Edwards of the powerful Illinois family. One of Lucretia's cousins married the sister of the wife of the future president, the hero of the North. Another cousin married the son of the "great nullifier," godfather of secession and hero of the South. To what extent French would ever use the Lincoln family connection is undocumented. He would definitely use his connection with Duff Green.

Raised by an elite slave-owning uncle in Kentucky and now living with an elite Illinois family who still owned slaves in Kentucky, French must have had an early and reinforced notion of class, racial superiority, and the associated links to opportunity. Southern boys were raised to become bold, independent, and self-sufficient. Dependence, submission, and subordination were distasteful, and that distaste sometimes got out of control in a tendency to disregard and defy authority. Willful, unmanageable, and independent young men were common. However, they still generally maintained a commitment to social obligations, as they saw them, and fostered mutual loyalty amongst extended family, friends, and acquaintances. Their future wealth, power, and social status hinged on that loyalty. Perceived honor was central to the stereotypical Southern manhood. Character attacks, alleged disgrace, humiliation, or indignity often generated a vociferous, if not violent, response. Cultivated and engineered from youth to treat slaves and lower classes as unequal and subject to exploitation, that characteristic often turned to similar treatment of all they considered subordinate or inferior.[29,30]

Did Parker French take on those stereotypical characteristics which would impact the rest of his life? Had he developed any conscience, empathy, or moral qualms? Or were those qualities so weak he could rationalize any guilt or feign any remorse as he used his relationships for his own benefit?

Good, bad, or indifferent, the young man was now ready to be launched into the world to make his own way. With the education, background, credentials, and experience to make a very successful and reputable life, he was tooled for better or worse. The next stop for Parker Hardin French was in St. Louis, where he would start a life mostly "for the worse."

4

ST. LOUIS: YOUNG ENTREPRENEUR

By the spring of 1848, Parker French moved to St. Louis, where he would quickly build a business as a commission merchant, make a small fortune, and launch an ocean-going ship. He would also build relationships with key business leaders, steamboat operators, bankers, lawyers, and journalists.

"French is a Kentuckian by birth, and distantly related to the Hardins, the most distinguished family in that State. He has some of the family characteristics, talents and energy of character; but lacks the integrity and similar admirable traits which has also justly distinguished many of the name."[31]

Birdseye view of St. Louis, circa 1850. Held by the Missouri History Museum, Photograph and Prints collections.

When St. Louis became an American possession in 1804, it was a small town supportive of, and benefitting from, the French fur trade throughout the west. The settlement included just two taverns, three blacksmiths, two mills, a bakery, and a doctor. After the Lewis and Clark expedition, mountain men, explorers, and settlers penetrated the continent and advanced the frontier. As westward migration increased, the town slowly grew into a small city of 5,000 by 1830. Then immigration surged, and by 1840, the population was almost 16,000.

Sitting on the Mississippi, with the Missouri River to the west, the Illinois River to the north, and the Ohio River to the east, St. Louis was ideally situated as a great center of commerce. Until about 1840, most manufactured and imported goods reached communities along the Mississippi via New Orleans. Manufactured goods from the east were offloaded in New Orleans and moved up the river by steamboats and keelboats. Eastern commission merchants necessarily kept close ties with their counterparts in New Orleans.

Everything started to change with the construction of northern canals. The canals linked the city through the northern river system to cities on the Great Lakes, as well as to the eastern merchants and manufacturing centers. The blended network transformed commerce in the northern interior, having a tremendous impact on the growth of St. Louis and spawning substantial prosperity for the city. At the confluence of the Mississippi and Missouri Rivers, the city became the principal center of commerce for western markets. It also competed with New Orleans as a distribution center for customers south along the Mississippi River. St. Louis was a center of the "Golden Age of Steamboats"; as many as fifty vessels could dock on the wharf.

Some projected that the city would become the "New York of the West." Merchants, investors, manufacturers, and migrants flowed into the city, quickening the pace of growth and multiplying the economic effect. The expanding transportation system increased the profitable opportunities for farmers throughout the agricultural heartland. The local economy surged, stimulating construction of commercial, residential, and infrastructure projects. Residents prospered and enjoyed an increasing class of retail merchants, who provided all manner of consumer goods and luxury items.

Thousands of settlers followed the trade routes and took advantage of the low-cost water passage to get to the "Gateway of the West." Mormons in their long exodus to Utah, settlers moving westward, and military expeditions all used St. Louis as a base and had to be provisioned. The St. Louis Arsenal was a key supply and principal staging point for support of forces in the Mexican War, adding enormous sums to the local economy for supplies and contractors.[32]

As Parker Hardin French arrived in St. Louis, circa 1848, the economic boom continued to spiral. Becoming the eighth largest city in the United States, and the largest west of the Mississippi, St. Louis's population had exploded to around 75,000. French joined an increasing group of commission merchants; he was now a "middleman." These businessmen provided an essential service and were significant figures in the commercial life of St. Louis and the region. Responsible for all elements of exchange of commodities, French would store, transport, and dispose of products from throughout the region, including such commodities as wheat, corn, lard, pork, furs and hides, whiskey, hemp, and lead. He could also have been an agent for purchasers to buy manufactured goods. Either way, he would advance money on credit and take a commission for products consigned for sale. Both farmers and manufacturers were unfettered from the expense and details of selling and could devote their resources and energy to production. There was a risk when the accounts did not balance, though. If farmers and manufacturers could not accommodate the debt, French, as a commission merchant, could be left in the lurch.

Through his commercial dealings, he must have struck up relationships with prominent men. Thomas Yeatman, the owner and editor of the *Intelligencer* newspaper, would be helpful in publicizing and marketing his business operations. His brother, James Yeatman, was a fellow commission merchant and cofounder of the Merchants Bank. Cornelius (C.K.) Garrison made a fortune in St. Louis from owning, building, and commanding steamboats. Thomas and Cornelius would both play significant roles in later exploits.

Then, in January 1848, discovery of gold at Sutter's Mill in California triggered gold mania. It took several months for the news to work east, first both rumored and discredited in August newspapers and later confirmed by government announcements. Reports rapidly spread throughout the country. St. Louis likely heard the news relatively early through the telegraph, which had reached the city in December 1847. Throughout the fall, the press reported on the shortage of and soaring prices for all types of provisions, clothing, tools, and equipment. Ships were reported heading to California with massive quantities of food, cotton goods, tents, boots, and hats. Spades, shovels, hoes, pick axes, and sieves were reported as favorite investments. Parker French would not be left behind when there was such a lucrative opportunity.[33]

According to McGowan, French gathered provisions and other supplies, shipped them to San Francisco and, by fall 1848, received the sizable proceeds from his venture. With the requisite months-long round-trip to California, the only way he could have so quickly realized the reportedly immense profit was through the commission merchant network.

With the tidy profits, the young entrepreneur decided that he was going to cut out the middlemen, build a ship, and transport supplies and equipment directly to California. He had access to the provisions, supplies and equipment from his supplier network. Because of his early success, he had likely established credit with banks and fostered credibility with partners, vendors, and shipbuilders. He was going to attempt the construction of a full rigged, ocean-going ship, the first such vessel built on the upper Mississippi. After launching and fitting out, French's plan was to sail down the Mississippi, through the Caribbean, down the coast of South America, around the Horn, and up the west coasts of both South and North America to San Francisco. He honored his betrothed Lucretia's sister by naming the prospective ship *Matilda*.

French acted quickly. He contracted with steamboat builders Emerson and Thomas, the company started modeling on December 16, 1848. Construction started soon after, at the foot of Cherry Street where French established the Messrs. French and Company Shipyard.

The 470-ton ship would be impressive. Built entirely of oak, copper sheathed and fastened, the hull was planked with 4-inch lumber and paired with a 3-inch ceiling. She would be 132 feet long, a beam of 28 feet, and a depth of 17 feet. It would have accommodations for 28 passengers and be able to transport up to 6,000 barrels. French hired a locally famed supervisor, E. Lufton, and rigger, Alex Clemons. Two lumber firms were contracted to provide the milled wood. West, Field & Vandeventer, with their well-established pine mill, provided all the

finish pine as well as the spars and decking. Gordon
and Brotherton, who owned a mill, provided the oak
for the planking and ribs. Mr. L. Jackson, who ran a
small manufacturing company, provided all types of
general rigging, blocks, and tackle.[34,35,36]

Sailing ship *Matilda*.
Photograph of a
daguerreotype,
1849. The first and
only full-rigged ship
built in St. Louis.
Held by the Missouri
History Museum,
Photograph and Prints
collections.[37]

After an initial delay due to harsh weather and a
shortage of labor, construction rapidly progressed.
Announcements and advertisements began to
appear in local papers as early as March 5 and were
published across the nation. "FOR CALIFORNIA, SHIP
MATILDA OF ST. LOUIS, Now building at this place,
will be dispatched for San Francisco the 1st of April …
enquire of French & Co., 21 Washington Avenue."

Prospective customers were informed that *Matilda*
would sail without delay under Captain John Evans,
an old and experienced navigator of the Pacific. Clients
were offered cargo space for sending parcels to friends
or for commercial shipping of provisions or goods.
Those who planned to cross the continent could send
their baggage and supplies in advance. Passage was
also offered in the twenty-eight berths.

Part of the deck cargo space was already filled
by Parker French. He was shipping forty "portable
houses" (each 320 square feet) and one large
warehouse. It is likely he would use the prefabricated
buildings to set up a commission merchant operation

in San Francisco. He had probably already surmised that the smart money was in providing the picks and shovels, pants and boots, rather than digging for gold.[38,39]

As early as March 15, the shipbuilding effort garnered national attention. The *Boston Herald*, in a short blurb entitled "Ship Building at St. Louis," extolled the *Matilda* as "a superior vessel of her class." Related articles appeared in cities such as Trenton, New Jersey, and Richmond, Virginia. The *Richmond Whig* expressed fear of danger for cross-continent travelers and cautioned them not to miss the chance of shipping in the *Matilda*: "An opportunity is afforded to a few, both as regards safety and comfort by taking passage ... that will not present itself again this season."

The first of April came, and the expected launch did not occur. On Tuesday, April 10, French would take time out from his busy construction schedule to get married. He and Lucretia Edwards were wed near Alton, Illinois at her father's Wood River estate. Officiating at the ceremony was Minister of the Gospel Washington Leverett. He was a good family friend and President of Shurtleff College, where Cyrus, Lucretia's father, was on the Board of Trustees. The party continued that night at the Virginia Hotel in St. Louis. Lucretia's siblings and spouses, as well as many of the couple's friends, were noted in "Hotel Arrivals" the next day. Parker's older sister, Mary Jane French, even traveled from Kentucky to help celebrate the event.[40,41,42]

The work on the ship continued, but delays confounded the expectations of an early departure. Finally, to public acclaim, the *Matilda* was launched on May 3. A huge crowd gathered and greeted the "new era in the growth, prosperity and mechanical improvement of our city":

"A multitude of our citizens assembled last evening at the shipyard of French and Co. to witness the launching of the first ship ever put upon the ways in this city ... we found difficulty getting a position to see, so dense was the throng, including a large number of ladies ... she soon launched and glided off in majestic style into her native element, with colors flying without any accident to mar the scene. As she struck the water the force of the current caused her to career to the starboard, to the terror of a number of persons on board not acquainted with the cause, who rushed to the opposite side of the deck to the infinite delight of those on shore, but as soon as her full length reached the water, righted with her bow up stream and sat upon the river as graceful as a swan."[43]

Investors, customers, partners, vendors, and bankers would all soon regret their involvement in the enterprise. Parker French and his new wife absconded, leaving debt behind in both Missouri and Illinois worth approximately $90,000 (in 2017 terms, $2.75M). It is likely that the whole affair was not planned as a bunko operation but was a legitimate business arrangement gone awry. It either got out of hand and failed, or French just lost interest in the time-consuming endeavor. Either way, the venture was likely French's first lesson in the profitable opportunities afforded by manipulation and fraud.

Great Fire at St. Louis, 1849. Color lithograph by Nathaniel Currier. Held by the Missouri History Museum, Photograph and Prints collections.

Two other events also may have hastened the couple's departure. On May 17, the *Matilda* narrowly escaped destruction in the historic St. Louis fire. The paddlewheel steamboat *The White Cloud* was also moored at the foot of Cherry Street, but probably downstream. The boat caught fire, the moorings burned through, and the steamboat drifted downriver, setting on fire twenty-two other steamboats as well as flatboats and barges. Soon the entire waterfront levee was burning. The fire leapt the street westward, completely gutting a large city area. Investigation originally centered on suspected arson, but the final determination was accidental: sparks from a passing boat had landed on fresh paint. At the same time, St. Louis was enduring a massive cholera outbreak from fouled drinking water. The death toll hit 120 in April, some 700 in May, and reached 2,200 in July. By the time the emergency ended, the official death toll was 4,317—more than 5 percent of the population. Many residents escaped the city.

The story of the ship *Matilda* continued. The debtors sold her in a sheriff's sale, and in July she was towed to New Orleans. Some historians wrote that she sailed to San Francisco and sunk in the harbor, but that story is not supported by the record. The ship languished in New Orleans for several months until sold in December for $27,000 (2017 estimate, $830,000). On her maiden voyage in January, the ship was reported in distress from uncontrollable leaks and returned to New Orleans. In February, she was on her way again with a load of cotton for New York. Over the next four years, news reports suggest that she proved to be a very reliable ship. Making several round trips to San Francisco, her last reported sail was in September 1853, when she arrived in Baltimore with a load of guano from the Peruvian Chincha Islands. Along with a cargo of 620 tons of fertilizer, she was sold for 20 percent of the original fraud ... $18,000 (2017 estimate, $540,000).[44]

By early 1850, Parker and Lucretia were in New York City, where Lucretia delivered the couple's first child. In the city, Parker French would plan and organize his next adventure; he would be a "captain" leading a grand expedition across the continent to the California gold fields.

5

CALIFORNIA GOLD RUSH: FRENCH'S EXPRESS PASSENGER TRAIN

By Sea to Texas

As early as the fall of 1849, but certainly by February 1850, when daughter Matilda Strong French was born, Parker French and family moved to New York City. Since French expected to take several months on the expedition to California, Lucretia and newborn daughter, Matilda, moved to Berks County, Pennsylvania; they were to stay with Lucretia's sister, Matilda, and her husband, Newton Deming Strong. Both Lucretia and Matilda were counted in the 1850 census living with the Strongs.

Having granted himself the rank of "captain," French took an office in Tammany Hall and started advertising what he called a sixty-day pleasure trip to the gold diggings in California. The ads promised the hardy and adventurous a "happy combination of novelty, romance and adventure with bushels of gold lying about loose in the distance." Michael Baldridge, who was hired as a personal secretary, kept extensive notes for the entire trip. His reminiscence would be published more than a century later:

"Readers have doubtless heard of the notorious Parker H. French, who left New York with an expedition which was gotten up on a grand scale, in the spring of '50, destination the new El Dorado of the west. Of all the schemes originated to enable the eager gold seekers to reach the Sunset Land even in those days of gold fever and thrilling adventure, this was the wildest and most desperate both in conception and detail." [45]

Captain French soon transferred operations to 41 Wall Street and into the office of Thomas Douglass, who was an agent of the U.S. Mail Steamship Company, owned by George Law. Visitors who called on French found him to be pleasant, sociable, and capable. He spoke with certainty about his plans, equipment, livestock, provisions, and security. French likely also mesmerized them with his family ties, past adventures, and financial resources.

After the discovery of gold at Sutter's Mill in January 1848, it took several months for the information to reach Waukegan in Lake County, Illinois. Like everywhere else in the country, the news triggered gold mania and compelled Lake County citizens to head for the gold fields as part of the great forty-niner relocation. Newspapers reported steamships bringing large gold shipments to the east, along with startling news extolling and hyping the scope of the opportunity to strike it rich. Those same steamships brought mail and stories from the now flush Lake County forty-niners. Farmers and brothers Richard Goodbody and the author's great grandfather Francis Alexander (Frank) Goodbody must have felt some envy, thinking they were missing a fantastic opportunity for wealth.

Along with fourteen other Lake County friends and neighbors, Richard and Frank planned their trip to the gold fields. Leaving Waukegan on April 26, 1850, they intended to board the daily steamship in Chicago, cruise to Buffalo, and catch the train to Albany. From there, they would take a steamboat down the Hudson to New York City, completing the entire trip in as few as three days. In New York, they expected to buy passage on a steamship to Chagres, Panama, then they would cross the Isthmus and catch another steamer to San Francisco.[46,47,48,49]

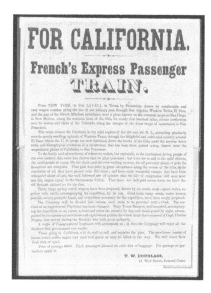

French Expedition Handbill, 1850. Courtesy of Yale University, Beinecke Library.

Getting impatient, twenty-year-old Frank Goodbody headed out early "on his own hook." When he reached New York, he found that steamship tickets were completely sold out and passage was not available for months. Discouraged and frustrated, Frank picked up a newspaper and soon saw a solution to his problem, Captain Parker H. French was offering passage on his French's Express Passenger Train.

"FOR CALIFORNIA: French's Express Passenger Train

From NEW YORK to Port LAVACA, in Texas, by Steamship, thence by comfortable and easy wagon coaches along the line of our military posts, through San Antonio ... the route crosses the Continent in the mild regions of the 29th and 30th latitudes ascending gradually over the gently swelling uplands of Western Texas, through the delightful and cultivated country around El Paso, where U.S. troops are now stationed, down the banks of the Gila amid the ancient Aztec ruins and hieroglyphic evidence of a civilization that has long since passed away, thence over the magnificent plains of California to San Francisco. ... Thirty large spring wagons have been prepared, drawn by six mules ... with everything necessary for the expedition, have been prepared."

The advertisement sounds like a modern tourism promotion! Of those who were marooned, frustrated, and anxious, some perhaps despairing, some just daring, who wouldn't jump at the chance?

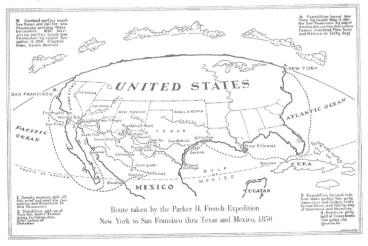

French Expedition Route Map from drawing by J. Goodman and Michael Baldridge, 1852.

At the office on Wall Street, the pleasant and informative "captain" explained the advantages of his route while emphasizing the dangers of disease and difficulty associated with the alternative of crossing the Isthmus. The captain further promised security provided by sixty Texas Rangers, armed with two mountain howitzers, commanded by a Mexican War veteran. He proposed to loiter in the Gila River valley for just enough time to prospect for gold; there might not be, he said, a reason to go any farther. He committed to getting the expedition to San Francisco in sixty days or forfeit $5 per day over that time. Frank was convinced by the charismatic, knowledgeable, and obviously competent captain. Fully confident, Frank joined the expedition for $250 (2017 estimate, $7,500). Upon leaving the office, Frank telegraphed brother Richard in Waukegan and gave him the news, both bad and good.[50]

On April 29, Frank Goodbody boarded the steamship *Ohio* of the U.S. Mail Steamship Company. Under the command of Lieutenant J. F. Schenck, the ship left at 3 p.m. that afternoon with 346 passengers, reportedly with fifty members of the French expedition. With mail stops in Charleston and Savannah, the *Ohio* would make port in Havana and then finish the trip in New Orleans. Many of the expedition passengers were "enlisted members" who had paid a reduced price of $100 in exchange for working on the trip. Parker French was scheduled to be on the ship, but after a few days at sea, their leader had not been seen. A man with the obvious alias of "North West" appeared and told everyone he worked for French. He said that the captain had been detained as a witness in a court case and would follow on the steamship *Georgia*. West said that he had been charged with taking care of the men and paying any bills. Hearing this, the men grew suspicious of a malicious scheme to rob them and called the situation an egregious swindle. West was able to mollify the men and the rest of the trip apparently went smoothly; after the stop in Havana the ship berthed at its wharf in New Orleans on May 8.[51,52]

On May 10, the North West-led party left New Orleans on the U.S. Mail steamship *Palmetto* under the command of Captain Smith. When they got to Galveston, they boarded the light draught steamer *Jerry Smith* for the 120-mile trip southwest to Port Lavaca in Matagorda Bay. Port Lavaca was one of the prime gateways to San Antonio and interior Texas. Encamped at Lavaca three days later, the party found no mules or wagons as expected. Their suspicions of fraud were again provoked, and they feared for their money. The situation became so volatile that North West abandoned the group, went to San Antonio, and awaited the arrival of Parker French. Since the rest of the expedition would not leave New York on the *Georgia* until May 13, the group at Lavaca would have to anxiously persevere for at least two more weeks. As time went on, the frustration, apprehension, and angst must have fed an ever-increasing vortex of distrust, fear, and anger. Frank Goodbody, if his later personality is any indicator, was a tough young man of action and not very tolerant and patient at all.

U.S. Mail Steamship *Georgia*. Sister ship *Ohio* was identical. Sidewheelers of 2,727 tons completed in 1849 with maiden voyage in January of 1850. Maximum speed 10 knots. Wheels were 36 feet in diameter. Engine had 90-inch cylinders with an 8-foot stroke. Sketch held by National Archives, Maritime Collection.

Having arrived in New York, Richard Goodbody and the rest of the Lake County Illinois boys signed on with the Express Train. Richard had placed a mortgage on his farm for $300 and left his wife with two daughters under four years old, as well as a namesake son who had just been born in April. They were ticketed on the steamship *Georgia*, owned by George Law. Law was a major financier, railroad, and steamship entrepreneur who owned the U.S. Mail Steamship Company with mail contracts from the government. Under the command of Captain Porter, the *Georgia* left New York on May 13 with the second contingent of the expedition, including the Lake County men. The voyage started badly with crowded conditions and heavy seas, inevitably causing sea sickness. As soon as the seas calmed, Parker French became a hero to the expedition by providing them 150 bottles of champagne. The brilliant move motivated additional recruits to join the "train" and triggered multiple toasts "To Parker French and the success of his expedition."[53,54]

Photo of Morro Castle Havana Cuba. Library of Congress, Prints and Photographs Division.

Arriving in Havana on May 19, the party transferred to the steamship Falcon, bound for New Orleans. But, under the guns of the commanding Morro Castle and surrounded by guard boats, the French expedition became involved in an international incident. A New Orleans-based operation under revolutionary Narciso Lopez had just invaded and captured Cardenas, less than 150 kilometers to the east, along the north coast of Cuba. After initial success in capturing the city, the invading force was hemmed in by a Spanish response and forced to evacuate. Spanish consulates in New York and New Orleans ran very effective intelligence operations so the Lopez operation was an open secret. The Spanish also knew that George Law was a heavy financial supporter of expansionist operations and

Cuban "freedom" adventures in particular. His federally subsidized mail ships regularly transported arms, propaganda, and men for Mexican, Central American, and Caribbean operations. New York newspapers had speculated that French and the *Georgia* were really part of the Lopez expedition; it was known that the party had a large number of weapons, including the mountain howitzers. So, with good cause, the Spanish government suspected the men on the three U.S. Mail steamers in port, the *Georgia, Falcon,* and *Ohio*, were a possible threat as part of the Lopez force. The captain general of the port would not let anyone go ashore, nor would he let the ships depart. The Spanish commander declared that he intended to inspect the *Falcon and* its contents. The ship's captain, Lieutenant Hartstene, refused, saying that the passengers and crew were peaceful United States citizens and that he would resist a boarding. If fired upon by cannon from Morro Castle, Hartstene said, he would haul down his flag, surrender the crew as prisoners of war, precipitate an international crisis, and perhaps instigate a war.

French's supply of arms and ammunition were distributed, and the party readied for action, likely with thoughts that their chance of reaching the gold diggings had been drastically reduced. The American Consul intervened, the Spanish relented, and the *Falcon* left Havana on the morning of May 22. The Spanish, to make sure there was no landing on the Cuban coast, provided an escort of two gunboats, which accompanied the *Falcon* for twelve hours. The Spanish concerns were probably justified. In a letter about the incident, the commander of the *Falcon*, Lieutenant H. J. Hartstene, wrote to Mississippi Governor John Quitman, a southern Fire-Eater who was also a leading proponent of Caribbean expansion—with specific sights on Cuba. In a later attempt on Cuba, Quitman would refuse the Lopez's offer for command of the revolutionary army. Hartstene wrote: "If the

invaders had only made a descent upon the City after
their diversion at Cardenas, they would have received
assistance from over twelve hundred well-armed
Americans, on board the *Georgia, Ohio, & Falcon,* and
carried with ease this most important point." Hartstene
likely embroidered the situation; it is doubtful that
the three ships carried enough men prepared and
committed to Lopez to make a difference.[55,56]

Because of the detention in Havana, the *Falcon*
arrived too late on May 25 to connect in New Orleans
with the steamship Palmetto for Galveston, Texas.
There were eighty-seven members of the French
expedition, which the Times Picayune noted as
arriving: "A fine set of men, and are all well-armed
with rifles and revolvers."

Captain French, at his expense, lodged everyone
in some of the best hotels and told the men to charge
meals to him. Many of the men had rooms in the
prestigious St. Charles Hotel.

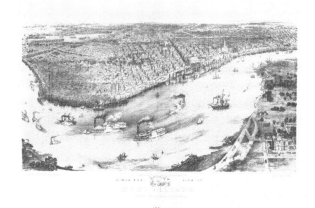

Birdseye view of New Orleans, circa 1851. Drawing by John
Bachman. Library of Congress, Prints and Photographs
Division.

The turmoil in Cuba did not end with the
failure at Cardenas; another effort was planned.

Returning to New Orleans after his defeat, Narciso Lopez established his headquarters near Lake Pontchartrain; French went to meet him. The captain came back from talking to Lopez and gathered the men in the St. Charles Hotel. Offered juicy inducements, including large Cuban farms, they were stridently urged to join the revolution under Lopez. All declined, even though French opined that success was a foregone conclusion.

Rumors started amongst the expedition that the plan from the beginning was to land on the Cuban coast. Expedition passenger Charles Lockwood noted: "The question of whether French's scheme was to land us in Cuba has never been settled and probably never will be; but when the whole story is told, it does not seem improbable."

Lopez was eventually arrested on June 6 for violating neutrality laws. Shortly after being released on bail and arriving at the St. Charles Hotel, he gave a short speech from the portico to loud cheers. Bolanos-Geyer, in his book entitled *Gray-Eyed Man of Destiny*, asserts that in attendance were Achilles Kewen, Colonel Chatham Roberdeau Wheat, William Walker, and Parker French. By June 6, however, French would be in Texas. In a future adventure, they would all be colleagues. Lopez would be executed by the Spanish in 1851 in another failed attempt to foment a revolt. His expeditionary banner is the model for the present flag of Cuba.[57,58,59]

Captain French and his team spent several days recruiting new members and buying provisions and other supplies. New Orleans merchants, restaurateurs, and hoteliers were likely very happy with the visit. There is no record of how French paid for the expenses, but he was carrying a letter of credit from Howland and Aspinwall. The firm owned the Pacific Mail Line, which ran passenger steamships from Panama to San

Francisco and was subsidized by a U.S. mail contract. The firm was well known and respected because of its long-time dominance in China trade, as well as for their steamships plying the Panama and San Francisco mail and passenger route. Coincidentally, the Howland family had extensive commercial interests in Cuba. They owned the El Dorado Sugar Plantation, as well as the Ontario and Mt. Vernon Coffee plantations.[60,61]

At last, on May 31, the expedition boarded the *Palmetto* for the trip to Galveston. French had previously gathered everyone together and explained that the price of cabin passage was exorbitant, so he had taken deck passage for all, paying the captain $150 with a draft. With the savings, he said, he purchased such good provisions and supplies that they would be willing to sleep on deck; the men were all pleased with the plan. That night it started to rain, and French went to the ship's captain to ask where his men were to sleep. The captain replied it was French's job. "Thank you," French said, "I will attend to it." He opened the door to the cabins and proclaimed, "Go in and occupy the land boys." Objecting loudly, the captain asked French if he intended to take over the ship. "Call it what you please," French said, "I propose to see my men properly treated." Charles Lockwood reported that he expected a fight but noticed that Parker French had his hand on his revolver—the men slept comfortably out of the rain. Upon arrival in Galveston, French told the men to go ashore and "eat, drink and be merry," adding, "Charge it to French." Morale and French's stock amongst the men rose accordingly. French paid the bills with more drafts.[62]

When the group finally arrived at Lavaca in the early evening of June 3, Richard Goodbody was reunited with his brother Frank. The joyous occasion included news of the birth of Frank's nephew, who had just been born in April. For Captain French, it was a less cheerful occasion. He was presented with a very irate and mutinous crew who felt abandoned for the last three weeks: no leadership, no information, no mules, no wagons, and little food. Parker French's charisma and magnetic personality came out to play; he charmed his passengers, calmed the emotions, and blamed others for the tribulations, errors, and omissions. Smooth talking the men, he convinced them that he would take care of everything. Confidence and order restored, at least temporarily, French determined to prepare for the next stage of their long journey. Arms and ammunition were distributed, tents and other camping gear were broken out, and the encampment was organized to prepare for the rest of their "pleasure trip."[63]

The wagons were beautiful, some obtained from famous circus masters Dan Rice and Isaac Van Amburgh. They were in good condition with a coat of bright paint and names of famous men in brilliant colors on both sides. One of them was Ben Edwards, named after French's wife's grandfather. The mules were another story—there were none. Again, the men got bitter and vocal. French, appearing completely calm and unperturbed, responded: "Gentlemen, the parties with whom I have contracted for mules have failed to come to time. It is no fault of mine. The best and only thing I can do is to proceed with all possible dispatch to secure such animals as I may be able to find, and the best thing you can do is to wait patiently until they come." For some men, including the Goodbody brothers, the situation further diminished their faith and trust in the captain. The boredom of inactive camp life crept in, bringing the associated rumors, speculation, and gossiping so disruptive of cohesion and morale.[64]

After disappearing for several days, Parker French returned on June 10 with a herd of mules, though all unbroken and wild. He bought them in Victoria and the surrounding areas from Burns and Taylor and other local ranchers; he paid at least $10,000 with drafts on a New Orleans merchant.[65]

On the same day French joined in a "compact" with the men, a form of written expedition governance that was to further unity, order, and justice while the expedition was removed from "wise laws and civilized communities." Signing the compact were 180 men to include French, passengers, and enlisted men. For the first time, there is a solid record of the men on the expedition. Various newspapers, personal diaries, and published journals are of little help in determining the size of the outfit. For instance, on the *Georgia* there were 250, 112, or 87. On *Ohio*, and initially in Lavaca, there were 59 or 50 or maybe 100. Some members were probably recruited on board ship, in New Orleans, or in southern Texas. Andrew Steele from Lake County kept a detailed journal of the trip. He listed friends and neighbors as: Richard and Frank Goodbody, James and John Cole, James Conlan (Quinlan?), John Crover, Peter Gray, Patrick Kennedy, James McBride, John McClory, Michael McGuire, Thomas Mackin, Roger McCormick, Michael Mines, and George Simpson. Part of the compact was the designation of a standing panel of thirty-two jurors. As necessary, selected juries of thirteen members would resolve internal disputes as well as adjudicate discipline for administration by the captain. Amongst Lake County residents, Richard Goodbody, Michael McGuire, and Andrew Steele were selected for the jury.[66,67]

The next day, the men started breaking the mules for pulling the wagons—it must have been quite an experience, even for the tough farm boys. The men assigned to each wagon were responsible for breaking, harnessing, and hitching their team. The Goodbody boys joined a wagon group with many of their Lake County friends and neighbors. From Andrew Steele's diary, it appears that the Goodbody pair, Michael McGuire, George Simpson, and Steele were particularly close, working and traveling together. Day after day, it took all hands to break the mules. A hired vaquero would lasso the legs, trip the mule, and bring it to the ground. The men would rush in, hold him down and attempt to put on the harness. They would then lead the mule to the wagon and hitch him up. The process would continue until six mules were hitched. The diaries and journals all have consistent mule breaking stories: lots of cursing, crunching kicks, broken harnesses, broken wagons, and amazing feats of mule dexterity. Baldridge states in his journal that "there was kicking to the right of us, kicking to the left of us, and in front of us, and the man who was not an artful dodger was compelled to take a back seat." When it was all over, Baldridge also noted that "As an amusement it was one of the worst failures on record." John Bartlett, who led an expedition of the United States and Mexican Boundary Commission, wrote about similar experience with the animals: "There is no species of defense belonging to the horse, no stubbornness peculiar to the ass, but are concentrated in the mule. He possesses the bad qualities of his paternal and maternal progenitors, with the good traits of neither. The gentleness, docility, and instinct of the horse, are not found in the race; while the capricious obstinacy of his paternal ancestor is exhibited to the fullest extent." They were still better than horses. All the difficulties with mules were countered by their few positive traits. Strong and sure footed, they could endure fatigue and privation from long, tough trips with little food and water.[68]

The train was now ready to travel in "comfortable and easy wagon coaches along the line of our military posts, through San Antonio ... the route crosses the Continent in the mild regions of the 29th and 30th latitudes ascending gradually over the gently swelling uplands of Western Texas, through the delightful and cultivated country around El Paso."

6

CALIFORNIA GOLD RUSH: FRENCH'S EXPRESS PASSENGER TRAIN

Across Texas to El Paso

On June 15, the train lined up for departure. It must have been quite a sight to a passing traveler or nomadic Indian. There in front of them would have been brightly painted circus wagons with badly tamed, untrained, and probably skittish wild mules. Exhausted, bruised, and battered passengers tried to control the uneasy critters. "Imagine the scene," Lockwood said, "six wild mules harnessed and hitched to the coach, the driver on the saddle of the wheel mule, with a long rope around the neck of each of the six mules, and three men on the ground at the end of each rope." The train started its trek to El Paso del Norte on what was described as a wretched muddy road.[69]

"French was an engaging scoundrel, a complicated figure, something out of the picaresque past. He belonged to the generation that bred the buccaneers of trade, the Vikings of the stock exchange. He could well have tried conclusions with the freebooters of the Spanish Main had he not been born out of season. As it

was, his quarter-deck was the wagon box of a prairie schooner; his Caribbean was the dusty plains and plateaus of the Southwest; his towns for sack were the remote villages of the Sierra Madre. [70]

The Express Passenger Train immediately encountered difficulties with beast, man, and nature. Some recalcitrant mule teams had to be driven and couldn't keep up. Other more exuberant teams, despite the men on the ropes, could not be controlled. As stated by Baldridge: "We had runaways galore and smashups." Some wagons were destroyed and left behind. The train was widely separated and spread across the countryside. With little discipline and control, men wandered, went hunting, and lost track of time; they had to catch up or walk back. The wagon with the Goodbody men found itself well ahead of the caravan and had to wait for the others to catch up.

Everyone who separated soon went hungry; they also learned to stay with the commissary wagon. To add to the misery and torment of the tired and bruised bodies, it rained hard for most of the first three days. The overall progress was morale-sucking slow: just a few miles a day through the rain, swollen creeks, knee-deep mud, and missed routes, all compounded by suffering the attacks from millions of swarming mosquitos. Every day it took terrific effort just to get the green mules hitched to the wagons. Many of the poor animals were not used to work and were easily fatigued. Thinking it would be hard to get the mules started again in the abysmal conditions, the men were afraid to stop. The entire train finally reached Victoria on the night of June 22, having covered thirty some miles in eight days of brutal travel. The trip now takes about thirty minutes along route US 87.

French was not the only one who had problems with the unusually heavy rain, which made the already terrible terrain virtually impassable. Just weeks before, a train of 150 wagons and 250 Mexican carts tried to make their way along the same route; they negotiated the same quagmire and experienced similar delays, breakdowns, and frustrations. The merchant Benjamin Franklin Coons, leading the train, observed that "During the past ten days we have seen more water fall than I ever witnessed in the year previous." Within a couple of months, French would catch up to Coons and transact some business.[71]

After two days of rest and refitting, the expedition left again on Monday, June 24 to travel the more than 120 miles to San Antonio. Trumping his previous descriptions of terrible road conditions, Steele declared this one the "worst road we ever traveled." After crossing the Guadalupe River near Victoria, the men had to push their wagon most of the first day. Food ran short and teams were sent out to purchase provisions, but they were far from a market and none were available. Happenstance intervened as they discovered a small train of carts taking flour to market. Four barrels were bought, enough to get to San Antonio. For the next several days, they made good progress traveling over the rolling prairies.

The mostly uneventful days were punctuated with notable events. They broke more mules, which French brought into camp; the jury decided an assault and battery case; and there were rest days with hunting, fishing, and relaxing. After crossing Coleto Creek and passing through rough country and "dreadful" roads, Steele reported the men and mules were again exhausted and "jaded out." A day of rest and recovery was spent encamped on "a handsome little hill."

On June 29, they started again, over "one of the

most magnificent rolling prairies ... that man has
ever beheld ... the most beautiful country in the
world." Over the next several days, the trekkers
were fortunate to have cool weather and good travel
conditions through an area of increasing population
with scattered farms. Stopping in the village of Goliad,
they noted the scene of the 1836 massacre of Colonel
Fannin's surrendered force by the Mexican Army. The
expedition made great time, and there was little for the
men to do except ride in the wagons or walk alongside.
Andrew Steele, the Goodbody brothers, and Michael
McGuire had time to visit farms, buy meals and
snacks, and have "an interesting conversation with two
beautiful young ladies on the pleasures of matrimony."
The only comedown for the expedition was the injury
to Captain French after he was thrown from his
horse and laid up. On July 4, Steele, McGuire, and
the Goodbody boys left on horseback for San Antonio
through more fine country. Their conversation turned
to home and family, how they might be spending the
Fourth of July, and the "fond hopes" they would be
able to join them the next year. After staying the night
at a Mexican Rancho on the banks of Salado Creek,
the men arrived in San Antonio on July 5, a city Steele
described as a "miserable assemblage of ruinous half
built dirty houses." He then described the river as the
"most beautiful stream of water I have seen since I left
Lower Canada." On July 6, the train caught up, passed
through San Antonio and encamped two miles west
of the city at San Pedro Springs: "a great curiosity ...
the most voluminous springs I ever have seen." It took
a full thirteen days to complete the trip from Victoria.
One can now drive from Victoria through Goliad to San
Antonio in a little more than two hours.

Soon after reaching San Antonio, an agent
representing New Orleans creditors arrived; he
intended to arrest Captain French for presenting
worthless and rejected drafts. Parker French was

horrified at whom he said was a swindling New
Orleans merchant with whom he deposited a large
sum of money. He was an "injured, persecuted man"
who offered to give up temporary custody of his whole
train—lock, stock, and barrel—while he straightened
out the mess. Still displaying great disbelief and
indignation at the failure of his backer to pay the
drafts, he presented a sweeping letter of credit
from Howland and Aspinwall, one of the wealthiest
merchant and shipping firms in New York. French
also showed an order from the War Department
urging commanders of all posts in Texas to provide,
at cost, supplies he might require. Now convinced of
the captain's honesty and legitimacy, and that a great
injustice had been done, the man from New Orleans
accepted new drafts on Howland and Aspinwall,
offered profuse apologies for the embarrassment and
inconvenience, and left satisfied at the completion of
his mission.[72]

While in San Antonio, the open and wide-ranging
letter of credit from Howland and Aspinwall, as well
as the War Department authorization, would open
more doors and ingratiate French with city fathers.

"Parker H. French Esq.

Dear Sir—Your favor of this morning has
been received and duly considered. In reply,
we authorize you to draw upon us at any time
within the next six months, in sums to suit your
convenience. We have the confidence that you
will use this important trust discreetly, and with
many wishes for the success of your enterprise,
we remain,

Your friends, (Signed) Howland and
Aspinwall"

French's Express Passenger Train took some time in San Antonio to reorganize, resupply, refit, and rest. For French, business and socializing were an important and complementary mix. With his impressive documents, he became a "hail fellow well met" with the merchants of San Antonio, as well as the army officers posted at the headquarters of the Department of Texas, the largest and most important command in the army at the time.

The way French treated his challenger from Victoria impressed his new partners in San Antonio and completely satisfied them of his integrity, business acumen, and ability to comply with his contracts. The letter of credit from the well-known and respected firm Howland and Aspinwall further reinforced the impression. And because the New York backer trusted French with virtually unlimited drafts, those drafts suddenly rose in importance and value. Everyone sought to obtain French drafts. Merchants were anxious to sell goods for them; the army officers were willing to receive them for what they could spare.

The biggest San Antonio merchant and freighting enterprise was named Lewis and Groesbeck; the firm had a very lucrative business line supplying army outposts, accommodating travelers venturing along the El Paso trail, and supplying northern Mexico. Brothers-in-law Daniel Lewis and John Groesbeck were old hands who arrived in Texas in the 1830s and built substantial businesses before partnering in San Antonio. Lewis served as a scout in the Texas Army and was a member of the Congress of the Republic of Texas. He established San Antonio's first gristmill, was an early real estate promoter and developer, and was the first large-scale cattleman in the region. He owned herds from San Antonio to the coast. Groesbeck was a banker, merchant, and supplier to

several army frontier posts. He and business partner
Lewis published the first San Antonio newspaper, the
West Texan.

John Groesbeck was famous for lavish
entertainment and would have been right in the
middle of wining and dining French. His house
was magnificent with terraced gardens, Dutch
tile fireplaces, massive antique furniture, carved
wooden doors, and stained-glass windows and
decorations. French drew extensively on the Howland
and Aspinwall letter of credit to buy supplies and
livestock sold by the firm, at preferential government
prices. Most importantly, he filled his commissary
wagons with food, remounted his security force,
and restocked his herds with both mules and cattle.
Newspapers reported the total drafts as valued at
$10,000 (2017 estimate, $301,000).[76,77,78]

The army officers, including Commanding Officer
Major General Brooke, wined and dined French as
well, loaned him a carriage, and partied with him
and the merchants. Three of the officers would play
prominently in Parker French's future: Ordnance
Officer Lieutenant James Benton, Assistant Chief
Quartermaster Major E.B. Babbitt, and Commissary
of Subsistence Major James Longstreet, of later
Confederate fame. With the concurrence of Major
General Brooke, under the Department of War
authorization and with the letter of credit, the three
sold French excess weapons, supplies, and surplus
food. As the ordnance officer, Lieutenant Benton
sold, likely happily, some obsolete weapons along
with buck and ball cartridges. What little French
did get in the way of food was the source of some
disappointment; scattered western posts typically had
little enough for their own use. The army provided
and French accepted condemned hardtack, which
came alive with weevils; it was, Baldrige said, "old

enough to have died a natural death" but "was full of life and particularly objectionable to those who were opposed to a mixed diet." French paid for it all with three drafts totaling almost $1,990 (2017 estimate, $60,000).[79,80]

For the first couple of days encamped near San Antonio, everyone was busy repairing wagons, wheels, and leather gear while preparing for the long trip to El Paso. With lessons learned from the arduous, unorganized, and ill-disciplined trek from Lavaca, Captain French acted and established rules and regulations for the rest of the trip. To centralize and control the food supply, he established a commissariat to buy, store, and distribute food to the wagons. Knowing the expedition would soon enter territory controlled by Comanches and Apaches, he established rules for standing guards, scouting, and patrols. It appeared they would need the increased security. Just a few days before, Major General Brooke had received a message from Major Sprague at Las Moras springs, west of Fort Inge, reporting "hostile Indians are all around us, requiring vigilance to avoid surprise and to prevent their stealing our cattle and horses."[81]

Map of the Southern Military Road between San Antonio and El Paso del Norte. The French Expedition followed several days behind the United States Army expedition led by Major John Sprague on the southern route. Ben Pingenot, *The Great Wagon Train Expedition of 1850.*

Everything was soon in order for restarting the trip, but day after day the expedition remained encamped. The men started grumbling about Parker French having a grand time, conducting business, and socializing with the community leaders. The mules were fine; they were just contentedly grazing. The men, however, were again angry and frustrated at the prolonged delays. The train had now been gone almost sixty days from their departure from New York City; they were still some 650 miles from El Paso and half a continent from San Francisco. The men started wondering if they would ever get to San Francisco and pondered the $5 per day default that French would owe them. There may have been a good reason for the delay. Just a couple of weeks ahead of them, an army resupply train commanded by Major John Sprague followed the same intended route. The Sprague outfit was huge: 1,800 mules, 500 cattle, 450 civilians, and 175 soldiers heading for El Paso. The train included a contingent of merchants from San Antonio such as Benjamin Coons, who had partnered with Lewis and Groesbeck. The watering spots they would need, many supplied by weak springs, would require time to replenish before French's train could pass through.

The planned route to El Paso was already well-known and heavily traveled. After Texas was annexed to the United States as the twenty-eighth state and the Treaty of Guadalupe Hidalgo established the Rio Grande as the international border, the transportation link between San Antonio and El Paso became critical. The gold rush increased the requirement for protected immigrant travel and commercial freighting. Early immigrant groups entered a mostly unmapped area, pioneering new routes; San Antonio businessmen, Texas Rangers, and army survey parties also reconnoitered. After a relatively short time, the best route was established by the spring of 1849.

French's Express Passenger Train would follow in the footsteps of these pioneers. After leaving San Antonio, the train would head due west through Fort Lincoln and the settlements of Castroville, Quihi, and Vandenburg, cross the Frio River near Sabinal, and stop at Fort Inge on the Leona River. Crossing the Nueces River, the route took them some seventy-five miles to the Devils River crossing, now flooded by Lake Amistad. Snaking up the Devils River and its eighteen crossings, they would follow the general path of current Texas Route 163. Then crossing some eighty miles of mostly dry country, they would reach the Pecos River Crossing. From there it was another 350 miles to El Paso, following the route through Comanche Springs, Leon Springs, Wild Rose Canyon, and Painted Comanche Camp (later the site of Fort Davis). After traversing dry and desolate terrain with undependable springs, they would head to the Rio Grande River through Eagle Spring and Canon de los Lamentos (later known as Quitman Pass). They would then visit all the small riverside communities on the way to El Paso. The army would have likely provided meticulous directions along with detailed locations of watering holes, good grazing areas, and river crossing sites.[82]

Just the previous year, a huge train under the command of Major Jefferson Van Horne had proven the viability of the route for large expeditions. The Van Horne command included six companies of the Third Infantry, 275 wagons, and 2,500 animals and completed the 650-mile trip in exactly 100 days. Smaller trains had negotiated the route in as little as sixty days.

For the first 200 miles, French's train transited a splendid hill country, rich with productive farms and prosperous communities, mostly of hard working and thrifty German immigrants. The residents concentrated in small villages and farm settlements, primarily for protection against raiding Comanches. The slowness of the pace, caused somewhat by damaged wagons, still angered some men, especially on a road Steele described as "smooth and handsome." Along the way, when they were delayed in camp, they enjoyed fresh fruit, eggs, and butter peddled by the local German women. Periodic alarms were raised, and livestock was stolen.

Albert Pettis died near Quihi, apparently of natural causes, and Abraham Goodrich was severely injured when he became entangled getting off a wagon and was run over by the wheels. On July 25, the train reached Fort Inge and encamped in an oak grove on the banks of the beautiful Leona River. The train had traveled seventy-eight miles from San Antonio in about ten days. Twenty men decided to leave and make their own way to Mazatlán.

Back on the Seco River, about sixty miles from San Antonio, Parker French wrote a letter to the *New York Herald.* He wrote:

"You will much oblige me and my company of two hundred and twenty-five men, if you will give this letter an insertion in your valuable paper. We have had many adverse circumstances to overcome—the irregularity of the steamers in reaching Texas, the bad faith of agents sent out to prepare the way before us, and the prolonged heavy rains that are unusual at this season, are the main causes that have retarded our progress. All those we have overcome and are now on our journey thirty miles beyond Castroville, the frontier town on this route. We average twenty miles every day. The health of the company is good. We have had one death thus far—that was Albert

Pettis of New York, who died yesterday of an affliction of the heart; his health had been bad since he left home. We buried him by the wayside, at a place called Quihi. My company, when I left New York, numbered one hundred and twelve men; it now numbers two hundred and twenty-five. If we find gold on the Gila, we will colonize, and at all events we will winter there. I will write you again from El Paso.

Yours, Parker H. French"

The expedition had not averaged "twenty miles per day." French reported being 30 miles past Castroville which is less than 30 miles from San Antonio, but French wrote the letter on July 22, eight travel days after leaving San Antonio. Perhaps French was forecasting what he wanted to accomplish. For the first time, rather than discussing possibilities, he was much more definitive about the Gila. "We <u>will</u> colonize" and "we <u>will</u> winter." None of the journals indicate that he ever communicated that decision to the men or asked for their input. He held it close to the vest.[83]

French was sitting near his headquarters tent on the banks of the Leona River with the cook and dining tents nearby. A dusty and obviously angry traveler rode up. French recognized the man immediately, rushed forward, and shook his hand: "Why Burns, my dear fellow, I am so delighted to see you and know you have decided to go to California with me. Here, cook, get Mr. Burns a nice meal, I know he must be tired and hungry. Pedro, take the gentleman's horse, unsaddle and water him and stake him in good grass. I declare, Burns, this is an unexpected pleasure." (Burns was one of the stock raisers from whom

French bought mules in Victoria.) After dinner, Burns brought up the subject of payment: "Mr. French, I sent your draft to Messrs. Burbank and Fisher, and it came back protested, stating that you had no funds there."

French was flabbergasted. "Why Mr. Burns," he said, "I will show you their letter to me, authorizing me to draw on them for any amount needed to equip my expedition."

French promptly produced the letter, saying he was hurt and mortified over the "conduct of these gentlemen." Assuring Burns that he would not lose anything, French then produced the letter of credit from Howland and Aspinwall. He provided a new draft to the very happy and satisfied Burns, who was soon on his way back to Victoria.[84]

After a day of rest and refitting, the train crossed the Nueces and made good time over the next couple of days as they headed for Devils River. Many of the men were sick from "Bilious fever and the ague," likely showing symptoms of nausea, vomiting, diarrhea, chills, fever, and sweating. A doctor who French had recruited in San Antonio proved useful.

Two men were caught sleeping at their posts; they were brought up on charges in front of the jury, who adjudicated the punishment of six lashes each. Captain French had the sentence executed.

For the first time, the men noted that there was poor grass near the campsites because of Major Sprague's huge train just a couple of weeks ahead of them. Soon they had their first Indian alarm. At Las Moras Springs, the train was woken at daybreak by gunfire all around the camp; Indians were attempting to steal livestock and were driven off by the guards. A good part of the day was spent gathering up scattered mules and cattle; Baldridge described seeing Indians in "great numbers." This was the same area from which Major Sprague had sent his alerting message to Major General Brooke in early July. The train arrived at Devils River the night of July 31, crossed it, and camped on the west bank. From San Antonio, the train had traveled about 160 miles in fifteen days.

For the next six days, they would twist and turn crossing and re-crossing Devils River. On the first day, the men did a little touring, visiting the Painted Caves (now submerged by the Amistad Reservoir). Continuing up what Steele called the "most God-forgotten rockiest road man ever traveled" along the river, the livestock had a terrible time walking on the sharp flint rock, ruining their hoofs and leaving a trail of blood. Some had to be left behind. A one-day break was had, for resting repairing wagons and fishing (fishing broke the monotony of the travel in the deep canyon with barren rock walls). It had been a trip through, as Steele described it, "mountainous dreary looking country." Soon, they crossed fresh Indian trails, putting the men on alert. They reached the head of Devils Canyon at Beaver Lake on August 6.

With the next water some forty miles away at Howard Springs, the train traveled in the cool of the first night to help the mules tolerate the heat. By the time the springs were reached on August 8, the normally enduring mules were suffering badly. The expedition paused at what was called a first-rate watering place, though the feed was poor due to the train in front of them.

After a two-day rest, during which they hunted for twenty-eight stolen mules, they again passed over waterless country with the mules having no water for two days. Live Oak Creek, with great water, provided a respite from the harsh trip. While there, Captain French wrote a letter to Lewis and Groesbeck, it was published nationwide:

*"I have at length got within a few miles of
your train and tomorrow expect to pass the
Pecos on your bridge. We are all well and
contented, except myself. I am discontented
because the thieving Lipans (Apaches) night
before last stole twenty-eight mules and four
horses, besides some cattle. I sent my ranging
company after them and recovered three; I think
we will recover all of them as they are still in
hot pursuit. They were stolen from us while at
Howard's Spring. We are now able to make
our twenty miles a day and will travel from
the Pecos onward much faster than we came
here."*[85]

French never found the rest of his twenty-eight
mules. The Indians raided for livestock again but
were thwarted by the guards' alarm and the response
from the camp. On August 11, Captain French left
the train and caught up with Sprague and Coons
on the west side of the Pecos River. French brought
welcome mail from home and induced Sprague to
authorize Coons to sell him flour, coffee, and sugar.
French paid Coons a draft of $500. Coons also agreed
to sell French all the provisions he needed until the
expedition reached El Paso.

The Pecos River crossing was just a few miles
away, and it was crossed on August 12. The
expedition had now traveled almost halfway from San
Antonio to El Paso, completing 300 miles in twenty-
eight days. Using an iron bridge left by the army, as
well as a ford downstream, they were able to cross the
river in about three hours rather than the expected
three days. The river had been held up to them as
the only formidable obstacle between Port Lavaca
and El Paso. The expedition traveled along the course
of the brackish Pecos and, on August 13, caught up
with the Coons train. Coons was no longer traveling

with army protection. Fearing a lack of water on the southern route, he decided to make his own way to El Paso along the northern or "upper" route.

One morning a tragic accident resulted in the death of a young man named Chamberlain. Caleb Thurston returned from overnight guard duty and was removing the percussion cap. The weapon went off and the ball hit Chamberlain in the stomach, lodging in his spine. The well-liked young man died quickly and was mourned by all in the camp, including his father who "wept most bitterly ... with convulsive sobs." A jury was empaneled and gave a verdict of accidental death with which the father concurred.

The expedition continued to travel slowly along with Coons, hampered by damaged wagons, exhausted, lost, and stolen livestock, and bad water. On August 19, after moving at night to avoid the heat, the train finally reached Comanche Springs, the present city of Fort Stockton. It took eight days to travel the eighty-one miles from the Pecos River crossing. Taking advantage of the abundant fresh, clear water, the expedition remained for the next two days, repairing wagons and resting men and livestock.

Parker French visited Coons again and came back to camp with eighteen wagons, 176 mules and two horses; he had bought them from Coons the previous day for $17,721 (2017 estimate, $530,000) with a draft from Howland and Aspinwall. French also made a deal with Coons for 125 mules deliverable in El Paso at $100 each. They also contracted for delivery of corn for another $8,500. To secure against default on the drafts, Coons demanded what amounted to a lien on the entire French train; French gave Coons a bill of sale for his Express Passenger Train with the understanding that the train would be transferred back to French when the drafts were honored. The provisions of the transfer are interesting since it details an inventory of the expedition: 20 wagons, 148 mules, 3 horses, 214 harnesses, 120 rifles, 100 revolvers, a portable forge, and miscellaneous supplies and provisions. French kept the bill of sale secret from his men.[86,87]

About the same time back in New York, newspapers exploded with news of a great fraud and forgery. On August 17, drafts for expenses in New Orleans as well as for the mules and supplies in Texas were presented to Howland and Aspinwall. The firm rejected the $30,000 draw, saying the letter of credit was a forgery. The firm had neither given Mr. French any such letter nor authorized him to draw upon them in any manner. More drafts arrived from Texas and were likewise rejected. One telegram reported a stolen draft of $20,000 and requested a stop of the payment. New York City newspapers reported the fraud the next week, and the news spread rapidly by telegraph. The shock was soon keenly felt in New Orleans as early as August 27 when it was reported in the *Times Picayune*. Merchants and ranchers in Galveston, Lavaca, Victoria, and San Antonio, as well as the army officers, would all have to wait for their shock later in September as the jolting news was couriered into Texas. The abused captain of the steamship *Palmetto* was out his $150. The total reported drafts to August 18 were over $92,000 with a 2017 value of about $2.75 million. There must have been additional unreported frauds.

While in camp on the night of August 20, Lipan Indians attempted another raid; one was killed by one of French's rangers. Return fire from the Indians, indicating a large party, initiated a wild turmoil in the camp. "All hands rushed furiously in every direction, discharging their rifles and pistols into the tall grass and clumps of bushes. They killed no Indians, however and strange to say, did not kill each other." Fearing continued attacks, additional guards were positioned, but the rest of the night was peaceful.[88]

The expedition broke camp on August 22 and traveled with no incidents through Leon Springs, Barilla Draw, and Limpia Creek to Wild Rose Pass. The train made good progress over the next three days, traveling fifty-six miles. At midnight of August 24, the expedition arrived in beautiful Wild Rose Pass where they camped in a narrow valley, the "highest and most picturesque" of any they had yet seen. Texas Highway 17 now follows the historic route through the pass. The men passed the next four days, resting and refitting as well as lolling about and grumbling about the slow pace.

Wild Rose Pass, 1857. Photo of print held by Library of Congress.

Leaving the Wild Rose Pass encampment early on August 29, the train passed through the narrow gorges of the rest of the pass to Painted Comanche Camp (site of the future Fort Davis). For the next several days, the train moved mostly at night to avoid the scorching sun, traveling through rough country with few water holes that frequently were not sufficient. With food supplies running low, necessitating rationing, the men resorted to hunting prairie dogs. The sixty-day promise well past due, the slow pace fed continuing and increasing disgruntlement, and more Indians were stalking their route. The expectation of the "pleasure trip" had finally turned to anger and resentment, especially at Parker French with his arbitrary and dictatorial manner. He would not accept any suggestions about movement plans or organization nor listen to any complaints. The unhappiness was deep and intense.

On September 2, the situation came to a head with a tough Texan named Durand, who was the wagon master of the train French bought from Coons. Instead of traveling at night, French wanted Durand to press forward under the blazing sun to the next water. Durand refused to move before the cool of the evening, and French could not tolerate any question of his authority. An argument started, and French dropped his hand to his revolver. Durand drew his weapon "in a flash"; French feigned being the injured party and rebuked Durand about the drawn weapon. "Mr. French," Durand said, "we have lived a long time in a country where we are never without these playthings, and we never allow a stranger to take the first shot if we have half a shot. If you want to talk to me, you must take your hand off your pistol. We never make such a move as you made just now unless we mean business."

Captain French left temporarily but returned, determined to reclaim his authority. He stood over a reclining Durand with a drawn pistol, again directing him to immediately move out. "You must be a brave man," Durand said with a deadly look, "if you came here to assassinate me, why don't you shoot? But if you do, see that you make sure work, for if I live two seconds you are a dead man." Adding, "I have had enough of this nonsense," Durand then challenged

French to a gunfight to settle the matter. Of course, French declined but then attempted to discharge Durand from his job; the teamsters refused to move without their leader. French had to have the last bombastic word: "I have with me a large company of men whose welfare depends upon me. I must attend to them at present; I will attend to you at the earliest opportunity."[89]

That afternoon saw the departure of some Illinois boys, including Andrew Steele, Michael McGuire, and the Goodbody brothers; they were also tired of the "nonsense" and decided to continue to California on their own hook. They would have their own adventures before meeting back up with the expedition at the little community on the American side of El Paso Del Norte. Some called the little settlement "Franklin" after Benjamin Coons's middle name.

After the Illinois and Goodbody boys left on their own, the train would continue through Eagle Springs and the almost impenetrable mountains to the Rio Grande River. There was a false warning of 900 Indians waiting in ambush. Friendly Indians came to the camp to trade, and Captain French illegally traded liquor for a horse. The trail covering some sixty miles to the river crossed a mostly waterless landscape with little forage. To get to the river they had to negotiate the last obstacle of the "pleasure trip," Canon de los Lamentos. Exhausted men had to drive emaciated mules, pulling worn out wagons over the nearly impassable road. After reaching the river, the expedition slowly moved up the north bank of the Rio Grande.

French proposed that the expedition cross into Mexico early before reaching El Paso. He was likely planning to evade all his creditors and the clutch of the law; he especially did not want to meet up with

Coons. But acting to guard against this eventuality, Coons had given clear written instructions to his men to follow the lower route to El Paso and not deviate from it. On the way up the Rio Grande, French purchased supplies and provisions worth several thousand dollars with worthless drafts. He also concealed a large amount of supplies, which he had diverted from the Coons-owned stocks.

The Express Passenger Train, now with 230 men, struggled into El Paso on September 18. It had now been over four months since leaving New York City and a little over sixty days from San Antonio. The frustration, dissension, and exasperation on the trail exposed a common problem when leaders overpromise, forecast fanciful progress, and engender unreasonable expectations; immutable reality intrudes, resulting in low morale and loss of confidence in leadership. French had promised a sixty-day schedule for transport all the way to San Francisco; at the time, it would take at least sixty days just to trek from San Antonio to El Paso. The rough terrain, shortage of watering and grazing spots, need to rest the mules and the repair of damaged wagons all conspired to constrain travel at no more than an average of about ten miles per day. The sixty-day trip from San Antonio to El Paso should have been expected.

Andrew Steele described El Paso or "Franklin": "There was a garrison of 2 companies, the barracks are composed of mud walls, the roofs are flat as in Mexico. There are several other houses built adobe fashion with soldiers' tents scattered ... there is only one store at the station. Altogether it is a very mean looking concern and as we had heard so much talk of the place our anticipations were considerably blasted. Provisions clothing and everything for sale goes at enormous prices. We bought some of the most delicious grapes and peaches I ever ate. They grow here to perfection and on the Mexican side of the river in every quantity."

French had ridden ahead of the train and reached El Paso a couple of days earlier; he wanted to make deals to try to reconstitute his tired and broken outfit. He was met by an angry and suspicious Coon who had received word that French had tried to cross the Rio Grande. Coons was still willing to deliver the contracted mules and corn and complete the complex deal for wagons and mules, but now he wanted to defer delivery until he received a confirmation letter from San Antonio. French knew that if he waited for the letter, the jig was up.

He tried another approach to salvage the situation by targeting James Magoffin, a long-time southwest and northern Mexico merchant. Impressing both army officers and Magoffin with his demeanor of confidence and competence, French reinforced those notions with his apparently unlimited line of credit from Howland and Aspinwall. Baldridge asserted, repeated by some historians, that French made a deal for $20,000 worth of supplies and equipment as well as a purchase for 125 mules from Magoffin for $80,000. He was also allegedly trying to negotiate a deal for $200,000 worth of mules, possibly to drive them to California for sale. These amounts were either apocryphal or hyperbolized, or a simple publication error misplacing a decimal point. If French bought 125 mules for $80,000, the cost per mule would have been a wildly exorbitant $640 each. For comparison, during the period 1849-1861, the army bought 1,609 mules for $84,700, an average of $52 per mule. Contemporary newspapers later reported the attempted fraud in El Paso was for $35,000, rather than $100,000 as published by Baldridge.[90,91]

(In one of those fascinating twists of history,

James Magoffin and Parker French would become relatives by marriage. James Magoffin was a native of Harrodsburg Kentucky, one of the centers of Parker French's maternal Hardin family. James' brother, Beriah Magoffin, was the future Kentucky governor; his daughter would marry Charles A. Hardin. Charles was the son of French's namesake Uncle Parker Calhoun Hardin, and French's younger foster brother.)

Expedition passengers soon learned of French's machinations with Coons, especially the bill of sale for their train; the troubling information fed the growing fear and nervous distrust of the captain. Then the gigantic scheme was exposed. The foundation of chicanery, fraud, and forgery buckled, and the whole rotten edifice collapsed.

On September 19, after riding hard for six days from San Antonio, express rider Henry Skillman galloped into town carrying an arrest warrant for Parker H. French and an order to seize the train. He also carried a letter from Howland and Aspinwall denying the legitimacy of the letter of credit and rejecting all drafts against them. Creditors had come out of the woodwork with letters protesting the fraud and demanding payment. The total known claims amounted to almost $170,000 with a 2017 value of over $5 million. Many more drafts may have been rejected at each locality as the fraud against Howland and Aspinwall was made public. A new name was added to the lengthy list of creditors from New Orleans, Galveston, Victoria, San Antonio, and the trail. James Fisk of San Antonio had a bill of sale for the entirety of French's train; Fisk's claim predated that of Coons. The news of the second lien on the train must have really dismayed and riled the already alarmed passengers.

After being arrested, Parker French escaped and

slipped across the Rio Grande; he was safe from both future arrest and the pursuit of creditors. Staying in the Mexican town, French would continue to cause trouble with demands for "his" property.

Both Magoffin and Coons moved immediately to try to seize their property with limited success. Newspapers reported losses of $4,000 for Magoffin and $12,000 for Coons. Expedition members immediately returned the recently purchased 125 mules to Magoffin while quickly moving to protect their interests. They elected Goodbody's friend and neighbor Michael McGuire as the "sheriff" and appointed three others as his assistants. McGuire gave two options for the expedition members: they could cross into Mexico or place themselves under the protection of Major Van Horne. The company chose going into Mexico and quickly moved what they could of the train and livestock across the river. Major Van Horne was released from his disagreeable duty to seize the train from the exhausted men. Very sympathetic to the plight of the immigrants, who were "wholly destitute of means," Van Horne had told representatives of the expedition his position on the private conflict; a legal levy on the property could only be executed by a sheriff, and, there was no sheriff within 100 miles. As long as the expedition did not interfere with the execution of some legal process, Van Horne would not interfere. Now in Mexico without passports or customs clearance, the expedition was soon detained by the Mexican Army and customs officials who impounded all the property as contraband. The problem was resolved quickly by one of two means, or perhaps both: a Mason in the expedition talked to the local Alcade who was a fellow Mason fraternity member; and/or Michael McGuire, as a Catholic, got help from a Father Ramon Ortiz.[92,93]

McGuire also secured a strongbox that was

expected to hold expedition fee proceeds in gold worth at least $37,000 (2017 estimate, $910,000). The box was found to be empty; French's servant said that it had been empty for a long time, the cash presumably in a New Orleans bank.

After receiving multiple demands from French to return all the property, as well as the herd of mules and cattle, the company decided to gather all the train property, corral the mules and guard the cattle. They would have a public auction. A committee was appointed to hold the sale and properly distribute the proceeds to creditors. The men asserted the right to have priority of payment ahead of all other creditors. The claims from the 230 men who reached El Paso may have been as high as $50,000, just for their payment to French for passage. The committee first had to determine the claims of the men. Each had paid an expedition fee of either $250 or $100; French had borrowed money from some men, so claims ranged from the minimum of $100 to $700. The property was then appraised and the items marked, even mules were chalked on the shoulder with their appraised price. The committee reserved all the property that might be used by the men, such as tents, harnesses, tools, saddles, and packs. All mules, some of them emaciated and worthless, were also held back from the auction. Everything left was sold at public auction. There was actually little of value after the three-month trip from Lavaca; wagons and equipment were worn out, and the remaining livestock emaciated and exhausted. After the auction was complete, the returns were meager. Only about 20 percent of the passenger claims could be paid. Each man had proceeds of about $40 to buy mules, at $15 to $40 per mule, as well as equipment and provisions. The narratives are silent on what livestock, equipment and supplies were left after the auction and distribution to the men. Perhaps most of it was worthless.[94]

The expedition broke apart. As the men received their new property, they left as quickly as they could and scattered. Some remained in El Paso or other places in Texas; some returned home; others continued to California along the original route, and others headed to Guaymas on the Gulf of California. Others, like the Lake County Illinois boys, including the Goodbody brothers, traveled through Mexico to Mazatlán and then to California by sea. Still others, including French's lieutenant North West, remained loyal to French and joined him.

In Mexico, Parker Hardin French would undertake a new multifunctional period in his career. For the next twenty-two months, he would be a predator on his former train passengers, a bandit robbing Mexican travelers and silver shipments, an inmate in a Durango prison, and a celebrated military leader fighting against Comanche and Apache Indians.

7

ADVENTURES IN MEXICO

With his letter of credit fraud exposed, his credibility shattered, and the "French's Express Train" defunct, the "captain" was left with few assets and little to command. Seven men remained loyal, and they were both train members and recently recruited frontier toughs: mysterious and stalwart second "North West," Joseph Dawson; Robert Trimm, a shipmate of French as a youngster; Harry Britt; Chris Steiner; Bob Lockridge; and "Ramrod" Harris. Harris was credited by Dawson for bringing the order from San Antonio to arrest French; perhaps he rode with Skillman. French convinced the men that he had been badly treated by his sponsors in New York and New Orleans. He reassured his new gang that he had shipped a lot of merchandise to both Mazatlán and San Francisco and had money he could access in both places. And, if awkward news did not reach the cities of Mexico before him, French still had the letters of credit from Howland and Aspinwall, as well as the merchants of New Orleans. French's little command left the El Paso area to exploit any opportunities he could find in Mexico.

Newspapers would follow his exploits over the next twenty-two months, even merchants got involved as they advertised their products:

"Parker French the now noted robber of Texas and Mexico, is not dead but alive and off again. If people of irritable temperaments would use good tea, in the place of vile brandies and gins there would be fewer robbers and villains generally. A good cup of tea is a great luxury, if you only get a fine article and for this purpose, go or send to Reddings & Co.'s China Tea Store. Their Hyson, Ningyong, Oolong and Imperial teas are great luxuries for a little money."[95]

Captain Parker French's first task was to reclaim "his" property. He knew that anyone continuing to California would likely pass through Corralitos, a little town about 160 miles from El Paso that had grown up around a mining operation. Shortly after leaving El Paso, according to Baldridge, French started robbing small parties of his former passengers, taking mules, weapons, and the little money they had. He purportedly declared himself "Captain of the Guerilla Band" and said he was "above all law, for here there is none; and is determined to wash his hands in the blood of the officers of the 'distribution'." He even stole a mule from Abraham Goodrich, still crippled from being run over by wagon wheels. Arriving in Corralitos in the first week of October, the guerilla band reclaimed some of French's "property" with intimidation, at the point of a gun. Spafford Rounds was stripped of his coat, which French auctioned off to his men.[96]

Late in the afternoon of October 9, another twelve-man party, led by David Cooper, set up camp near a small creek about a half mile from the town. Cooper had found the site and triggered a single gunshot, which signaled the rest of the party that he had found a good place to bed down. What happened next is an interesting study in witness testimony; there were multiple stories recounting the event, which became known as the "Gunfight at Corralitos."

Spafford Rounds heard the sound and came to the camp to warn the group of French's predations. The shot also alerted French of their arrival. The twelve men in Cooper's party were well armed, all with revolvers and all, except for one, with rifles.

The French guerilla band, which was also well-armed, suddenly rushed the camp: "On they came, charging upon us at full speed, whooping and yelling like so many savages." In their journals, Charles Cardinell, David Cooper, John Holmes, and Michael Baldridge all reported different accounts of how the skirmish began, how it progressed, and who shot whom. Another account by French loyalist Joseph Dawson, gives a completely contradictory version. He asserted that French had been approached by some of his Express Train passengers, who protested that Cooper's group had taken an unfair proportion of the train. French, as Dawson claimed, merely visited Cooper's camp trying to peacefully arbitrate the dispute; Cooper, Dawson asserted, had fired the first shot and wounded French, instigating the melee.

There were several who claimed to have shot French: David Cooper shot him in the side, the same one-ounce ball shattered French's arm above the elbow, traveled through his forearm and hit his wrist on the way out; John Holmes shot him through the wrist, or the palm of the hand, with the ball exiting near the elbow, or he shot him in the side and broke his arm with the same ball; Daniel Wright was trying to kill French with a Bowie knife when he was killed by the shotgun, or the pistol, of "Ramrod" Harris, which also destroyed French's arm. What was consistent amongst all the stories was the ferocious fight, heavy and rapid gunfire, the lead flying in all directions, the mayhem and the deadly results. From the Cooper party, two men were killed and two wounded: Daniel E. Wright of Vermont rather than being killed by Harris' shotgun, was probably killed by French with a head shot; William J. Nelson of New Hampshire died from a bullet to the stomach; David Cooper of Ohio was wounded in the hip; and, John Holmes of Maine was shot in both arms. Cardinell noted: "French robbed us of our animals, and left us destitute. Graves were dug and our departed comrades were rolled in their blankets, and buried side by side on the spot where their blood was shed."[97]

There are two totally contradictory accounts of the post-clash situation and the treatment of Parker French's wounds. Fearing further trouble, the Alcade of Corralitos asked for help from the Mexican Army Post at Janos, twenty-five miles to the north. A detachment soon arrived to deter any further trouble. Cardinell reported that the Cooper group stayed around Corralitos for three days due to lack of mules; they were protected by a part of the Mexican unit posted at the entrance of the town to prevent a clash. With the help of the Alcade, the French band was convinced to return some of the seized mules. Joseph Dawson related that French was taken to the Corralitos hacienda of Don Jose Maria Zuloaga to be given rudimentary treatment. Dawson also declared that after the gunfight, somehow all the previous enemies in the gunfight became friends; the mules of the Cooper led group were returned voluntarily, with a measure of grace and reconciliation. He also purported that the former enemies organized together, fearing that the Mexican Army force from Janos would detain them all. A purported threat of a battle between the Americans and the Mexicans was only calmed by the intercession of Zuloaga, who vouched for the Americans.

An interview published in 1871 provided another storyline. Parker French was moved by his men to the Hacienda La Barranca Colorado owned by Don Louis Flotte. His wife Refugio McNight Flotte took French in and tried to make him comfortable. By chance an unnamed traveling adventurer arrived; he was a sometime Texas Ranger, Indian fighter, and former superintendent of mines for Flotte. He had some elemental medical skills that probably saved French's life:

> *"He was on a bed, with his right arm done up in a bloody sheet, evidently suffering, but suppressing the signs of it with astonishing power. I went to him and took a look at his arm, which he said must be amputated. All the while I was handling the shattered limb he kept his eyes fastened on me with a devouring eagerness which made me nervous ... I never saw fortitude like that man's."*

The samaritan worked on French's arm, which had been shattered above the elbow with torn bone and flesh extending into his forearm. He cut away the shredded tissue and tied up the artery but left several inches of protruding bone because he did not have an adequate saw. He bound up the stump with pulverized charcoal. The whole operation was completed with rudimentary painkillers, including quarts of mescal.[98]

At some point, the amateur surgeon showed French a document that a nearby group of his former passengers had prepared. It laid out the charges of forgery and fraud, describing him as a swindler. French told him a different tale: "I am not the forger and swindler there represented, as I can prove to you." He flavored the "proof" with a smattering of truth surrounded by creative fiction. French explained that he had been an officer supporting the Lopez expedition to Cuba, an operation aided by the influential and wealthy and "winked at" by the government. He had been given letters of credit by firms in New York and New Orleans to be used as needed. After the failure of the Cuban invasion, French claimed, he outfitted the expedition to California in New York, using the letters of credit and that the wealthy merchants dared not protest for fear of exposure. He also claimed that he had letters directing military posts to furnish him equipment. He left out the part that he had to pay for any excess and obsolete supplies. Of course, he averred the merchants tried to have him arrested, but they were only trying to reclaim the implicating documents, bring him back, and pay him off to keep quiet. Needing to escape from arrest forced the "temporary" abandonment of his train, and later, he was only trying to recover his rightful property from his thieving passengers. Then French blamed the Corralitos Alcade for not opening the gate of the corral holding his mules; when refused, French shot the lock. The fictional gunshot which destroyed the fictional lock prompted the gunfight. Of course, there was no corral, locked or otherwise. French claimed he "fought like a demon" and was immediately wounded. With his right arm shattered, he dragged himself along the ground, and while supporting himself on the mangled stump, he continued firing his revolver with his left hand. He had to at last give in, French lamented; the stronger party prevailed and went on with their spoils.

The Texas Ranger, Indian fighter, mine superintendent, and proud amateur surgeon was paid for his life-saving efforts by a worthless draft on Howland and Aspinwall.[99]

Whichever medical treatment was provided, French still needed to have more expert medical care, so he was packed off by mule to Chihuahua, almost 200 miles away. Zuloaga provided letters of introduction to the governor in Chihuahua, giving an account of the clash at Corralitos, absolving everyone of any illegality and asking that the party be given kind treatment. On the several-days-long trip, the pain was reported to be terrible with severe inflammation and swelling. Upon reaching Chihuahua and presenting their letter of introduction to the governor, they were directed to a Doctor Roger Dubois, a Frenchman who was also the French Consul in Chihuahua. The wound was badly gangrenous by the time they arrived and to save French's life, the doctor amputated French's arm.

The group stayed four to five weeks in Chihuahua waiting for French to recover. The stay must have been very pleasant. Dawson and Steele both extolled the city for the kindness of its citizens, the impressively massive Gothic cathedral, and the beautiful plaza with its living fountain of water—as well as its beautiful women, lively music, and dances.

News of French's fraud and forgeries in the United States had not yet reached Chihuahua, so the one-armed man was able to get some spending money on a Howland and Aspinwall draft. He negotiated additional drafts for $10,000 and waited for the money. Then there was unexpected and disturbing word that the drafts were refused; suspicions had been aroused. French found out that Ben Coons had freshly arrived from El Paso and had exposed French's previous frauds. The band hastily left for Durango the next day, carrying with them letters to the governor in Durango asking that the party be well received, and that all assistance be made to facilitate the journey to Mazatlán.[100]

On the over 300-mile journey from Chihuahua to Durango, French and party were reported as "making free use of the rancheros' mules, hogs and poultry" as they passed through what was described by several as a verdant and beautiful valley. Upon reaching Durango, he yet again produced letters of credit, but this time from merchants in Chihuahua. He defrauded merchants of some small amounts for spending money and was negotiating larger payouts against the Howland and Aspinwall letters of credit. With the letters of introduction from both Don Zuloaga and the governor in Chihuahua, he gained entry to the Governor and had several interviews. The subject became the settling of a colony of American immigrants on the Gila River. French agreed to protect the frontier from the Apaches and establish 2,000 American families within two years. The governor promised to exert his influence and to recommend providing $600,000 (2017 estimate, $18 million) for the grand project. Intending to visit the governor one day, French was refused entry, was informed that the governor would not see him, and was told not to return. Seeking his promised money, French next visited those who held the drafts. Payment was refused because unfavorable information had been received.

Upon investigation, French found the source of his troubles; it was his nemesis Benjamin Franklin Coons, who had just arrived in Durango. Vowing to shoot Coons the moment he could "set eyes upon him," French went looking. Meeting in a street, the pair exchanged shots, slightly wounding French in the already useless right shoulder; Coons' hat was holed.

The group left for Mazatlán but, as Joseph Dawson reported, a courier caught them and asked for their immediate return to Durango. The governor wanted their help in an operation against a Comanche raiding party of about 100 warriors, who had penetrated to the edge of Durango and had plundered large amounts of money, goods, horses, and mules. The French party joined a troop of Mexican cavalry and a number of American mercenaries. The pursuit caught the Comanches about twenty miles north of Durango; a skirmish resulted in three Comanche dead and many wounded. The raiders fled with their wounded and abandoned what was described as an immense herd of horses and mules. The resultant celebration, with "dances and bullfights galore," especially honored the one-armed Parker French, who was noted as leading the charge. His bravery and boldness won "the plaudits of the men and the hearts of the women." The governor asked the Americans to stay on, with offers of $100 a month and $350 per Comanche scalp. The French party declined and departed again for Mazatlán.

The 200-plus-mile route through the Sierra Madre mountains to Mazatlán was passable only by mules, horses, and men on foot. Andrew Steele described part of the route: "The narrow paths over which we had to travel today were of the most dangerous character, the least slip of our animals would have precipitated them into an abyss below, the bottom of which I dared not venture to look down." The modern route is called the "Espinazo del Diablo—the Devil's Backbone." The road is considered one of the most dangerous in the world.

El Espinazo del Diablo, "Devil's Backbone." The modern route through the Sierra Madre mountains between Durango and Mazatlán. The dangerous road is known for its steep slopes, hairpin turns, and deadly drop-offs.

As he was traveling, French noticed a choke point on the trail; a narrow pass had been cut for about a mile, through which men and animals could only pass in single file. Mexican Army guards and customs officers were posted at each end to control smuggling. French would use that intelligence soon.

Upon reaching Mazatlán, French found about 140 Americans with many men from his Express Train; they were waiting passage by ship or were marooned for lack of money. French deceived sixteen of his previous colleagues again. His ability to perform serial scams on the same men was astounding. He had an ability to appeal to the irrational in his victims— he met what they wanted to believe. Gathering all the money the men had, he announced that he had arranged ticketing on the steamship *Panama,* commanded by Captain James Watkins. Former personal secretary to French, Michael Baldridge, and two others, with no trust in French, made their own way to the ship and signed on as hands. The others, ecstatic to get passage, rowed small boats for the ship and produced their vouchers for passage. Captain Watkins informed them that he had made no such arrangement. Ironically, and probably to French's great gratification, the vessel was owned and operated by the Pacific Mail Steamship Company of which William Aspinwall and Gardiner Howland were the controlling owners. Probably thinking he had time to get away with the men's money, French had not yet left town when the men accosted him for his deceit. He apologized profusely for the "misunderstanding" and chartered a schooner. Since there would be a delay, he also agreed to pay for expenses, paying 25 cents per day per man to provide for meals and lodging (meals were only 5 cents each). Lockwood said, "In payment for the charter and provisions, French had given drafts on San Francisco. He was still at his old tricks; a combination of rascality and generosity I have never seen equaled."

The saga of the Lake County and Goodbody boys continued; they were not victimized by the latest Parker French scam because they were no longer in Mazatlán. The group had stayed together since the breakup in El Paso and had arrived in Mazatlán in mid-November but soon left. A group of eleven boarded the Mexican Bark *Guaymas* under Captain Saldonado for the four-week journey to San Francisco: Andrew Steele, Richard and Frank Goodbody, Michael McGuire, John McClory, Thomas Mackin, James and John Cole, James McBride, James Conlan, and John Crover; staying in Mazatlán were Michael Mines, Peter Gray, Patrick Kennedy, and Roger McCormick. Ten days out of San Francisco, on December 3, Richard Goodbody (the author of this book's great-great uncle) died after being sick for six days. Andrew Steele wrote that the last twenty hours, Richard was "totally insensible, his eyes would wander from object to object without any apparent consciousness, he heard nor heeded nothing that was said or done around him." He died with all his comrades gathered around his bed: "it was to me one of the most melancholy occurrences I ever had occasion to witness."

On December 6, Frank (the author's great grandfather) had the same symptoms and rapidly deteriorated. December 8, Steele wrote that Frank could not sit up and was not expected to recover. He lived to arrive with the *Guaymas* when it anchored in San Francisco bay on December 13, eight months after Frank Goodbody left Lake County, Illinois. Frank spent the next two years in the gold fields, being credited with a major discovery: the "Whiskey Diggings." He returned to Illinois with enough money to buy productive farm land in Lake County, as well as city property and a hotel in Waukegan. And he had some great stories.[101]

Parker French then turned to his next daring exploit. Some contemporaneous stories reported that he turned bandit against travelers, mail coaches, villages, and ranchos and was eventually run down and captured by the Mexican Army after a desperate and deadly fight. According to Joseph Dawson, French had a much more profitable target in mind. Remembering the narrow defile he had noted in the mountains, French resolved to plunder a mule train transporting silver, reported to be worth $200,000 (2017 estimate, $6 million).

He gathered twelve toughs, including the loyal North West, and headed into the mountains. He timed his attack on the defile to gain possession of the gap just before the mule train was to arrive. Surprising the guard at the west end, he took possession of the mouth of the cut. The intense fight resulted in multiple Mexican casualties including several killed. Leaving a rear security, he then moved to the east end and captured that guard with no shedding of blood. When the silver mule train arrived, they unknowingly walked into an ambush and were captured with no fight. French left the established trail and started for the west coast near Mazatlán, where he had arranged for a vessel to meet him and the silver. Managing to escape, some of the guard alerted the Mexican Army, which soon had a strong force of cavalry in pursuit. French had a sixty-mile head start, but he did not anticipate how slow a pack mule moves through rough terrain, especially when the animal was on an unknown route. The mule drivers also likely had a role in purposely delaying movement to the sea. After a forced march, the cavalry found and surrounded the bandits, and a brief but desperate struggle ensued, compelling French to surrender. Two were killed, including North West; French and three others were wounded.

Supporting Dawson's account, Michael Baldridge cited discussions with a physician who he had met in Mazatlán; the doctor confirmed the attack on the silver train. Both the detailed description in Dawson's account, and the consistent report by an independent source, support authenticity.

But, as in many times in Parker French's life, there is another story. A correspondent from Durango reported that French decided that the silver train was too well protected Abandoning his plans, he resorted to attacking small bands of travelers, ranchos, and villages.[102,103]

In mid-April 1851, based on a February 14 letter from a correspondent, the *New York Herald* reported that French and two others were hanged from the nearest trees, and the rest of his gang were shot. Newspapers throughout the nation picked up the story. The *Louisville Courier* especially lamented French's criminality and his death at the "hands of lynchers in Mexico." The paper reviewed his life to include his admirable start as a youth, his prospective potential, and his unfortunate descent into crime:

"The Late Parker H. French ... commenced those depredations upon society which has resulted in his paying the penalty ... by a death as ignominious as it was tragical. He seems from the beginning to have thrown off all moral restraint. ... To the crime of forgery, he soon added that of robbery and finally ended the catalogue of his transgressions by becoming a murderer. There survives him a wife, whose hopes on earth are crushed forever, and a lovely infant daughter, upon whom ... a cold and heartless world will cast its frowns on account of the sins of its father."[104,105]

The *New York Herald* soon corrected its own story and reported that Parker French and the rest of his gang were alive and in a Durango prison.

They reported that in fact "North West" had been killed; French and three others (Thomas Parker, William Arnold, and Peter Floyer) had been seriously wounded. Others incarcerated were John Jones, John English, Francis Lelay, and a "Negro George." There was speculation that the whole party would be sentenced to a long imprisonment, but others reported that result was considered doubtful given the uncertainty of the Mexican Justice system: "The noted Parker H. French has been killed twice by reports from Mexico, but it is now said that he is in prison at Durango. He is studying Spanish and had proposed to the Governor to fight the Apaches and Comanches if liberated."[106]

Parker French was also lobbying newspapers in the United States trying to rehabilitate his shattered reputation. He wrote a long letter to the *New York Herald* which declared all the charges against him were false; the calumnies had been concocted by his enemies on Wall Street, as well as other sponsors of the Lopez expedition against Cuba.[107]

Joseph Dawson returned to Texas through Durango, accompanying the ever-present Benjamin Coons. When Coons visited French in prison, Dawson refused to go along, saying: "No, he has robbed me and deceived me and I will have nothing to do with him."

Even though French was technically incarcerated, he had so charmed the prison commander and a visiting priest that he was allowed substantial privileges. He had especially enchanted the local women: "Such was the wonderful charm of this talented man's manner that he had become a lion among the pretty senoritas." By this time, French had been separated from his men and had comfortable quarters in a private house near the prison. Two soldiers were tasked to be his guards, and they turned into his servants. French kindly received his old enemy Coons in what was described as an ostentatious style with the nicest food, drink, delicacies, and flowers. Dawson also reported that the Mexicans seemed to have rationalized French's crimes, since French had fought with the Mexicans against their ancient enemies the Comanches: "they did not consider he had committed such a great moral wrong in trying to capture $200,000; and as to smuggling, that was a fascinating and a quite legitimate profession."[108,109]

After months of incarceration, probably sometime in the spring of 1852, French and the rest of his jailed compadres were released by the governor. All his companions headed for California, while French was intent on following up on his plan to battle the Apaches and Comanches.

By then, French had mastered the Spanish language and had convinced all who would listen to him that he was a great military leader. He knew that the raiders were an increasing threat and had become bolder; 1852 was a peak year for Apache and Comanche raids, which reached 700 miles south of the U.S border to the city of Jalisco, south of Durango. They had secure bases in the mountains, would raid ranches and villages at will, and then retreat to the safety of their mountain sanctuaries. After release from prison, French wrote a long rambling letter, in Spanish, to Governor Don Jose Maria del Regato. He recognized that he came "before your Excellency under most unfavorable auspices since I have just come forth from imprisonment with a reputation much defamed, without friends and without influence to recommend me."

He ingratiated himself with the governor by fawning over his wisdom, judgment, impartiality, and upright manner. French then proposed a plan to the

governor: if given a contract, he would organize a
force to campaign against the marauders within six
weeks. As the core of his force, he would recruit 150
to 200 warriors of the Seminole Indians who were
living along the southern banks of the Rio Grande.
They had become discontented in Indian Territory
and immigrated to Mexico. The Seminoles, French
wrote, were "the most proper to pursue constantly
the savages even to their most secret retreats in
the mountains—wrest from them the fruits of their
depredations, destroy their Rancherias and by this
means give entire security to the state."

French praised the Seminole bravery, intelligence,
and gift of languages. They especially knew guerilla
warfare and "use with admirable precision the death-
dealing rifle and the revolving pistol." French went
on to claim that he could save the State of Durango
at least half a million dollars annually and be very
beneficial to mining, agriculture, and commerce.
There is no record that Parker French ever received
a contract, but Joseph Dawson later asserted that
the governor gave French $10,000 (2017 estimate,
$300,000) in gold and authorized him to organize
a company to fight the marauders. French himself,
almost two decades later, would claim that the
governor offered a substantial contract but did not
mention any performance against it. The governor's
offer was: $500 in gold to French per month; each
man would receive $5 per day; each rescued Mexican,
$500; each captured Indian, $300; and, each killed
Indian, $250. McGowan also wrote that French drove
the marauding Indians away from the city and out
of the state, "killing and slaughtering them in large
numbers, giving no quarter and taking no prisoner."

A report from a traveler through Durango
corroborates and embroiders the story. Parker French
was not only released to fight marauding Indians,

he had utterly routed them, caused terror amongst them, and driven them out of the state. "Many of the Mexicans desire to make him Governor ... His exploits have rendered him almost as famous in Durango as El Cid is in Spain, and the people hail him wherever he appears as their deliverer." The *St. Louis Reveille* went a step further, making the farfetched claim that "in consideration of his bold, fearless and daring deeds," he was actually made governor of the province.[110,111,112,113]

As in almost all things French, there are other versions of the Durango prison story. Baldridge cited a third person in his account, with both consistency and contradiction and a smattering of probable fictitious embellishment. The governor had agreed to pay French a sizable bounty for Comanche and Apache scalps. As despicable as that policy was, Baldridge also alleged that French was indiscriminate in his choice of victims; he was just as likely to bring in a scalp of a peon as that of a marauder. For his crimes, the source said, at least three different dates were scheduled for French's execution. The sentence of execution was suspended and held over his head to ensure French's loyalty and compliance. A wealthy Spanish girl whose "affections he had won" bribed the jailor and provided $700 for French's escape to Mazatlán. French and his comrades deserted and escaped to the coast, according to McGowan.[114]

Because of French's terrible reputation, it was easy for newspapers and ostensible witnesses to pile on. In an 1877 article in the *Arizona Sentinel*, French was falsely accused of predations and crimes against a village in Mexico. The writer asserted that French and his men had entered Cieneguita, a village in western Sonora near Guaymas. Finding all the men gone to the mines, they purportedly hanged the priest to force him to give up the church's money, ravished the women, and plundered the town. If it happened at all, perhaps it was a contingent of French's train heading to Guaymas or another American group. But based on other chronicles, French himself was never near the town.[115]

Whether officially released by the governor or deserted and escaped through the talent and loyalty of a loving senorita, Parker Hardin French again made his way to Mazatlán. He was there by early July 1852 looking for a way to sail to San Francisco for the next chapter in his life.

8

CALIFORNIA: LAWYER, LEGISLATOR, JOURNALIST

In Mazatlán, French sought a ship to take him to San Francisco, a place where he was not likely to encounter an entirely friendly audience. Since December 1850, expedition members had been arriving in the city. Their descriptive and inflammatory stories of the notorious Parker Hardin French and his failed Express Passenger Train were well distributed in the newspapers. The accounts were reinforced by eastern newspapers, which detailed his fraud and forgeries as well as his predation and banditry in Mexico. Regardless of his questionable history and shameful reputation, French viewed California as a wide-open opportunity. Parker Hardin French would become a probate lawyer, district attorney, California legislator, newspaper owner and editor, backroom political brawler, and Know-Nothing Party principal. He would also engage in his typically questionable business dealings; French would torment wealthy land owners, cattle barons, and politicians alike.

Historian William Scroggs wrote:

> *"Parker H. French had arrived in California ... under very suspicious circumstances. No one in California in those days, however, scrutinized too closely his neighbor's past, and as French was a clever*

and polished individual, he secured a seat in the legislature. All who had financial dealings with French had cause to regret it, and he soon acquired the reputation of being one of the cleverest rascals on the Pacific coast. With his oily tongue easily persuading large numbers of people to enter into his schemes, he lacked the honesty and strength of purpose to carry his plans to a successful conclusion, and usually abandoned the undertaking as soon as he had filched from his associates all the money they were willing to entrust to his care." [116]

On July 1, 1852, Parker Hardin French boarded the brig *Hallowell,* Captain Gesenius commanding. Embarked as well were 111 other passengers, mostly Texan emigrants who had journeyed through Mexico to Mazatlán. Unable to resupply in Mazatlán, the Hallowell sailed on a very tough journey to San Francisco. Battling calms and the headwinds to Cabo San Lucas, she entered that port for a resupply of water. On the trip up the coast of Baja California, the ship encountered the prevailing northwest winds and the California current, which create one of the most difficult upwind boat passages in North America. According to a biographical sketch on John Jacob Simmler, a fellow passenger on the *Hallowell,* the vessel encountered very light northwest winds and periods of calm; she made almost no progress for days. The ship was totally unprepared for an extended time at sea with too many passengers. Shortages of food and water caused terrible suffering and distress; Simmler reported that seven of his fellow passengers died of starvation on the trip. On August 18, the ship was off the coast of Baja California southwest of Ensenada. She had only sailed about 1,000 nautical miles in about forty-seven days. Lookouts spotted a sailing ship, and Captain Gesenius signaled distress. The *North America*, Captain Artell Austin commanding, pulled alongside. Austin provided twelve days of provisions but refused Parker French's offer of $40 to take him on board. Perhaps Austin had heard the news of French's exploits. After another fifteen days, the *Hallowell* again needed provisions and struggled into Cave Landing in San Luis Bay, San Louis Obispo County. It had taken sixty-two days to sail about 1,335 nautical miles. All the crew and most of the passengers left the ship. Newspapers in San Francisco and Sacramento speculated that Parker French had bribed the captain to stop, fearing to continue to San Francisco. It was just as likely that everyone on the ship sought solid land and fresh food away from what was described as an arbitrary and capricious ship captain. For some newspapers, the landing of more than 100 probably peaceful Texan immigrants was hyperbolized into "Parker French landed with 75 Texas Rangers."[117,118,119,120,121]

Cave Landing or "Pirates Cove" in San Luis Bay, San Louis Obispo County, 1865. From U.S. Geological Survey.

Destitute with no friends, badly clothed, and "having the musty smell of a Mexican prison," Parker French headed to Los Angeles where this "most remarkable character hung up his hat at the Bella Union." Advertised as the best hotel south of San Francisco, the one-story flat-roofed adobe had six-by-nine feet "pigeon holes or dog kennels" for guest-rooms. Rain would percolate through the roof, turning the dirt floors a sloppy mess. If a distinguished guest sought lodging, he was offered to bed down on the billiard table in the bar. Parker French's dirty and damaged clothes soon went in the trash. They were replaced by elegant apparel, which made French a dashing hotel figure. Of course, French housed and clothed himself at the expense of the hotelier and merchants who were taken in by his demeanor and spiel. "I am sure that whoever arrayed the ragged French in rare cloth and fine linen never got so much as thank you for their pay."[122]

With the air and trappings of a gentleman, French next appeared in San Luis Obispo where he rapidly became a model citizen as a lawyer, providing legal services especially in probate and land cases. His gift of gab now included a strong fluency in Spanish, with which he endeared himself to the land grant Dons and their ladies. The newly formed County Board of Supervisors was very charmed by and impressed with the newcomer and was perhaps uninformed of his nefarious past. At their first meeting on December 13, 1852, the board appointed French as the district attorney at a salary of $500 per year. Most of the powerful board members, some of whom were Mexican land grant Dons, would eventually succumb to Parker French and get entangled in his schemes. William Dana, Francis Branch, and Samuel Pollard would all be stung.[123,124,125]

McGowan asserted that French, during 1853, plotted to defraud William Dana and Francis Branch of the proceeds of cattle sales. McGowan related that Dana made French an agent to sell his cattle in San Francisco. French was very successful and "proved himself a great help to the Captain (Dana) who became further impressed with the importance of French, and looked upon him in the light of a fast friend."

Based on the initial success, more cattle drives were agreed to. French reported by letter that everything was going fine and that he would soon send them money for the sale of the cattle. McGowan asserted that French swindled Francis Branch out of his cattle and his huge ranch; deeds for the land were purportedly filed in San Luis Obispo County. French, McGowan wrote, never paid Dana or Branch anything, and, in fact, caused Branch a great deal of trouble and money to gain his ranch back. Horace Bell hyperbolized: French "gave a great deal of attention to selling and mortgaging the ranchos of his constituents to San Francisco money-lenders and speculators." Kenneth Johnson in his notes to McGowan's *Strange Eventful History* stated there were no such deeds in the county records. A later search by San Luis Obispo historian Joseph Carotenuti was also negative. What is recorded are two suits in the District Court of San Luis Obispo. William Dana and Samuel Pollard sued French for repayment of loans; for Dana, $1,800 (2017 estimate, $54,000) and for Pollard, $1,300 (2017 estimate, $39,000). In Parker French's bankruptcy, adjudicated in 1870, William Dana was listed as a creditor. As a surety, he represented petitioners seeking $20,000 (2017 estimate, $600,000) for real estate and stock deals.[126,127,128]

In September 1853, while Parker French was still in the good graces of Dana, Branch, Pollard and the rest of the County power brokers, he was overwhelmingly elected to the California State legislature, representing the county of San Luis Obispo.

His time as district attorney satisfied, French returned for a brief time to his private practice. Most notably, he is credited by Joseph Carotenuti for defending and gaining the acquittal of the infamous robber Jack Powers. Robberies and murders by Powers and his gang had made the El Camino Real, which ran through the county, the most dangerous route in the state. There was a newspaper report of an acquittal, for insufficient evidence, of Jack Powers in Los Angeles; he had been indicted in Santa Barbara for "resisting the sheriff in the discharge of his duty." Since it was judged that an impartial trial could not be held in Santa Barbara, the venue had been changed to Los Angeles. The defense counsel was not identified.[129]

At some point during this time, French received distressing personal news: on May 16, 1853, his wife Lucretia filed for divorce in Alton, Illinois. She and her family had probably gotten sick of hearing of her husband's schemes, frauds, forgeries, and banditry. Lucretia and daughter Matilda had returned to Alton from Reading, Berks County, Pennsylvania upon the death of her sister, Matilda Strong, in February 1851. The now Honorable Parker French headed east, probably just after the election, to either save his marriage or, as McGowan related, to remarry Lucretia. The whole family, along with a servant, returned to San Francisco on December 31, 1853 aboard the Steamship *Sierra Nevada* from Panama. The honorable legislator's newfound status and prospects in California were likely instrumental in convincing Lucretia to take him back. They settled in San Jose, where son Hugh Murray French was born on August 7, 1854. Parker and Lucretia must have had a particularly joyous reunion in late October or early November 1853.[130,131]

When the fifth session of the California legislature convened in Benicia on January 2, 1854, the small town had little to offer, and over 100 men had no place to sleep except in saloons. Change came quickly; Sacramento offered the large Sacramento County courthouse until a new capitol could be built. The governor signed a bill authorizing the move on February 25, and the same day the whole operation was moved by steamer to Sacramento.

Parker French was naturally named to the Ways and Means Committee. He became immediately embroiled in the battle for senate representation in the United States Congress. At the time, senators were selected by state legislatures as representatives of the sovereign states. In opposition to sitting Senator William Gwin, French supported David Broderick, formerly of New York City, as well as a former state senator and lieutenant governor. Broderick had established a Tammany Hall-like "dictatorship" in San Francisco, corruptly fixing elections for lucrative, fee-bearing positions such as sheriff, tax-collector, and assessor. For Broderick's assistance and assurance in winning the election, the candidates had to fork over half of their fees, which sometimes exceeded $50,000 per year. Broderick probably lined his pockets with hundreds of thousand dollars per year; he was well funded for his drive to represent California as a senator. Parker French was a key ally in the legislature, pushing for an early election which would favor Broderick. The one-armed legislator was engaged as a "persuader" in the legislature and as an enforcer in the streets and bars. French was associated with journalist William Walker (soon to be of Nicaragua fame), Broderick political advisors George Wilkes and Ned McGowan, as well as with street toughs Billy "Snaggle Tooth" Williamson and Billy Mulligan. Having gained a Tammany Hall political education in New York, Mulligan brought those skills to California. Only a little over five feet tall, he was notorious in the ring as a prizefighter and in the bars as an enforcer. He and French teamed up, arriving in saloons and threatening to beat up any Gwin supporters. Ready for partying and dressed in a tuxedo, Mulligan once knocked out a Gwin supporter with head butts, ordered champagne and a steak dinner, and paid the bill by emptying the man's pockets.[132,133,134,135,136]

Sacramento County Courthouse, temporary state capital in 1854. Held by Sacramento History Museum.

When not in Sacramento, French was with his family in San Jose practicing law with partner and fellow legislator Freeman S. McKinney. In 1857, McKinney would be killed in Sonora, Mexico, when the survivors of the Henry Crabb filibuster incursion were massacred by Mexican troops. "Free" McKinney and Parker French were not averse to taking on the rich and powerful; they did so with James Lick on a property case. Lick was arguably the richest man in California. In San Francisco, he owned what was considered the finest hotel west of the Mississippi. From his estate near San Jose, Lick administered huge land holdings all over the state, including a good part of Santa Clara County, a large amount of land around Lake Tahoe, the whole Island of Santa Catalina, and a large ranch near Los Angeles. James Lick bought a large town lot in downtown San Francisco from the original Mexican owner, but a necessary power of attorney and the sale were never recorded. French and McKinney, in partnership with a William Stafford, also bought the very valuable lot from the original Mexican owner, who was still the owner of record. French and McKinney sued for Lick to be ejected but lost in district court. They would eventually win on appeal to the California Supreme Court. Of course, French's good friend Hugh C. Murray was the chief justice; fellow Kentuckian and political ally David Terry was an associate justice. Terry was elected in the Know-Nothing Party sweep of the 1855 election.[137]

In early 1855, French established a newspaper, the *Daily State Tribune*. He needed its capabilities to leverage a new opportunity. French realized some of the benefits of being a legislator, and he reaped the rewards by being awarded a lucrative government contract for printing official records.

Sensing a shift in the political winds, French soon turned his back on Broderick and the Democratic Party. The *Tribune* became a mouthpiece for the emerging Know-Nothing Party, and he was appointed as one of its secretaries.

The ascendant party was extremely successful. Following closely its overwhelming success dominating local elections throughout the state, the Know-Nothings had a clean sweep of the statewide elections: governor, attorney general, the reelection of Chief Justice Murray, the election of Associate Justice David Terry, and control of both houses of the state legislature. Governor elect Neely Johnson was a self-described "most startled man in the state."

A rival paper, *The Democratic State Journal*, edited by William Walker, was the mouthpiece of the Broderick faction of Democratic Party; the two papers engaged in sometimes bitter fights. In just a few months, Walker and French would be partners in a grand but outrageous undertaking.[138]

Being one-armed and of slight stature might have prompted French to avoid physical altercations. That was not the case, especially when his own honor, or that of a friend, was besmirched. Former Governor of California John McDougal was prone to drinking and quarrels and made a disparaging remark about Chief Justice of the Supreme Court Hugh C. Murray. Upon hearing the offensive remark, the one-armed battler confronted McDougal and "struck the latter with a severe blow to the face." French and Murray were close friends from Alton, Illinois, where Murray had studied law under French's brother-in-law, Newton Deming Strong; French's son Hugh Murray was his namesake.

There was plenty about the chief justice to disparage—Murray was the youngest in history and arguably the worst prepared; he was also an inveterate racist. In 1854, he ruled that Chinese immigrants had no right to testify against white men; his ruling freed a white murderer of a Chinese miner.

In another altercation, French was wounded in the leg, accidentally shot while he was trying to separate two friends who were in a steamboat bar fight.[139,140,141]

In mid-1855, seeking new adventures, Parker Hardin French looked south. Nicaragua was gripped in a brutal civil war. The vulnerable country also offered great economic potential for enterprising and ambitious men who were not stifled by American neutrality laws, or who were hampered by sympathy for the rights and aspirations of the local people. Parker French was to become a filibuster in support of William Walker as he attempted to take over Nicaragua, and perhaps, all Central America and Cuba.

CONQUEST OF NICARAGUA: PARKER FRENCH THE FILIBUSTER

Although it was front page news at the time, few Americans now likely know of the filibuster incursion into Nicaragua in 1855. The upheaval of a brutal internecine civil war offered an entrée to American adventurers; the history still affects United States and Nicaraguan relations.

Photograph of William Walker by Matthew Brady, Library of Congress.

The role of William Walker is well documented. Without the benefit of access to the digitization of newspapers, historians have portrayed Parker Hardin French as an interesting, minor, somewhat humorous and perhaps quixotic character. Research suggests that French had a much more central and vital role than has been previously recognized and documented. For several months in 1855 and early 1856, Parker French would be a principal in support of William Walker's quest to take over Nicaragua, all Central America, and Cuba. French would recruit and arm men to join Walker. He would be commissary of war, the minister of finance, defense counsel for a convicted traitor, and appointed ambassador to the United States.[142]

San Francisco and the rest of Northern California would be taken in by the Nicaraguan adventure of William Walker and Parker French. The *Daily Alta* opined:

"Some little excitement is rife about town among that very excitable portion of our population known as the Filibusters, owing to the report that Parker H. French is to start in a few days with a band of over thirty companions for Nicaragua. That unfortunate republic seems to have committed some terrible crime to judge from the numbers of expeditions on foot against it."[143]

The term filibuster is originally based on the Dutch word for freebooter or pirate. It was adapted by Americans who used the term to describe the private and unsanctioned attacks against countries at peace. All such operations technically violated American neutrality laws but were almost impossible to stop, much less prosecute. Violators became very adept at escaping the provisions of the laws, either by sidestepping enforcement attempts or gaining acquittal in front of sympathetic juries. The more sophisticated filibusters, like William Walker and Parker French, would haughtily declare that they were not filibusters; Nicaragua sought lawful and peaceful immigration, believing it was the right of every American to peaceably go where they wished.

William Walker already had an experience with a filibuster operation. In late 1853 and early 1854, Walker tried to wrest Baja California and Sonora from Mexico to form the Republic of Lower California and later the Republic of Sonora. His filibuster operation failed; a ship with all his supplies inexplicably sailed, and a large part of his band deserted. Mexican forces almost had him cornered when he retreated to California. Tried in San Francisco for violation of United States neutrality laws, he was acquitted in eight minutes by a sympathetic jury. He perhaps learned five things: gain political support and at least nominal cover from a local "democratic" faction; ensure money and supplies; recruit, train, and retain a committed force; manage the press and public opinion; and don't violate US neutrality laws.

Campaign map of Nicaragua, William Walker, *The War In Nicaragua.*

Nicaragua's geographic position astride one of the strategic transit routes across Central America was always of interest to the United States. After the Mexican American War, the acquisition of California and the Treaty of Guadalupe Hidalgo, access to the transit routes became critical for the security of, and commerce with, California and the rest of the west coast. Discovery of gold in California heightened interest in both rail and canal routes in Central America, specifically Nicaragua. The only alternatives were across the continent or around Cape Horn, both long and dangerous journeys. Nicaragua's significant mineral wealth and agricultural potential also attracted business interest.

In 1849, Nicaragua and the United States forged a treaty granting exclusive transit rights to the United States while providing protection to Nicaragua from other foreign intervention. With full knowledge of the diplomatic progress between the United States and Nicaragua, magnate Cornelius Vanderbilt was immediately postured to ink a contract with Nicaragua. He registered the Accessory Transit Company (ATC) as a Nicaraguan company and gained exclusive transit rights to build a canal within twelve years. The ATC also had exclusive interim rights to a land–water route to move passengers and cargo across Nicaragua. In September 1849, the Nicaraguan Congress approved the treaty, along with Vanderbilt's contract.

Vanderbilt meant to compete with the existing Panama route. The Nicaraguan option was assessed to be six hundred miles shorter, healthier, more efficient and less costly by half. Vanderbilt steamers delivered passengers to the port of San Juan del Norte (called by the British Greytown; now San Juan de Nicaragua). Boats traveled up the San Juan River to Lake Nicaragua (the largest lake in Central America) at an altitude of only 107 feet. Steamboats crossed the lake to the small town of La Virgen on the west shore. From La Virgen, just a twelve-mile well-maintained road brought travelers to the Pacific Coast and the port of San Juan del Sur; well-scheduled steamers connected to San Francisco.

In 1850, the Clayton-Bulwer Treaty helped create the conditions for continued good commercial prospects for the United States and Great Britain, as well as Nicaraguan development. The two powers agreed that neither country would claim exclusive rights to a Central American canal nor gain exclusive power over any part of the region or country. It also provided for British-American cooperation in the building of a canal. Both retained their portion of the transit route: Britain continued to control the nominally free city of Greytown; the United States retained the transit rights, including steamboats, hotels, restaurants, and land transportation.

Prospects were bright from a commercial and development perspective, but political instability and civil war threatened to retard all progress. Since independence from Spain in 1821, political disorder, civil wars, revolutions, and coups had tormented the country.

Such was the case in 1854, when civil war raged between the "Legitimists" and the "Democrats." The Legitimists were aligned with conservative elements, had friendly ties with Great Britain, and were closely tied with the Catholic Church. The Democrats were more liberal, anticlerical, and more favorably associated with the United States. The Legitimists controlled the southern part of the country with their capital and stronghold in Granada, on the northwest coast of Lake Nicaragua. Crucially, they also sat astride the transit route with the all-important transit fees and tax base. The Democrats controlled the northern part of the country with their capital in Leon.

In the autumn of 1854, Californian Byron Cole was traveling in Nicaragua seeking commercial opportunities. A journalistic compatriot of William Walker, Cole became friendly with the Democratic leader President Francisco Castellon in Leon.

Knowing that Castellon's army was struggling and at risk of losing, Cole proposed that Castellon seek aid from William Walker. Parker French would later assert that Cole recommended both Walker and French as men who would readily come to Castellon's aid if given the "proper inducements." Both were, Cole said, well known in the United States and were qualified to bring assistance. Walker and French were in fact "well known," but there was certainly a split of opinion on qualifications and reputation. Walker's resume included his failed Mexico filibuster; French had his well-documented nefarious exploits as well as a well-deserved reputation as a schemer and fraudster.[144]

Cole traveled to California with a proposed contract. Walker was to bring 300 Americans to Nicaragua to serve in the Democratic Army with monthly pay, and he was to get a grant of 21,000 acres of land. Rejecting the contract, Walker assessed that it would violate United States neutrality laws, and there was too much risk for any projected gain. A second trip by Cole to Nicaragua resulted in an acceptable contract, increasing the grant to 52,000 acres and designating the men as "colonists."

Parker French would later assert that Walker did not act alone in contracting with Castellon. In January 1855, French avowed, Cole met with both Walker and French in Sacramento with the initially rejected contract. The second approved contract had multiple satisfactory provisions: the Americans were to become naturalized citizens, have the right to bear arms, and each would receive 250 acres of land. An area of 52,000 acres would be set aside on which Americans could settle. Part of the deal, French said, was a commission as colonel for both men. French further asserted that the pair agreed to enter the effort as joint partners and would equally share in the benefits. French would take the lead in

California, since he had more means, connections, and influence. Walker would take the initial force to Nicaragua, and French would follow with another contingent as soon as possible.

There may have been discussion, as well, for the need for information on the Legitimist situation in Nicaragua—disposition of forces, strengths, weaknesses, and vulnerabilities. Subsequent activities by French suggest that he may have taken on that intelligence mission.

Claiming influence, French introduced Walker to Cornelius K. Garrison, the San Francisco manager of the Accessory Transit Company. In 1853, Charles Morgan and Garrison were officers in Vanderbilt's ATC. While Vanderbilt was on vacation in Europe, they colluded to take over the company and manipulate stock in their favor. They added cronies to the board, voted Morgan as the president, and removed Vanderbilt as the New York agent. Morgan then suspended payments from the ATC to Vanderbilt, which had been a hefty 20 percent of the revenue. Cornelius Vanderbilt reacted with rage: "Gentlemen: You have undertaken to cheat me. I won't sue you, for the law is too slow. I'll ruin you. Yours truly, Cornelius Vanderbilt." The press headlined the controversy "The War of the Commodores."

Parker French undoubtedly knew Garrison in 1849-1850 from business transactions in St. Louis. There, Cornelius made a fortune building, owning, and operating steamboats on the Mississippi River, while French was probably a customer as a commission merchant. French thought he could get Garrison interested in supporting the movement of "colonists" to Nicaragua since the effort was bound to affect the corporate situation. Initially declining to help, Garrison probably questioned whether

Walker and French could be victorious in Nicaragua and perhaps was unsure of the position of his boss, Morgan. He refused to issue tickets to San Juan del Sur and required the purchase of through tickets to New York, even if travelers got off in Nicaragua. He was obviously cautious in making sure the company could not be implicated in violation of neutrality laws.

By May 1855, everything was in order to launch Walker and his initial contingent. Legal hurdles were passed; S.W. Inge, the local United States Attorney determined that neutrality laws would not be violated. Major General John Wool, commander of the Department of the Pacific, said he had no authority to interfere.

Key officers were on hand. Veteran soldiers and filibusters like Collier C. Hornsby, Frank Anderson, and Achilles Kewen would provide combat experience for the initial fifty-eight-man force. Available resources were reported as paltry and money as pitiful. Support would remain in California to gain political support, press for enlistments, and to solicit funds. In support of the effort were lawyers and politicians Edmund Randolph and Kentucky native Alexander Crittenden, as well as Henry Crabb and Thomas Fisher, who were both principals in the California Know-Nothing Party.

With $1,000 from corrupt and shady bankers Palmer, Cook & Co., Walker had enough to purchase supplies and engage the ship *Vesta,* a vessel that historian William Scroggs described as a "leaky old brig." All set to sail on April 20, the sheriff intervened with a creditor's attachment against the ship; then the United States Marshal piled on with another writ, enforced by a revenue cutter. Two weeks were lost negotiating with the creditors and dealing with a sheriff who wanted his posse costs paid.

Finally, on May 4, 1855, with creditors satisfied

and a deputy sheriff distracted and entertained below with cigars and drink, a steam tug towed the *Vesta* away from the pier. The deputy was transferred to the tug, tow lines were loosed, and the *Vesta* was at sea on the way to Nicaragua. On June 16, after hazarding rough seas and high winds, Walker's force of fifty-eight men, who would come to be called the "Immortals," landed at the port of Realejo on the northwest coast of Nicaragua. Castellon welcomed them a short time later in his capital of Leon.

General Jose Trinidad Munoz, the Nicaraguan commander-in-chief, did not trust Walker and wanted to use the Americans to reinforce various units of his army. Walker refused, maintaining that if the Americans were to stay, they would operate as a separate force under Walker's command.

The democratic movement and army in desperate straits, Castellon agreed; he designated the new force as the American Phalanx—the "Falange." Newly commissioned Walker was its colonel, and Achilles Kewen was commissioned a lieutenant colonel. The first mission was to occupy and control the twelve-mile transit road from La Virgen on the west shore of Lake Nicaragua to the Pacific Coast port of San Juan del Sur. This task was especially important to Walker: he wanted access to potential recruiting from American travelers transiting the route. To augment the force, 200 Nicaraguan troops were promised, but 100 showed up under the command of Colonel Ramirez.

Back in California, Parker French prepared to reinforce Walker with the follow-on contingent. He claimed that he had already 150 and another 100 were required. French had posted notices for the "Central American Colonization Society." The society, said French, was to "cultivate and mine large tracts of land granted by the Government of Nicaragua to the <u>undersigned</u> (French) and others." Since the country was in such an unsettled state, he advised the "colonists" to go armed. There was no mention, of course, of any intention to participate in the ongoing civil war; Attorney Inge would have no cause to intervene. The fortunate colonists would leave San Francisco, French wrote, about July 20. He also opened a postal letter bag for the "Friends of William Walker." Already knowing of the land grant that Walker had previously made known, newspaper editors wondered if in fact French was part of the deal. Was French's land grant claim credible? Did he matter?[145]

In Nicaragua, events rapidly progressed. As a necessary step to control the transit route, Walker judged that the first operation required the capture of Rivas, about nine miles north of La Virgen. Walker attacked the town on June 28. The supporting Nicaraguans under Colonel Ramirez soon fled, allegedly due to a jealous General Munoz who induced Ramirez to treachery. Also suggested was that an opponent of Walker, perhaps General Munoz, leaked the operation to the Legitimists. The Falange was trapped in town, under attack by up to 500 of the enemy. Casualties mounted with six killed and twelve wounded, leaving only thirty-eight effectives. The only choice was to break out and leave five seriously wounded behind at the mercy of the Legitimist commander; they were executed. One of the losses hit Walker hard; loyal, effective, and reliable second-in-command Achilles Kewen was killed in action. Walker and his decimated command retired back to Realejo, and then moved to Leon to help protect the capital.

Because of the suspected treachery at Rivas, as well as further disputes with General Munoz, Walker feigned a threat to leave the country and go to Honduras. Knowing that his situation would be desperate without American support, Castellon induced the all-too-willing Walker to stay, and the

Democratic leader started acceding to Walker's demands. With the arbitration of Byron Cole, Walker gained a new contract. He was to enlist 300 men who would be paid monthly and given land rights. Much more far reaching and defining, Walker was given full authority to negotiate with the Accessory Transit Company. He rested and recuperated his force; gathered arms, ammunition, and other supplies; and recruited local troops. Importantly and essential to his Nicaraguan strength, Walker was able to recruit leaders he could trust, notably the capable and respected Jose Maria Valle. The Americans were getting ready for another attempt to occupy the transit route.

Back in San Francisco, Parker French prepared for his planned deployment in July by sending his family back east. Lucretia, Matilda (age five), and Hugh Murray (ten months) left on the Nicaraguan steamer in late June.

Then on July 14, shortly before French's reinforcing contingent was to leave, the steamer *Sierra Nevada* brought the very disturbing news of Walker's defeat at Rivas. Knowing the defeat could shatter everything, French shelved his immediate plans, left his "colonists" in San Francisco, and headed to Nicaragua aboard the *Uncle Sam* along with his mulatto servant, Tom. The *Daily Alta* noted his departure as: "Parker French will remain in Nicaragua for a few days on a peaceable tour of observation." Another newspaper declared that "his business is entirely disconnected from the disquieting question of filibustering."

The *Uncle Sam* arrived in San Juan del Sur on July 28, and French immediately made his way to Rivas, where he was taken into custody by the Legitimists. From there, on July 31, French wrote a remarkable letter to his paper, the *State Journal*.

A superficial reading of the document could be interpreted as complete and unexpected antipathy for everything that Walker was doing. It is more likely that it was a typically cunning and calculating attempt at ingratiating himself with the Legitimists. French's past actions, his gift of deceptive and fawning sincerity, and subsequent reports and letters reinforce the latter view. If intercepted or read by a censor, the letter provided substantial protection to Parker French from any suspicion or allegation that he was an agent of Walker:

"Rivas, July 31. I am now in the city of Rivas, but under arrest. I walk at large, but cannot leave the town, and will be sent to Grenada tomorrow under an escort. I have only time to write a few words and cannot say when I shall have another opportunity of communicating with you, as these people are very much exasperated against the whole American race, since the late attack upon them by Walker and his party. They now look upon us with hatred and aversion. Although I am their warm friend, and desire to serve them, yet they distrust me and fear treachery; hence I am hedged around with difficulties I never anticipated. These people know all that is going on in California as well as we do. They have so far treated me with studied kindness, in spite of all their suspicions. I am still in hopes of accomplishing my mission, and assist in establishing a permanent peace in the country."[146]

French was, in fact, escorted to the Legitimist capital of Grenada and held in loose arrest. In further editorial correspondence, he wrote two more reports that he held for publication until he returned to

California in mid-September. French wrote:

"The object of my visit to this Republic, is only known to but few, and those few are gentlemen associated with me in an enterprise of great moment, the success and welfare of which prohibits a public explanation at the present time; but in furtherance of my plans, and to give myself more weight with the government with which I wished to communicate, I procured the best letters and vouchers that the State of California could give me, to our minister, Mr. Wheeler, so that through him I might be introduced to the authorities of the country, on a respectable footing."

If the document would have been discovered and seized, it could only have been interpreted as supporting the then official and recognized government of the country, the Legitimists. In another letter, French noted the decay and ruin in the once great city of Granada, the impact of the civil war on the economy and populace, and the brother against brother characteristic of any civil war. He also reported that cholera was ripping through the countryside.[147]

Parker French would later claim that while he was in Grenada he spied for Walker. Further, he ostensibly provided intelligence and tactical advice that enabled Walker to make plans for the storming and capturing of the city. He noted the defensive works, assessed their strength and weaknesses, mapped the approaches, and gathered other information on the Legitimist position. French professed to have sent the intelligence by courier to Walker in the hollow of a bamboo cane. Also, purportedly in the cane was advice to immediately capture and fortify San Juan, and make it Walker's base of operations where he could recruit and receive supplies. French said that he even proposed the tactical plan to capture the capital.

Meanwhile, servant Tom had been spreading stories about the one-armed man's bravery and amazing skill as an artillery expert; he claimed his master could hit a man with a twenty-four-pound artillery ball at a mile's distance. The Legitimists, intrigued and wanting to secure French's valuable service, offered to appoint him chief of artillery. French rejected the position and countered with several colonization proposals, which were likewise rejected. There was agreement on a lucrative arrangement to supply gunpowder to the Legitimists.

What game was French playing? Was he now willing to play both sides against the middle and seek his own colonization charter? Or was he feigning interest just to cozy up to the Legitimists, a way to encourage discussion, a method to facilitate spying and intelligence gathering? Dependent on the way the contract for the gunpowder was structured, that deal could have been an elaborate ploy to increase Walker's depleted gunpowder stores while the enemy paid for it. Parker French had fabricated more elaborate schemes; whatever game he was playing, it was dangerous, and perhaps his most daring.

Back in Realejo, after almost two months of inaction, rest, recuperation, and refitting, Walker's force was spoiling for a fight. His hand with Castellon had also been strengthened and the Americans had become even more essential. Nemesis General Munoz had been killed at the Battle of Sauce, even though he was victorious against the "Butcher of Honduras," General Santos Guardiola. Walker would soon encounter the "Butcher," who earned his nickname by executing his prisoners via bayonet or fire. With the loss of the capable Munoz and his army reduced by both battle casualties and cholera, Castellon feared that Guardiola would attack Leon. He appealed to Walker to return and protect the city.

Walker desisted, and without political approval the "Immortals," backed by Jose Valle with his Nicaraguan battalion, sailed from Realejo. The force approached San Juan on August 29. When the defending troops spotted the *Vesta*, they abandoned the town and port without a fight. The way was now clear to control the transit route.

Parker French had just arrived in San Juan after being released (French said he escaped) from Granada and was waiting for the steamer back to San Francisco. French had himself detained and taken to the *Vesta* under arrest, possibly to allay any Legitimist suspicions if spies were lurking. On the vessel, as French related, he and Walker consulted all night long, presumably discussing the impending operation to capture the Legitimist capital of Grenada. Walker said French gave him observations on the strength and defenses of the city. Walker would later belittle the information, saying he *"attached no importance to his statements."* The Walker version of the meeting appears false on its face, or it exposes a complete lack of competence in intelligence matters by Walker— and he was not known to be incompetent in gaining information about the enemy. That statement was also written five years after the fact, and after a jarring rupture of relations between the two men.

Walker, despite his purported reservations about motives, actions, and loyalties, said he gave French authority to raise seventy-men upon his return to San Francisco. French claimed he was given more general authority to raise troops, grant commissions and to raise funds by selling bonds at ten cents on the dollar. On September 2, he left for San Francisco on the *Uncle Sam.*

Walker's force of about fifty "Immortals," reinforced

by 120 Nicaraguan troops under José Maria Valle, prepared to march to La Virgen. After a night march, the Democratic force occupied La Virgen by 9 a.m. on September 3. Musketry fire from the Nicaraguan pickets announced the arrival of "Butcher" Guardiola's Legitimist force of 600, which had marched from Rivas. The Nicaraguan pickets and main force performed admirably. The Americans, with their deadly rifles and revolvers, controlled the critical buildings, key terrain, and avenues of approach while maneuvering to reinforce threatened sectors. Jose Valle captured the Legitimists' entire ox cart train of ammunition reserve. Soon the enemy gave way, leaving sixty dead on the field; over 100 were wounded, many of them died during the retreat to Rivas. A valuable 150 muskets were collected from the battlefield. Walker's force had minimal casualties; the Falange had none killed and several wounded, most of them having minor injuries, including Walker. Valle's force had two killed and three wounded.

The captured and wounded Legitimists, who expected to be abused and executed, were surprised by the humane care Walker demanded of both American and Nicaraguan soldiers. That policy was to pay off handsomely in support from the populace, willingness of the enemy to surrender, and with recruiting.

The strategy was not to stay and hold La Virgen. Walker meant to demonstrate an offensive capability to intimidate the Legitimists, now under General Ponciano Corral, into staying on the defense to protect their critical position in Rivas. Walker marched his force back to San Juan to control that essential port. There, he would await reinforcements and supplies from Leon, allow Valle to strengthen his force from local volunteers, as well as to gain recruits from American travelers. Some local American residents and passengers on the way to California soon brought the Falange up to sixty men; ally Jose Valle's force swelled to over 200.

Walker soon learned that the Legitimists, in fact, could be paralyzed. When he heard that Corral had left Rivas intending to attack San Juan, Walker demonstrated toward La Virgen and feinted toward Rivas, compelling Corral to return to the city.

Since Parker French had sailed from San Juan the night before the La Virgen victory, he knew nothing of Walker's success or of his increased strength and position. *Uncle Sam* arrived in San Francisco with 106 dead from cholera, which he avoided by being in a first-class cabin.

French soon got to work, recruiting men, gathering resources, and spreading self-serving propaganda printed in his own newspaper: "Capt. Parker H. French, whom we believe, is destined to figure nobly in the future history of the Central American States, arrived in this city yesterday. Capt. French considers that Col. Walker is in virtual possession of Nicaragua, and he pictures a brighter day for a country whose resources, mineral and agricultural, are incalculable, but as yet completely undeveloped."

By no means was Walker yet in "virtual possession," but it was probably a good recruiting advertisement.[148]

Within a couple of days, French had fifty-five men ready to sail, under the command of Colonel Charles Gilman who had lost a leg in Walker's filibuster in Mexico. The second in command was Kentuckian and Know-Nothing Party San Francisco alderman George R. Davidson. French again tried to convince Cornelius Garrison to provide tickets on the steamer *Cortes.* Again, the ATC manager refused, knowing only of the defeat at Rivas and not knowing about Walker's subsequent victory at La Virgen. He was not about to support a losing proposition. French bought thirty-five through tickets to New York and embarked twenty others, betting that he could get them approved for Nicaragua. Before dawn on September 20, French loaded fifty-five muskets, twenty-one rifles, eight thousand rounds of cartridges, and eight kegs of powder, concealed as ordinary freight. Twenty men without tickets were booted off the *Cortes,* even though French said he was willing to buy through passage for them. Thinking he now needed direct information about Walker's situation, Garrison sent his agent C. J. Macdonald to Nicaragua with broad powers.

French remained in California, recruiting the next contingent.

The thirty-five men under Gilman landed at San Juan del Sur on October 3, increasing the Falange to nearly 100. The same day, Captain Ubaldo Herrera and a contingent of thirty-five volunteer Nicaraguan troops arrived from Realejo, bringing Valle's battalion troop strength to over 250. The force now had two cannons as well, one brought by Herrera and one purchased from a ship in the harbor.

With the reinforcements and cannon, Walker now felt strong enough to go on the offensive; he would attempt to execute the secret plan to capture Grenada. French would later claim the plan as his own. The night of October 11, the force arrived at La Virgen where they waited for the accessory transport steamer. The village and the lake front were put under heavy guard—no one was allowed to leave the village and no boat could be launched on the lakefront.

The lake steamer *Virgin* arrived the next day and was commandeered. The ship weighed anchor with the entire force on board and departed to the east as if on a normal transit. Out of sight of the western coast of the lake, the vessel soon turned north toward Grenada, exciting everyone on board. The ship was blacked out as it passed the defensive positions of the city.

The force landed about three miles north of the city and, after a night march, a dawn attack totally surprised the defenders. Only two or three of the defenders were killed, and Valle lost a drummer boy. Nearly 100 political prisoners were released. Walker had possession of the Legitimist capital; he also had important prisoners, and he had negotiating capital. He was set to bring Corral to terms.

Back in California, Parker French had tremendous success recruiting. Hundreds of men had swarmed into San Francisco to catch the steamer *Uncle Sam* departing on October 5. Cornelius Garrison still had not learned about the La Virgen victory because the scheduled steamer *Sierra Nevada* was overdue. And of course, he would not yet have heard from his agent Macdonald. He still was not willing to support the expedition or sell anything but through tickets to New York. Sixty recruits were allowed on board, but there were hundreds who were left on the wharf, disappointed and angry. Chaos ensued: "The wharf was densely packed with men, and at the first move of the steamer's paddles, a general rush was made to board her. The officers of the boat resisted and the body of the crowd was driven back, at the imminent risk of their being crushed between the vessel and the wharf, or launched overboard. The scene was frightful, indeed."

French's men were able to spirit crates of arms and ammunition on board, including twenty-nine muskets pilfered from the "San Francisco Blues," a militia outfit. A warrant-carrying sheriff was able to recover the Blues' property. Later it was found that the Sacramento Rifle Company had also been poached of every weapon and round of ammunition, and that theft was discovered too late to have the weapons recovered by the sheriff. Also secreted on board were 1,500 lbs. of lead, 250 lbs. of gunpowder, 2,500 percussion caps, and sixty-two Mississippi Rifles, five modified for snipers. The very deadly .54 caliber rifles were accurate, reliable, and somewhat waterproof. The stockpile had been bought from arms dealer A.J. "Natchez" Taylor; he was never paid and immediately filed suit against French. Taylor tried to attach all of French's assets, but the culprit had already disposed of everything valuable. Another sixty-four rifles were left on the dock; the merchants demanded payment before they would release the weapons.

Parker French slammed Garrison publicly in the newspapers for his "foolish" neutrality and opposition to his own best interests. He declared he was not going to leave on the *Uncle Sam* and would return to his editorial duties.

French did not return to his paper because he could not; he had sold his interests in the *Tribune* and the *State* printing contract—and fraudulently twice. French's declaration that he was not going to leave was an obvious ruse to obscure his intent and slow down the authorities and his creditors. The San Francisco Bulletin wrote: "From all we learn about Mr. Parker H. French, a late 'respectable' editor in this state, we think he is as precious a scoundrel as ever escaped from our shores. He stole about $1,200 worth of goods in this city before he left and under the assertions that he was not going to Nicaragua."

Of course, Parker French was on the *Uncle Sam*.[149,150,151,152]

On the morning of October 17, the sixty reinforcements under now Colonel Parker French and a newly recruited Colonel Birkett Fry disembarked at San Juan del Sur. "Colonel" Fry had that rank only through the claimed authority and promise by French. Walker would later be irritated by what he considered a presumption of authority.

Taking a brass six-pound cannon from the ship, which French "borrowed" (some articles labeled it stolen), the force headed to La Virgen. They commandeered a lake steamer, mingling with the peaceful passengers. Possibly wanting the glory of military success, French intended to capture Fort San Carlos, on the east coast of Lake Nicaragua.

On October 18, around noontime, French demanded an unconditional surrender of the fort, which was immediately refused. Finding the fort too heavily defended and intimidated by heavy cannon fire that thankfully fell short, they sailed to Grenada; the ship next took the peaceful and delayed passengers back to La Virgen.

Upon hearing the story, Walker was livid; he considered hazarding the civilians while threatening the fort a "most foolish if not criminal act." Fry was allowed to keep his unauthorized colonelcy; French was removed from troop leadership and made the "Commissary of War."

French's action at Fort San Carlos had unintended and deadly consequences; a lake steamer, with hundreds of passengers from New York, entered the lake soon after the engagement; the ship was fired on by the fort. A woman and her nine-year-old daughter were killed, and a son was badly wounded, requiring a foot amputation. The stranded eastbound passengers who were unexpectedly at La Virgen were later attacked by Legitimist troops, thinking they were the force that French had just landed. Soon, the Legitimists realized they were slaughtering mostly unarmed innocents and the attack was stopped, but not before five died and many wounded. The incidents served to bolster Walker's cause and inflame American public opinion.

Walker had his pretext to force negotiations with Ponciano Corral. He executed Interior Minister Mateo Mayorga, who was judged morally responsible for the "outrages and barbarities." A message informed Corral of the execution and implicitly threatened the remaining hostages; they would be held safe, dependent on the good conduct by Legitimist officers towards women, children, and other non-combatants.

The threat brought Corral to the negotiating table, a peace was forged, and a Provisional Government was formed, headed by a new President Patricio Rivas, who was inaugurated on October 30. Walker was made commander-in-chief of the army. The American "colonists" were retained in the army, and their promised pay and lands became liabilities of the new government. Shared between the parties, new ministers were designated. Corral was appointed minister of war, now formally Walker's boss. The ambitious Parker French was the new minister of hacienda, essentially the minister of finance or the treasury secretary. Americans were now installed in charge of the essential instruments of state power, the sword, and the purse. The Nicaraguans readily agreed to release from the army anyone who wanted a discharge; most Nicaraguans soon left the service. The American Falange became the primary protective, and coercive, force in Nicaragua.

Minister of War Ponciano Corral, wary of the Americans and distrustful of Walker, realized his authority was fleeting; Commander-in-Chief Walker was the government and President Rivas and native ministers were merely puppets. He signed his own death warrant by sending letters to allies in Guatemala and Honduras, including the "Butcher" Guardiola. Emphasizing Walker's danger to all Central America, Corral asked for armed intervention to oust the Americans. The minister of war trusted the wrong courier, an undercover Democratic partisan. He gave the documents to Jose Valle, who handed them to Walker.

Unsuspectingly called to a cabinet meeting, Corral was shocked when Walker used the letters as proof of treason and conspiracy to overthrow the republic. Rivas approved a court martial, composed of American officers at Corrals request; Collier Hornsby presided with Parker French as defense counsel. The minister of war was found guilty, sentenced to death and shot by a Falange firing squad on November 8.

William Walker had consolidated power and was now, effectively, the Dictator of Nicaragua. President Rivas was seen as a figurehead, by friends and foes of Walker alike.

United States Ambassador to Nicaragua John Wheeler soon announced the recognition of the Rivas administration as the legitimate government of Nicaragua. Upon hearing of the recognition, of which he did not approve, Secretary of State William Marcy was furious with Wheeler. Marcy's anger would soon have an impact on Parker French.

As commissary of war and then minister of hacienda, Parker French immediately started seeking funds for the new government, and very importantly, funds to pay soldiers and purchase supplies. French enjoyed the unqualified support of William Walker as represented in the government-controlled newspaper *El Nicaraguense.* It was noted with pleasure that Parker French had accepted the position: "Since he has been in office many of the capitalists of this city, native and foreign, have offered to advance the government all their ready funds; that the merchants to a man, have offered him all the facilities at their command, taking as their security for future payment the joint names and reputations of General Walker and Col. French. The Department over which Col. French presides is second only to that of Gen. Walker."[153]

The new Minister of Hacienda levied a 20 percent duty on imports and started working on the long-standing dispute on Accessory Transit Company fee payments. The agent of Cornelius Garrison, C.J. Macdonald, had arrived in early October with full authority to act; he now said that he was staying as the business agent for the ATC. French arranged a loan of $20,000, which went into French's coffers; McDonald pulled the gold from the latest California gold shipment. In New York, the bank of Charles Morgan and Company would refund the owners of the gold.

As a unique way of arming the troops, French was reported seizing personal arms from passengers arriving from San Francisco. His henchmen confiscated rifles and pistols, while giving receipts and a promise that French would give compensation. Passengers, who reported that French could not be found, were never paid for their loss.[154]

The minister of Hacienda also had other sources of revenue. According to historian William Scroggs, the vicar of Grenada was induced to lend the parish 963 ounces of silver, netting perhaps $1,250. Author Bolanos-Geyer considered the silver "loan" as a confiscation. Bolanos-Geyer also identified some more resources that French extracted. The previous government had a monopoly on trade in tobacco, hides, and alcohol, and there were sizable quantities in storage. Then Minister French hit the merchants of Grenada, laying heavy fees of $200 to $12,000 each. If the merchants didn't have the cash, then goods were taken at half of the original cost. Within a few days Parker French shipped large quantities of both stored and confiscated goods to the United States. Walker, enabled by French, could now pay the troops and purchase arms and ammunition.

Transportation of migrants also became cheaper. Back in San Francisco, Cornelius Garrison learned that Walker was ascendant and became conciliatory about passage for "colonists"; he now started sending men free of charge and billing the cost against the money owed by the company.

One anonymous observer, whose byline was "By an Eyewitness," had an assessment—of both a laudatory and condemning quality:

> *"It was Col. Parker H. French, of Mexican notoriety, who invented and perfected the supply system; and since his day the officials of the so-called 'Hacienda' Department of the Walker government have been only feeble imitators of that illustrious financier. He could charm gold from its hiding place and applied the financial thumb-screws to terrified proprietors with a grace that elicited the admiration of his victims and the enthusiasm of the bystanders. To drink with him might cost five hundred, but a walk arm in arm, in public, was an honor for which the astonished Don Carlos paid five thousand dollars."* [155]

Undoubtedly, "Eyewitness" was alleging graft and corruption by French, taking bribes from merchants. The mention of "Don Carlos" was probably a reference to Don Carlos Thomas, a major importer/exporter to whom duties and other fees and taxes would be of significant importance. Likely, Don Carlos also wanted to make sure he was part of the plans for import and export of goods.

The Accessory Transit Company, partly because of the Nicaraguan civil war, had been losing money, which led to a depressed stock price. Company directors Morgan and Garrison knew that Cornelius Vanderbilt had been buying cheap stock and that he was likely going to be successful in taking majority control of the ATC; Vanderbilt would then terminate both as directors. Walker also learned that Vanderbilt, upon taking over the ATC, would try to execute his threat to "make the Nicaraguan government suffer," if Walker did not settle the ATC debt dispute on company terms. Walker, Garrison and Morgan now had a joint problem with Commodore Vanderbilt; they also had a common cause against him.

Everyone acknowledged the problem. In San Francisco, Walker's best friend Edmund Randolph and Cornelius Garrison came up with a solution. They reckoned that Morgan and Garrison could retain the transit right, freeze Vanderbilt out of Nicaragua, and provide stability for Walker. Edmund Randolph, accompanied by Garrison's son William, left for San Juan on the next steamer. Before the pair left San Francisco, father Cornelius pleaded with Randolph: "For God's sake. Randolph, keep William out of the clutches of Parker H. French."

Upon arrival in Grenada, Edmund Randolph, the young Garrison, and Walker made a closed-door deal without the knowledge or consent of President Rivas. The plan was ingeniously simple but with complex and time sensitive steps: Cornelius Garrison and Charles Morgan would guarantee a shipping line to and from Nicaragua; Walker would influence Rivas to revoke the ATC contract on the grounds that the company was in breach of its financial obligations; Rivas would then reassign the charter to Edmund Randolph who would, in turn, assign transit rights to Garrison and Morgan; the Rivas administration would seize all Transit Company assets in Nicaragua; the administration would lease the transit assets to Randolph and then he would sublease the assets to Morgan and Garrison. The ATC assets were extensive: lake and river steamers, lighters, depots, accommodation buildings, employees' houses, jetties, roads, and other fixed facilities, as well as coaches, horses, and mules. The conspiratorial plan had to be secretly executed with precise timing. Vanderbilt had to be kept completely unaware, and critical manpower had to be transported while Morgan and Garrison prepared their coup. The conspirators hoped a deal would be complete by February, when they would drop the hammer on Vanderbilt.

Parker French soon resigned from his position as minister of Hacienda, publicly citing health reasons. A short time later he was, at the recommendation of Walker, appointed by President Rivas to be "Minister Plenipotentiary to the United States with Extraordinary Powers." More simply, he was to be ambassador. He would replace the Legitimist incumbent Jose de Marcoleta and gain United States recognition of the new Nicaraguan government. French also had the mission to settle the long-standing fee dispute between Nicaragua and the ATC.

In his book *The War in Nicaragua*, Walker would later assert that he had to replace French as minister of Hacienda and send him out of the country since "French's rapacity made him dreaded by the people of the country, for which reason it was necessary to get rid of him." The notion that Walker did not know or approve of the purported loans, coerced contributions, duties, fees, taxes, and property confiscations seems implausible. The anonymous observer "By an Eyewitness" declared that Walker knew, and approved all along: "These are the fruits of that robber policy instituted by Col. French and carried out with all of its confiscations, oppressions and extortions, under the guidance and sanction of Walker himself, always with the unanswerable plea of necessity—always with resistance, disaffection, hatred and revenge for its legitimate consequence."[156,157]

As "Minister Plenipotentiary to the United States with Extraordinary Powers," the next stops for Parker Hardin French would be New York and Washington

D.C., where he would soon be the center of attention and controversy. The new ambassador would be the subject of lively and spicy press coverage ... AGAIN!

10

AMBASSADOR TO THE UNITED STATES

As the new "Minister Plenipotentiary to the United States with Extraordinary Powers," Ambassador Parker Hardin French headed east to catch the next steamer to New York. He would not be accepted by the Pierce administration and Secretary of State Marcy. He would also fail to attain recognition of the Rivas/Walker administration as the legitimate government of Nicaragua. The failure would buttress Central American allies in their opposition to Walker and help lead to his downfall. French would have success in adjudicating the disagreement on the Accessory Transit Company fee claims and ensure cheap passage of migrants to Nicaragua. His recruiting efforts would help harvest over 1,000 recruits for the Walker cause. Charged and indicted with breaching neutrality laws, he would use his legal knowledge and audacious gall to frustrate the United States legal system. French's notorious past, especially his defrauding of army officers at San Antonio, would hamper all his efforts and solidify Marcy's opposition. A failed and rejected Parker French would return to Grenada, there to be fired by Walker and ejected from the country.

The Sacramento *Democratic State Journal*, in a mixture of seriousness, humor, and sarcasm, reviewed his exploits in Nicaragua and his elevation to ambassador:

"We have laughed immoderately over the adventures of
Parker H. French, at Washington and New York; the story is
so piquant and refreshing! ... One fine morning we find him
in Sacramento ... enlisting an army for the Central American
expedition. Next, we hear of him is that he is Minister of
Finance ... Presto! Again, he is at Washington, aspiring to be
the arbiter of the destiny of nations. ... He would almost baffle
a Bonaparte by the rapidity of his movements, and shame a
Richelieu with the vigor of his policy. We suppose we shall
hear of him next at Paris or London settling the quarrels
of the crowned heads of Europe. He has gone upwards like
a rocket; but we hope he will not go out as suddenly, for we
confess that we relish his impetuosity and are amazing tickled
at the sensation he creates."

On December 11, Parker French arrived in New
York aboard the *Northern Light*; he carried a treaty
between the nations, already ratified by the previous
Legitimist government and newly confirmed by
President Rivas. While in New York, his wife's uncle,
General Duff Green, helped him maneuver through
the New York networks.

One of French's first acts was to negotiate
settlement of the Accessory Transit Company debt
claim. As an easy fix, the ATC agreed to a French
proposal that they would transport migrants to
Nicaragua for $20 per head and deduct those sums
from that owed to Nicaragua. In return, the ATC got
what French knew to be an irrelevant and worthless
extension of their transit charter. It was agreed
that 500 passengers would go out on the next two
steamers, *Northern Light* on December 24, followed by
the *Star of the West* on January 9.

If Vanderbilt would have known about the Walker-
Randolph-Morgan-Garrison trap awaiting him, he
certainly would have tried to intervene and stop the
action. But at that time, the commodore assessed the
agreement as a very positive step for continued ATC

success in Nicaragua. From December to when the trap was sprung in February and made public in New York in March, the ATC carried about 1,000 Walker recruits to Nicaragua.

French quickly turned to recruiting, posting newspaper ads offering grants of land and cheap passage to those wanting to migrate to Nicaragua. Hundreds of visitors came to his suite at the St. Nicholas Hotel. Prominent expansionists like General William Cazneau were especially noted; he was implicated in plotting the annexation of the island of Santo Domingo. There were representatives of the Cuban revolutionary junta led by Don Domingo de Goicouria; Walker would pledge common cause and support with the junta "for the purpose of overthrowing the Spanish tyranny in the island and of insuring the prosperity of Central America."[158]

ST. NICHOLAS HOTEL, BROADWAY, NEW YORK.
TREADWELL, ACKER & Co., PROPRIETORS.

St. Nicholas Hotel New York City, 1853. Print from *Frank Leslie's Illustrated Monthly.*

In Washington on the diplomatic front, events were not going well. Undoubtedly instigated by leaks from the State Department, the press speculated Ambassador French would not be received and recognized by Secretary of State Marcy. Newspapers also reported that Secretary Marcy had earlier sent a notice to Ambassador Wheeler to deny recognition to the Rivas/Walker's regime, but the direction had not been received in time. Some of Parker French's nefarious background caught up with him. Major Babbitt, whom French scammed in 1850 at San Antonio, wrote a letter to Secretary of War Jefferson Davis, who forwarded the letter to Secretary of State Marcy. Babbitt outlined the San Antonio scam, not only on himself but on Benton, Longstreet, and local merchants. The press quickly picked up the news, remembered the forgeries of the Howland and Aspinwall letter of credit, and started questioning how such a fraudster could be recognized as an ambassador.

Parker French's ambassadorial dreams ended on December 21. In reply to French's request for an appointment to present his credentials, Marcy wrote a scorching letter: "The President of the United States sees no reason for establishing diplomatic intercourse with the persons who now claim to exercise the political power in the State of Nicaragua; those who were chiefly instrumental in suspending or overthrowing the former government of that State were not citizens belonging to it."

United States Attorney General Caleb Cushing wrote United States Attorney for the Southern District of New York John McKeon, saying that French was entitled to diplomatic privileges only in a limited way: "He is not an accredited Minister, but simply a person coming to this country to present himself as such ... any diplomatic privileges accorded to him is of mere transit, and of courtesy, not full right; and that courtesy will be withdrawn from him so soon as there shall be cause to believe that he is engaged in ... any act not consonant with the laws, the peace or the public honor of the United States."

McKeon directly informed French that the extended courtesy of remaining and traveling in the country was short lived "in the hope that no further complaint be made against you." French replied that he would go where he pleased, when he pleased. It would not be the last time Caleb Cushing would torment Parker French; over the next sixteen years, Cushing would be a three-time nemesis.[159]

In the meantime, Parker French had been recruiting "colonists" and preparing to send them to Nicaragua aboard the steamer *Northern Light*. On December 24, Attorney General Cushing directed McKeon to prevent the vessel's departure; he was to seize any weapons and remove any passengers bound for Nicaragua in violation of the neutrality acts. McKeon and deputy marshals found the ship ready to sail with hundreds of passengers suspected of being Walker recruits. The authorities boarded the ship and announced its seizure in the name of the United States government. There was a serious but nevertheless humorous order of events: a riotous crowd on the pier, dispute with the captain, legal argument with the ATC counsel Joseph White, an unauthorized departure from the dock, a chase by a cutter towed by a steam tug, a warning from the cutter firing a blank charge, and finally a live warning shot with a cannonball, which one observer described as soaring "over the bow of the Northern Light, plopping into the gray water and creating an impressive plume." The captain gave up and hove to. Over 230 passengers were removed, suspected of being in violation of neutrality laws. Among them was Parker French, but after initial questioning he was released.

The record of a follow-on interview is instructive as to French's knowledge of the law, his gift of gab, and the palpable frustration he caused the United States Attorney McKeon. McKeon decided to visit French at his hotel, the exclusive St. Nicholas. French was talking to Generals Cazneau and Green of Texas, as well as Colonel Jack Hays of California and Texas Ranger fame. At first McKeon asked Cazneau if he was Parker French, Cazneau directed McKeon's attention to the one-armed man. Requesting a private interview, McKeon started asking leading questions, obviously trying to get French to implicate himself. To every question the Nicaraguan minister would answer with a claim of diplomatic immunity, explicitly deny any wrongdoing, or assert that he was exercising legal rights. After being asked if he was recruiting soldiers for Walker, French responded that he was not; he was inviting settlers of "good character and industrious habits to come out and cultivate the rich unoccupied domain of Nicaragua." When challenged about possible illegal inducements, French said that each settler would receive 250 acres of fine land and the privilege of the most favored residents. McKeon confronted him on the fact that the passage was only costing $20 per passenger. "Precisely" French said, "for it is the anxious desire of my government to induce emigration to Nicaragua." McKeon protested by saying that the United States government would not allow it. French responded that he doubted whether the United States would want to keep citizens from "going where they please, when they please, in a proper and legal manner." And for the rest of McKeon's complaints, well, that was an entirely internal Nicaraguan matter. McKeon then declared that he would arrest the emigrants and stop the vessel. French replied, "Whatever you do in the violation of your own laws and the freedom of your own citizens is the affair of the United States. ... Nicaragua will do justice to all that reach her soil." Upon hearing McKeon threaten to seize and sell the steamers, French responded, "When you take that extreme measure, be kind enough to notify me, that I may buy the steamers for my Government."

Next French asked in multiple ways for McKeon to put all his questions in writing. McKeon refused, spouting that "the law must take its course." Finally, French had enough and asked McKeon if he had traced any violation of the neutrality laws to his door. McKeon strongly declared that he had undoubted proof of French's criminality.

French was then reported as resolute, saying: "You shame the office you represent by coming here to tamper with me and trying to entangle me when you say you have already proofs in your hand that will justify my arrest. You should have come with a warrant; but as you have forgotten your own duty by not bringing it, I will waive the formality and allow you to arrest me without it. If I have violated the neutrality laws of the United States, I have done so by doing nothing at all and I must require an immediate investigation of the matter ... otherwise I must request you to retire."

In a huff, McKeon left.[160]

McKeon then sent a letter to French charging him with violations of the neutrality laws and on the account that French had "begun, set on foot, provided and prepared the means for a military expedition ... carried on from this country against the ... Republic of Nicaragua." French dismissed the letter with a short denial of any criminality, saying, "You will perceive therefore, that it is not necessary that I should give your letter any further consideration."

Newspapers openly splashed reports of the McKeon charges and the ensuing grand jury indictment. Soon a marshal executed a warrant for French's arrest; the warrant was swiftly rescinded just a half hour later "without bail, parole, or recognizance of any kind." The press speculated that the government did not want to give Parker French the publicity. Because breaches of neutrality law could be extremely difficult to prove, McKeon and Cushing also probably recognized the weakness of their case. French took great pleasure in openly responding to the charges and indictment, in newspapers and in court. He likely drove McKeon to distraction by publicly demanding a speedy, fair, and public trial; there was never a trial, but French kept noticeably protesting the open indictment and persisted in demanding a hearing.

For a while, the emerging controversy would create sympathy for the rejected minister and make him a hero amongst Walker supporters. Most of that sympathy and hero manufacturing was probably wasted. The press kept alive the incriminating stories, including French's 1850 use of the Howland and Aspinwall forged letters of credit and especially the defrauding of army officers Babbitt, Benton, and Longstreet. The continued press interest was likely fed by prompting from the State Department, as well as resolutions in Congress, giving relief to the officers from the pecuniary responsibility.

Neither the inability to get diplomatic recognition nor McKeon's threats kept Parker French from his other duties. He kept on recruiting and arranging passage with the ATC at $20 per head. McKeon investigated again on 9 January; he removed a few passengers from the *Star of the West* but could not identify any other filibuster suspects. Parker French bid fond farewell to 125 migrants listed as "mechanics and laborers" needed to complete the wharf at La Virgen. When they arrived in Nicaragua, the men transmuted into army recruits and would form the core of a New York regiment for Walker.

In the first week of January 1856, Parker French was back in Washington, living the high life at the National Hotel. With the expert guidance and excellent connections of his uncle Duff Green, he was in the halls of Congress lobbying members. The

New York Herald reported that "the representative of Nicaragua was warmly received by a strong majority" in both houses of Congress, and "His firm bearing and brilliant style of conversation captivates even the old fogies."

There were plenty of expansionists and supporters of Walker for Parker French to buttonhole, especially such senators as Slidell, Mason, Cass, Weller, and Douglas. Virginian James Mason and Louisianan John Slidell, as southern champions of Central American adventures, were a given. Northern expansionists Lewis Cass of Michigan, Stephen Douglas of Illinois, and John Weller of California were particularly important to Walker's cause and French's mission as ambassador. Lewis Cass was strident in his support of Walker: "I am free to confess that the heroic effort of our countrymen in Nicaragua excites my admiration, while it engages all my solicitude... He who does not sympathize with such an enterprise has little in common with me." On the floor of the Senate, Weller slammed the Pierce administration for rejection of French on purely personal grounds, attacked the arrest of emigrants, and explicitly supported Walker. He said, "It is a great mistake to suppose these men are desperadoes and freebooters!"

Author Robert May in *Slavery Race and Conquest in the Tropics* described Stephen Douglas as a long standing and fervent apostle of Manifest Destiny, supported expansionism into Central America, Mexico, and Cuba, and had been crowned the "prince of Fillubistierism"—a descriptive term, even if misspelled. The senator argued that the Rivas/Walker regime was more stable than any other in Central America since the end of Spanish colonization. He considered the Rivas/Walker government as "... legitimate as any which ever existed..." in the region. He even compared Walker's military command to the

Revolutionary War commissioning of Lafayette.

Trying to save his ambassadorship, Parker French made a late run at Douglas, imploring him to influence Secretary Marcy. French even recommended that Douglas sponsor an amendment to the Neutrality Act of 1818, which expansionists described as "the most efficient aid and support to European interference and dictation in American affairs."[161,162,163]

French's extravagant living, both in New York and Washington, certainly did not please his family in Kentucky and Indiana, especially his sister Juliet French Banks who lived with her husband Henry near New Albany, Indiana. A local newspaper, *The Ledger,* ran a piece which Juliet likely prompted: "We see that Parker H. French is still trying to get the President to recognize him as Minister from Nicaragua. French is living in clover at New York and Washington while his father is an inmate of the poor house in Mason County, KY." There is no record if Parker French ever reconnected with his father Hiram, who died in 1872.

On February 7, Parker French was rebuffed again as he tried to present his credentials and seek formal recognition from the Pierce Administration and Secretary of State Marcy. At about the same time, the State Department received Nicaraguan President Rivas' signed decree suspending relations with the United States; he recalled French, citing his treatment received from the cabinet at Washington.

French left New York and traveled through Alton, Illinois to see his family. By February 29, he was ensconced in the St. Charles Hotel in New Orleans recruiting emigrants. He left for Nicaragua on March 12 on the *Daniel Webster;* aboard were 200 recruits for Walker.[164,165,166,167]

The conspiracy against Vanderbilt worked like a

charm. On February 18, 1856, President Rivas signed the decree revoking the charter of the Accessory Transit Company and granting the charter through Edmund Randolph to Morgan and Garrison. The timing worked perfectly to trap Vanderbilt. In New York on March 12, Accessory Transit Company stock was priced at $22 per share; after the news of the revocation reached New York by telegraph from New Orleans, the stock plunged to $13. Morgan had been selling short and made a killing. Parker French would later assert that he was an integral part of the plan.[168]

The man who sought an empire in Central America made a huge and defining blunder by alienating Commodore Cornelius Vanderbilt; it would be the biggest mistake that William Walker made. The richest and most powerful man in America was soon out for blood; the Commodore would have his revenge in a little over a year. He made common cause with Britain, Central American countries and the growing anti-Walker forces in Nicaragua. All Vanderbilt steamers on the Nicaraguan route were idled at their wharves in New York, choking off Walker's reinforcements and supplies.

In May 1857, the isolated and extensively weakened Walker forces were defeated by the Central American allies, led by Costa Rican President Juan Rafael Mora. The allies had been encouraged, as well as partially funded and equipped, by the Commodore.

Some observers believed that Marcy used French's notoriety, especially the fraud against Army officers, as an excuse to reject French as an ambassador and a ploy to withhold recognition from Walker. They remembered that worse ambassadors had been accepted in the past. Their view was reinforced just a few months after French's rejection. The same Rivas/Walker regime that was unacceptable in February became acceptable in May; Nicaraguan Padre Agustin

Vijil was received, and the government recognized.

Some historical documents imply that Walker did not then know, or appreciate the potential impact, of French's nefarious background. But Walker was an astute man. In 1850, Walker was in New Orleans when French arrived on his ill-famed gold rush expedition; he undoubtedly knew about French's well-publicized meeting with defeated Cuban revolutionary and filibuster Narciso Lopez. As a California newspaper editor, Walker was likely aware of French's negative press during late 1850 and early 1851. Stories about French's frauds were steadily arriving from eastern and southern newspapers. He was probably attentive as angry and talkative victims of French arrived in San Francisco. Walker certainly had to know of French's tough-minded approach to the backing of California politician David Broderick when Walker was supporting that same man.

Walker was probably a good judge of character; perhaps he actually prized French's basic Machiavellian nature more than he worried about his background. He probably assumed that the cunning, audacious, and sociable Parker French could readily maneuver through the duplicitous landscape of international diplomacy. French would be the right man, for the right job, at the right time, representing Nicaragua in the halls of power. Walker himself gave partial credit to the rejection of French for his ultimate defeat; the rebuff encouraged the Central Americans to ally against him. But Walker did not see it as his own flaw; he blamed President Pierce and Secretary of State Marcy. He should have sent a natural born Nicaraguan.

Upon return to Walker's headquarters, French was immediately fired after what was labeled an "angry scene and a definitive rupture." There was conflicting press speculation on the cause. Conduct in New York and failure in Washington, treatment of immigrants, and alleged embezzlement were possible reasons. Perhaps internal enemies in the Walker cabal had poisoned Walker against French. The unhappy merchant class could have turned him in for pay-to-play graft and corruption. If Walker was truly angered at some disloyalty, French was lucky to escape with his life. Some just said that Walker quietly declared. "Parker French, I will give you twenty-four hours to leave this country."[169]

For the next several years Parker Hardin French turned up all over the country. His established notoriety fostered the compulsive need of editors and their readers to follow his exploits.

11

HE "TURNS UP" AGAIN
AND AGAIN

After dismissal by William Walker and expulsion from Nicaragua, Parker French moved around the United States for the next five years at a frantic pace in the era of sail, steam, and horse transportation. He engaged in a bewildering mix of commercial interests and activities, as well as the expected instances of deceit and fraud. After summarizing his multiple moves and engagements, one editor wrote:

> "Parker H. French, of whose erratic movements it is almost impossible to keep the run, left very suddenly, and to his anxious creditors very unexpectedly on the steamer Sonora. Within the period of eight years he has been a stock dealer on the plains, editor of a Know-Nothing organ, filibuster in Sonora, diplomatist in Nicaragua, applicant at the national capital for the plenipotentiariship (sic.), real estate operator in Minnesota and editor of an ephemeral Republican sheet in this city. Who dare say he will not next 'turn up' as a coral hunter on the reefs of Madagascar."

The editor was wrong on just two counts; French was not just a stock dealer on the plains and neither was he involved in any Sonora, Mexico, filibuster operation.[170]

For the next five years, Parker Hardin French continued to "turn up" in newspapers. By this time there was an allure about the "delightful rogue," as some called him, who somehow represented a romantic if flawed heroic character. Disagreeable, offensive, and exasperating as his exploits were, there must have been some grudging everyman appeal as he echoed an American iconic character—hard working, independent, ambitious, audacious, and adventurous. Many articles took on the character and style of celebrity-watching supermarket tabloids with a mixture of truth, gossip, innuendo, and speculation. Some subscribers might have read the stories as a compilation of an interesting travelogue. Others probably read the articles looking for report of a train wreck and chuckled about his latest endeavor.

In the spring of 1856, when French was fired from Walker's headquarters, he met two emancipated black Americans, James Thomas and his nephew John Rapier Jr. They were seeking permission from Walker to return to the United States after just a few months in Nicaragua.

Before immigrating to Nicaragua, both Thomas and Rapier had become disgusted with growing racial tensions, as well as the North-South intersectional turmoil. John Rapier feared losing his freedom in the south. Uncle Thomas was also frustrated and angry at the bigotry, segregation, and second-class citizenship in the North. They were looking for somewhere to start a new life; they were looking for a promised land. Rapier showed his uncle a news article about William Walker and the expedition to Nicaragua. Walker's forces had just captured Granada. The new government promised immigrants 250 acres of free land and free passage to Nicaragua. Thomas, a lifelong resident of Nashville, had known Walker since boyhood, always had positive experiences with him, and described him as a "quiet, modest, and unobtrusive young man." They even attended the same church, which allowed both white and black members to take sacraments at the same time. With high expectations of new land and new freedoms, Thomas and Rapier both resolved to migrate to Nicaragua, their "Canaan." Thomas would later recall that people would ask him why he was going to Nicaragua. "I thought it strange to put that question to me when such grand opportunities were presented," Thomas said.[171]

Traveling down the Mississippi to New Orleans, they worked through restrictive travel checks, armed with their emancipation documents and letters of introduction from reputable white citizens. With the help of a New Orleans merchant, they gained passage, along with dozens of recruits, on the steamship *Daniel Webster* bound for Nicaragua. They carried with them a letter from Walker's father. Upon meeting with Walker, Thomas and Rapier were impressed with his quiet, modest mannerisms, absence of pretentious clothing, and the simple furnishings of his headquarters. Thomas said that Walker perused his father's letter quietly and without any apparent emotion.

Quickly, Thomas and Rapier recognized that their dream of a promised land of equality and opportunity was, in fact, a terrible nightmare. They discovered the death, destruction, and disease in the tropics of Central America. They also quickly learned that Walker had no plans to improve the circumstances and prospects of native peasantry. Worse, it became clear to them that Walker intended to conquer all Central America, and perhaps Cuba. They suspected that he would reintroduce slavery as well. Indeed, later in September, Walker decreed that slavery be reintroduced to Nicaragua, which would "furnish a supply of constant and reliable labor requisite for the cultivation of tropical products." Dismayed and betrayed, Thomas and Rapier left the country less than two months after arrival.[172]

After receiving permission from Walker to leave the country, Thomas and Rapier made their way to Aspinwall, Panama (now Colón), which was the Caribbean terminus of the Panamanian transit route. At Aspinwall, Thomas and Rapier boarded the steamer *Illinois* bound for Havana. They discovered that George Wilkes of the *New York Herald* and Parker French were fellow passengers. What they did not know at the time was that French had been canned by Walker. They also did not know that French had penned a letter to Walker insulting him for his leadership and actions. French threatened to help overthrow Walker's government and labeled Walker's actions as suicidal. The *Los Angeles Star,* in reporting the letter, clearly showed its support of Walker by finishing the article "Proh Pudor"—"For Shame."[173]

By the time the ship reached Havana, the young John Rapier Jr. had agreed to be the personal secretary to French. They departed for New Orleans on the steamship *Granada*. Rapier's Uncle James Thomas headed for New York to seek new opportunities.[174,175]

Upon arriving in New Orleans, French and his new secretary checked into the St. Louis Hotel, a luxurious and prestigious gathering place for New Orleans elite. On the night of April 28, 1856, a large number of politicians, merchants, shippers, property owners, and slave owners gathered in the hotel's rotunda. They assembled to discuss the situation in Nicaragua and hear a speech on the subject from Pierre Soule, former Louisiana senator. Soule was a long-standing supporter of filibuster operations in general—Cuban "freedom" in particular—and

Walker's operation in Nicaragua. As the ambassador to Spain in 1854, Soule had co-authored the Ostend Manifesto. The document proposed buying Cuba from Spain and, absent a sale, stated that the United States was justified to use force in seizing it. Soule gave a rousing and eloquent speech in support of William Walker to a receptive crowd. He spoke about the commercial and political characteristics of the Nicaragua situation and stated that William Walker had the wisdom, courage, and efficiency to handle the affairs of Nicaragua in accordance with Southern principles: "truth, justice, righteousness and wisdom." When Soule was finished, the crowd started to yell "French, French, French," to whom Soule turned over the speaker's platform. French urged that the United States absorb the whole of Central America. He warned of war if the US did not act, since another country might attempt an occupation in violation of the Monroe Doctrine. Both Soule and French asked for money, ships, war materials, and men to come to the assistance of William Walker and what they called the "legitimate" government of Nicaragua.

It was doubtless confusing to some that French would still be in such hearty support of Walker given the growing understanding that French had been sacked. Despite widely publicized accounts of the breach with Walker, French asserted that he had reconciled with Walker and that he was empowered to take care of business for the Nicaraguan government. French's speech and actions were clear, and he appeared to be sincere and solid in his enthusiastic support for Walker. One editor defended French, claiming that personal quarrels did not indicate a violation of principle, and "his conduct ... and the handsome manner in which he spoke of General Walker, show that he is a man of upright and generous impulses and will not allow his personal feelings to interfere with his sense of public duty."

Rotunda, Old St. Louis Hotel, New Orleans, La.

St. Louis Hotel Rotunda in New Orleans.

After the speeches, men were recruited to go to Nicaragua and help settle the country with the "bone and sinew of the South." Several attendees came forward and subscribed to a fund to advance "the great movement which had for its object the expansion of the South and the establishment of New Orleans as the capital of an empire." Over $4,000 was collected just at this one meeting; over $18,000 had been collected the previous four days. The combined $22,000 is the equivalent of over $660,000 in 2017.

Other newspaper articles asserted that Walker had entrusted French to negotiate with the Accessory Transit Company. He could settle their differences and had the power to reinstate the Transit Company because Morgan and Garrison were unable to perform their contract. That information likely came from deceitful comments French made himself.[176,177,178]

They didn't stay in New Orleans long. On May 17, French and Rapier arrived in New York and settled into the Mansion House Hotel on Chambers Street near Broadway. French immediately came to the attention of the press by recruiting men and soliciting funds for Walker's cause. He was also a speaker at a large rally in support of Walker. More money flowed, and Parker French seemed on top of the world again.[179]

But bad news had already arrived. By April 30, the *New York Tribune*, edited by Horace Greeley, had reported that French was accused of fraud and theft in Nicaragua and owed thousands of dollars. Immediately after arriving in New York, French saw the article and countered with a long letter to the *New York Herald*, declaring all the assertions and implications false and giving an unqualified denial. He complained bitterly about the "slanderous and libelous falsehood." He further declared that, rather than owing anything to the Nicaraguan government, the government was indebted to him: "I furnished from my individual pocket near the entire means that carried the revolution successfully forward." He further attacked Greeley for calling Walker a robber and for gloating over what French called the "rumored rupture." French expressed continued loyalty for Walker's cause and declared his intention to return to Nicaragua.[180]

In early June, another shoe dropped. In a special correspondence from Nicaragua dated May 26, a reporter from the New Orleans *Times-Picayune* discussed the morale boost in Walker's government because of the supportive rallies around the country, especially those in New Orleans and New York. But, as he also reported, French's support and his enthusiastic praise of Walker were seen as bizarre by most observers in Nicaragua. It was well understood that French was in "decidedly bad odor with the government." French reportedly had been unable or unwilling to account for funds entrusted to him. He was considered a defaulter on the order of $10,000-$15,000 (2017 estimate, $273,000 to $410,000). Although the supportive rallies and fundraising were said to be very much appreciated, French "would hardly do as treasurer of the funds." The "special correspondence" was probably written by Charles Callahan for the *Picayune*; Callahan had just arrived in Nicaragua. He was described in the Walker newspaper *Nicaraguense* as "sympathetic," and would soon become Walker's collector of customs.[181]

Nicaraguan government announcements soon appeared in newspapers around the country. French had no connection to the government, had not been entrusted to conduct any government work, and was "engaged in doing the Republic of Nicaragua all the injury his genius is capable of."

With all his increasing notoriety and newspaper publicity, French's past dealings came back to haunt him. The Sheriff arrested him for old debts associated with a ship purchase scheme a year earlier; he subsequently skipped bail. Rufus Tilton, a passenger on the California expedition, sued him. Tilton's lawyer laid out the facts of the case: French had borrowed hundreds of dollars from Tilton and promised to pay it back when they reached Franklin, Texas (now El Paso). Instead, French "discarded his passengers, disbanded the company, some of the members were shot, others robbed, and the balance left to roam about the plains of Texas and Mexico." The judge stopped the lawyer and marveled that French had luckily escaped with his life; he then granted the plaintiff's motion for court costs.

No further reports of the court cases emerged. French had skipped town. He and his secretary were on the way to Cincinnati, doubtless wanting to be near the center of power, money, and influence represented by the national Democratic Convention of 1856.[182,183,184,185]

By June 1, French and Rapier were in Cincinnati to attend the convention. Droves of delegates and visitors overwhelmed the city, crowding the streets and bars. The *Cincinnati Times* reported fifteen or twenty thousand strangers in the city packed into hotels and filling up boarding rooms as well as private houses.

Parker French probably saw the throng as a target-rich environment. He was ready to take advantage of the enthusiasm of Democrats, especially southern Democrats, for Walker's cause. It was also an opportunity to meet with key supporters of expansionist principles, who were directly linked to French in a *Baltimore Sun* article: his Louisiana ally Pierre Soule; John Appleton of Maine, advisor to the next president, James Buchanan; Representative Preston Brooks of South Carolina who famously cane-whipped Senator Charles Sumner just two weeks earlier; Ben McCullough, Texas Ranger, adventurer and secessionist; and, Isaiah Rynders, New York street tough and political organizer for Tammany Hall. Also available was fellow Kentuckian John C. Breckinridge, the next U.S. vice president, future Confederate general, and Confederate secretary of war.

Members of the Louisiana delegation had previously asked both Pierre Soule and French to help prepare two planks for the party platform: "These pieces of lumber were first, 'Nicaragua and her independence' and second, 'Indemnification in soil and territory for American blood shed at Panama!'" There is no mention of these in the convention records, but the convention did approve two planks: they expressed sympathy in the efforts of the people of Central America to regenerate "the passage across the Interoceanic Isthmus," and the Democratic Party would expect the next administration to ensure "our ascendancy in the Gulf of Mexico."

On the night of September 4, French gave a lecture at the Masonic Hall to enthusiastic applause. French ended his lecture by noting that Nicaragua sat at a strategic crossroads between the two continents, between the Atlantic and the Pacific, close to Cuba, adding that "Nicaragua only needs the life-giving energy of Americans to take a proud place among the nations of the earth." There were no reported efforts at recruitment or solicitation of funds, but it is unlikely that French would miss the opportunity to buttonhole subscribers. He was scheduled to give another talk on June 5, but it was cancelled with no explanation. Perhaps the news of his rupture with Walker had finally caught up with him.[186,187,188,189]

Over the next several weeks, French was reported in Louisville, Kentucky, southern Illinois, and St. Louis, Missouri, probably visiting family and friends. He did not get a friendly reception in St. Louis as debtors vainly continued attempts to recover their losses from his failed businesses, including the ship *Matilda* fiasco. His visit to St. Louis "was terminated prematurely by … writs requiring his presence in our courts to answer sundry actions on promissory notes," which totaled $90,000 (2017 estimate, $2.7 million).[190,191]

At some point, John Rapier must have considered his boss's questionable character and suspicious activities. There was plenty of evidence in newspapers that French had not disclosed being fired by William Walker, neither to his audiences nor to Rapier. He had to realize that French, as engaging and charismatic as he appeared, was a talented and convincing swindler. But Rapier stayed on, likely because French still owed him all his pay to date.[192]

French appeared next in St. Paul, Minnesota, aboard the side-wheeler *Alhambra*. Arriving on August 15, he arranged lodging in the Winslow House. The 200-room hotel featured luxury accommodations for southerners who came upriver via steamboat to escape the sweltering summers. Easterners also visited on business or as tourists. Parker French was pursuing a new career and targeting a new business opportunity. He was now a land speculator and real estate developer heading up the Mississippi to the little town of Watab, Minnesota. This time his party included his family: wife Lucretia, seven-year-old daughter Matilda, and three-year-old Hugh. Along for the adventure was the family of Lucretia's sister Ellen Metcalf. Ellen's physician husband Richard and his merchant brother James would help build the community.

At about the same time, papers all over the country reported that French had formed a joint stock company in Illinois for the purpose of land investment and development in Minnesota. There were no subsequent reports of the success of stock sales, the amount of money raised, or the number of investors clipped.[193]

The town of Watab had just been designated the county seat of Benton County. Considered the most important business center northwest of St. Paul, Watab sat on a critical crossing over the Mississippi. As part of the "Oxcart Trail" system, it serviced settlements in the Red River Valley and was the center of trade for Native American tribes.[194,195,196]

Minnesota was in the middle of a land boom. County seats and commercial centers were particularly fruitful targets for speculators and developers. Benton County commissioners approved building a courthouse, jail, and a building for county offices. They issued bonds to contractors with heavy rates of interest with no means of servicing the interest or retiring the bonds. The contractors, presumably including Parker French, resold the bonds to investors, probably at a discount. By the middle of September, Parker French was in Watab at the head of a company that erected frame buildings. A visitor reported that French was making a good impression on the town while "rushing the place ahead with great zeal." Even French's personal secretary, John Rapier Jr. caught the fever and bought a lot. The purchase was presumably on credit, since French had not yet paid his back wages.[197,198]

French also bought printing equipment and started the newspaper *Northern Herald.* First operating the paper in Watab, he then moved the paper upriver about twenty-five miles to Little Falls, the county seat of Morrison County. French described the *Northern Herald* as "the most northern paper in the Union." As any superb marketer and self-serving promoter would, Parker French effectively used the power of the press to report on the wonderful progress of the development company under this new man "Parker French."[199,200]

"Our Town—Watab—after a Rip Van Winkle sleep of two years has suddenly awakened to a sense of importance and commenced a work of progress as if desirous of atoning for her long inactivity. A company from Northern Illinois bought a third interest in the town, some six weeks since, and placed the management of their business in the hands of Colonel French. The company sent up twenty-two men, some of them with families, who have become citizens of our town and most of them become possessed of lots, and are building on and improving the same."

Construction came to a grinding halt in November. The winter of 1856-1857 was one of the worst winters in Minnesota history with early and heavy snows, violent winds, and brutal temperatures. With Parker French in Little Falls, John Rapier became very ill. He found that loyalty, empathy, and compassion were not Parker French characteristics. French fired Rapier, cut off his room and board, and refused to pay Rapier's back wages. Rapier survived the rest of the winter with the help of charitable Little Falls citizens.

Spring came with high expectations of further progress. But there was no effective tax base in the county and no means to pay the bondholders. Buildings were not complete, and there was no money for continuing operations of the county. French had already put his plan in place to abandon the project and leave the territory. Rapier approached French and demanded his back pay. French agreed, but only with a provision that Rapier would accompany him to California. But this time Rapier resolved to get the upper hand and leave French as soon as possible, "I will go with him to St. Paul & there bid him a final adieu, the dam Scoundrel."[201]

The *St. Paul Daily Pioneer* reported that French had failed to give a talk about Nicaragua to the Young Men's Association on March 12. He had left the territory, the paper said, "rather quietly and mysteriously." He was absent in St. Paul because he was, in fact, already in New Orleans.[202]

French was on the move to California through Panama, Benton County's money likely in his pocket. French left his wife Lucretia and children in the Alton, Illinois area with the Edwards family. He visited contacts in St. Louis, where again he had to hastily evade the clutches of the subpoena-bearing sheriff.

French was now without his personal secretary, who certainly did not need him anymore. Rapier became a journalist for a while and then was the first African American to graduate from a medical school west of the Mississippi River. During the Civil War, he was appointed as an assistant surgeon for the Freedman's Hospital in Washington, D.C.

Arriving in San Francisco on April 13 on the *Golden Age*, French immediately purchased the equipment for a new paper. Competing San Francisco and Sacramento papers announced that French anticipated an early start. The *California State Register,* he announced, would have "Republican proclivities." Parker Hardin French—pro-slavery Democrat, an anti-foreigner member of the Know-Nothings, a filibuster, and an attendee at the Democratic Convention—had apparently morphed into an abolitionist Republican. He either had a dramatic turn of principled convictions on the weeks-long trip or saw an opportunity in a new and underserved market with limited competition. Cynical people would probably think the latter. The paper was suspended after only three issues, and there was no positive critical acclaim.

What was not generally reported was that French, in partnership with another publisher, had obtained a lion's share of the very lucrative and profitable California state printing contract for 1856-1857. The bureaucrat who ran the state printing office was assumed to have "fallen among thieves." [203,204]

Due to French's notoriety, the advent and the demise of the paper did not go unnoticed. For one, the St. Paul Minnesota *Daily Pioneer* now knew the whereabouts of their missing land speculator, developer, schemer, and newspaper editor who had disappeared in mystery. Newspapers all over the country weighed in:

Boston Post: "Parker has not won much glory by any of his public acts, previously, and we do not believe his present undertaking will result more auspiciously than his previous labors."

Daily Ohio Statesman: "The notorious Parker H. French is an editor of a black Republican Daily Register."

San Joaquin Republican: "...paper is handsomely printed, but evinces a sad lack of mental capacity and professional skill. It will not set the world on fire."

Memphis Daily Eagle and Enquirer: French "a year ago was peddling filibuster sentiments." They further hoped that "he writes better English than he condescends to use when he lectures."

His newspaper having failed, French next turned to his dormant legal career and began representing clients.

One of his cases was the defense of an alleged murderer. At Whitlock mine, about ten miles from Mariposa, on December 28, 1856, John Lucas and J.D. Rose were drinking and playing poker for small amounts. Mrs. Lucas, without the intoxicated Lucas noticing, picked up about three dollars belonging to Rose. Rose demanded the money and Lucas refused to give it up. Reportedly, there was not much of an argument and no harsh language was used. After repeated refusals from Lucas, Rose quietly stood up and plunged a nine-inch Bowie knife into Lucas's chest up to the hilt, cutting right through the heart and killing Lucas instantly. Rose was soon arrested by the sheriff and jailed in Mariposa to await trial. The trial was conducted in June 1857. Parker French, along with local Mariposa lawyer Samuel Merritt, defended Rose. The act of homicide was admitted; French and Merritt based their defense on a plea of "delusive insanity." Many witnesses came forward supporting the insanity defense, which was asserted to be long-lasting and hereditary. Rose had a good family and a good reputation. The jury found Rose not guilty, and he was released.[205,206]

In May 1857, French learned that his old boss had been defeated in the final battle of what Nicaraguans

called the "National War." Walker had been besieged
in Rivas by a Central American allied army and slowly
overwhelmed. Commander Charles H. Davis of the
United States Navy stepped in and arranged a truce.
On May 1, 1857, Walker and his remaining followers,
escorted by a force of United States Marines,
evacuated Rivas, marched to the coast, and took
ships back to the United States.

French returned to San Francisco, and in early
July 1857, started playing hardball with the big boys
again. This time he targeted shipping and railroad
magnate Charles Morgan and accused him of fraud
during the Nicaraguan transit rights struggle with
Cornelius Vanderbilt. French filed a lawsuit in San
Francisco alleging that Morgan had cheated him
out of $66,000 (2017 estimate, $1.8 million). They
had formed a secret partnership, to speculate in
Accessory Transit Company (ATC) stock. French's
share was supposed to be 25 percent of the profits.
The conspiracy was brilliant; Morgan had the money
while French had inside information, influence,
and power in the Nicaraguan government. Morgan
also anticipated the plans of Cornelius Vanderbilt.
Vanderbilt had been buying up stock in ATC, took
control of the company, and forced Morgan out.
Meanwhile, Morgan and Cornelius Garrison had
secretly formed a counterattack. As discussed in
Chapter 9, the two had made a deal with Walker,
through Edmund Randolph, to cancel the ATC
contract and award a new contract to a company
owned by Morgan, Garrison, and associates.
Thinking he had the advantage, Vanderbilt had been
secretly buying stock. Morgan knew Vanderbilt's
plans and had been simultaneously selling short.
The conspirators struck at the same time as the
cancellation of the ATC deal by the Nicaraguan
government. The ATC stock tanked. The conspirators
made a killing by covering their short positions.

The profits, French asserted in the lawsuit, were a tidy $300,000. French accused Morgan of false and fraudulent representations. He claimed that Morgan had paid him only $9,000, rather than the $75,000 to which French was entitled. French also filed suit against Cornelius Garrison for $2,500. In the filing, French alleged that Garrison had promised to pay some of the debts of the Nicaraguan government; included was the previously discussed $1,343 claim by A.J. Taylor for weapons, including the famed Mississippi rifles.[207,208,209,210]

On Saturday, July 11, with lawsuits in hand, French sailed on the steamer *Sonora* heading for New York by way of Panama. California newspapers were baffled and humored by his unexpected and precipitous departure; his local creditors probably had different adjectives to describe their reactions. Based on experience, they had just cause to assume the worst. One newspaper called him a "rare bird" for departing just after filing the lawsuit five days before. What they probably did not appreciate was that the cunning French now had powerful ammunition against Morgan and Garrison.[211]

On July 20, 1857, French arrived in New York City on the steamship *Illinois* from Aspinwall, Nicaragua. He moved into a home at 106 West 22d Street between Sixth and Seventh Avenues. The residence had easy walking access to the centers of political, economic, and social power along Fifth Avenue and Broadway. The surrounding area was filled with the homes of the rich and powerful. Just a couple of blocks away, the exclusive Fifth Avenue Hotel was under construction, scheduled to be opened in 1859. On the corner of Twenty-First Street and Fifth Avenue was the mansion that housed the exclusive *Union Club*, a social organization with a membership of 400 of the city's most powerful citizens, including

Cornelius Vanderbilt. And, to facilitate pursuing the lawsuit against Charles Morgan, the mansion of French's adversary was on the north side of Madison Square, a short ten-minute walk; Garrison's home was just a little farther north on Fifth Avenue.[212]

There was no further news of the lawsuits. Perhaps Morgan and French settled out of court to avoid a public exposure of the speculation as well as insider trading, bribery of a government official, misrepresentation, and fraud. Perhaps Morgan just ignored French, but with the proclivity of Parker French to make his views publicly known, it is more likely there was an unpublicized out-of-court settlement. They agreed to partner again; Nicaragua was still a lucrative target for their conspiracy.

The situation in that country had grown more entangled. Nicaragua and Costa Rica both claimed rights to the transit route and were pressing their competing claims, sometimes threatening force. The United States government attempted to formulate a treaty in the area to ensure access through Nicaragua. British and French agents, both governmental and private, were pressing their own security and commercial interests. At least three American partnerships were scheming and competing for the transit franchise. Among them were Charles Morgan and Cornelius Garrison, who maintained they still had the legal rights to the transit route, which had been approved by President Rivas and William Walker in 1856. Reports that William Walker was readying a force in New Orleans and Mobile to again invade Nicaragua increased angst in Central America.

A secret deal by Charles Morgan, C.K. Garrison, and Parker French was exposed by the *New York Tribune*. Its correspondent in Costa Rica detailed an elaborate scheme to reprise a filibuster operation in Nicaragua. Morgan and Garrison sought to retain the

transit rights contract with the assistance of a small
sum of money—$50,000—a bribe to President Mora
of Costa Rica, the *Tribune* reported. More ominous for
Costa Rica, and all Central America, was information
that the conspiracy was possibly in "close league
and correspondence with Walker and his associated
land pirates." Once in custody of the lake and river
steamers, the men planned to deny Costa Rica control
of the San Juan River and Lake Nicaragua. The cabal
would contract with Parker French to provide wood
to the lake and river steamers. The labor-intensive
contract would require a large number of woodcutters
and laborers, who would be armed for their self-
protection. The deal was the perfect cover for moving
a mass of tough, armed men into Nicaragua and
taking over the transit route. There would be no legal
rationale for the United States government to prohibit
the movement of these contract workers under the
neutrality acts. French would become the commander
of a tough, well-armed force; Morgan and Garrison,
with control of the transit route, would become the de
facto rulers of Nicaragua.[213]

Right in the midst of all this turmoil, William
Walker attacked. With his force of 270 men, he
landed near Greytown. They immediately captured
the critical Costa Rican Fort Castillo Viejo on the
San Juan River, as well as lake and river steamers
owned by the Accessory Transit Company. The initial
success, which the filibuster force cheered, was
short lived. United States Navy warships moved in to
block any movement by sea; landing parties cut off
any movement up the river. With the threat of direct
naval gunfire and no possibility of escape, Walker's
situation was hopeless. He surrendered his force
to Commodore Hiram Paulding, the commander of
United States squadron.

Because of the political divide over Walker,

Paulding's actions came under intense Congressional investigation. There was an enduring public debate over Walker's alleged violation of neutrality laws and what President Buchanan described as Paulding's "overzealous" actions. Paulding was temporarily relieved of command and mildly censured. Walker was charged in New Orleans for violation of the neutrality laws. He was acquitted by the sympathetic jury.

In October 1857, an author using the pen name of "Veritas" warned against trusting Walker, using an exposé of the Nicaraguan incursion of 1855-1856. The real author was either Parker French or someone well informed and influenced by French. Introduced as "one who knows," Veritas was described by the editor as an active participant and direct witness to Walker's scheme in Nicaragua. He said the series was a warning to others who might contemplate service to Walker in the future: "they had better keep out of his clutches."

Veritas proceeded to excoriate Walker's character and capabilities. He cited unprincipled ambition, terrible leadership, deceitful promises, fatal overconfidence, and immoral lawlessness. Walker had "total indifference for human life and utter disregard of all the decencies and humanities of civilization." On the other hand, Veritas praised Parker French for being the head, heart, and soul of the original cause, which was just, honorable, and plausible. French alone, Veritas wrote, sustained and maintained the noble cause in the early days. He created the excitement in California; he recruited the entire list of the original principle officers; and he advanced his own funds in the amount of $20,000. French was also the tactical genius responsible for the early battlefield successes, presumably to include the surprise operation against Grenada. Veritas attacked Walker's ability to be a civil or military leader. Any victories were beyond the originality of Walker, yet Walker claimed all the glory and prestige. As Walker advanced his authority, he was more and more "overbearing, capricious and cruel." Walker alone was responsible for the illegal executions of Nicaraguan leaders, intense internal security and surveillance, and confiscatory taxation, as well as unwarranted fines on businesses and property owners. It was Walker's political, strategic and tactical missteps that led to his defeat, the death of thousands of Americans, the death of many more Central Americans, and the devastation of the country. He robbed Vanderbilt of his lawfully won transit rights and declared war on a peace-seeking Costa Rica. And what more evidence would be needed after Veritas explained Walker's unfair treatment of and spiteful quarrels with "the very man (Parker French) who created him." Perhaps it was not prudent for Parker French to openly have the byline.[214]

The governments of Nicaragua and Costa Rica, fearing more filibuster operations and the devastation of war, set aside their hostility and began negotiations to divide the transit interests between the two nations. Continued unrest and instability, combined with the devastation from years of war, would frustrate any further development of the Nicaraguan transit route. Besides, the Panama route with a cross-Isthmus railroad had become well established and cost effective, foreclosing any need for the Nicaraguan route.

French disappeared from public view for the next several months while he and his family continued to live in New York City on West Twenty-Second Street. Parker and Lucretia's third child, Nancy Reed French, was born July 9, 1858. Her name honored Lucretia's mother, Nancy Reed Edwards (1803-1834), the first wife of Cyrus Edwards (1793-1877).

Newspaper editors throughout the country wondered when French would "turn up" again. In

December 1858, a tiny four-line blurb in the *New York Herald* announced the publication of a new paper in the city. It was the "spirited and spicy" *Evening Sentinel* owned by Parker H. French and Mike Walsh. Seeming to belie the owners' backgrounds, the paper's lofty mission statement stated:

> "We are free from the trammels of partisan trill and the serfdom of political organizations, free from the bigotry of creeds and the scrofulous isms that now agitate society. We owe no allegiance to any of the enslaving parties that now disturb the harmony of the country and fill the land with slanderous clamor and fulsome flattery. We hate both prejudice and bigotry because they are tyrants ... destroying all free opinions, cramping the mind and withering every effort toward the advancement of our race."[215]

Mike Walsh and Parker French were neighbors, living just a couple of blocks apart near the center of power along Fifth Avenue and Broadway. French likely knew the powerful Mike Walsh from previous associations in the city, as well as Walsh's support of expansionist operations. Walsh was a notorious street gang leader, anti-Tammany Hall rabble-rouser, and Democratic Party insurgent. For all his bombastic rhetoric and willingness to resort to head bashing, he was not a violent revolutionary; he preferred to work within the political system. Elected as a New York legislator and United States representative, he vehemently criticized the system and supported a range of then "radical" policies, such as fair labor practices, ten-hour workdays, and the end of child labor.[216]

The public was so interested in Parker French that the story was reprinted in papers across the country, each with some variation of the headline "Turned-up." Through the paper, French and Walsh were expected to try to influence the politics of the "Bloody Sixth Ward," since votes in any quantity "...can be obtained there when needed." And, from a prospective competitor: "The names of the editors are notorious enough and perhaps somewhat odorous." Mike Walsh was probably not the ideal newspaper partner; in a previous journalistic endeavor, he had been sued for libel and twice jailed. The paper quickly shut down, reportedly from lack of newsprint and ink. The news of the "fizzle" was just as quickly and universally announced, in some cases happily and with sarcasm.[217,218,219]

Mike Walsh and Parker French probably had a closer relationship than just the newspaper. From his base in New York City, French could take advantage of any new prospect. The next opportunity came in the rise of the "Knights of the Golden Circle." French was likely involved in their quest to gain Southern power and expand slave culture. He also became entangled as the organization transitioned to support of disunion and Southern secession.

12

KNIGHTS OF THE GOLDEN CIRCLE

Press reports and contemporaneous information suggest a possible connection between Parker French and an organization known as the Knights of the Golden Circle (KGC). Because of a lack of surviving KGC records, there is no direct evidence that establishes French's membership, or even alliance, with the KGC. There was, however, during the period 1859 to 1861, a remarkable congruence in time, location, and activities between Parker French and the organization. That linkage could be explained away by pure coincidence; however, the circumstantial evidence suggests that Parker French was a member, or at least an ally, of the organization. It is also possible that French targeted the organization for a marvelous, extensive scam. French had always displayed chameleon-like characteristics as he sought adventure, power, fame, and wealth. His past proclivities for opportunistic exploitation, as well as conspiratorial scheming, reinforce the notion of an association with the Knights of the Golden Circle. Exposure and investigation of his later activities during the Civil War, which is discussed in Chapters 13 through 16, aroused official suspicions that he was an agent of both the KGC and the Confederacy. But even those records and reports cannot shed light on when or if he joined the organization.

The KGC is well chronicled by David C. Keehn in

his highly regarded and well-documented history. The organization was formed under the leadership of George Bickley as early as 1854, and it slowly and quietly grew through the South. It was an intensely secret organization, zealously faithful to the survival of Southern society, dedicated to Southern rights, and the retention and extension of slavery.[220]

The organization became more widely known and more powerful in 1859–1860 through the first part of the Civil War. The *New Orleans Courier* pronounced:

"The Knights of the Golden Circle was organized to cultivate the martial spirit of our people ... now it numbers 39,000 members, who are scattered over the Southern States, and holding within its charmed circle many of our most influential men and best soldiers. No organization of the kind has in this country ever combined so much talent with such immense financial resources ... the whole nation may soon become deeply interested in the ultimate labors of the Knights of the Golden Circle."[221]

The KGC meant to establish a slave-based political and economic empire in the "Golden Circle." The aspirational empire centered on Havana, contained the Southern slave-holding states, encompassed the entire Caribbean basin, and extended to Mexico, as well as Central America. Military security would be ensured by control of sea lanes through the Caribbean and the western Atlantic approaches. Transit to and from the Pacific would be enabled by control of Central America and southern Mexico. The economic potential was enormous. Farming production would focus on cotton, sugar, tobacco, rice, coffee, and indigo. Annexation of parts of Mexico and Central America would add tremendous mineral wealth. The combination of farming and mining industries, both labor-intensive, would require a large slave population. Dependent on future conditions, including the scale of northern oppression and intrusion, there were two options for the slave empire: The South could remain in the Union as a political and economic equal to the North, or it could emerge as an independent nation.

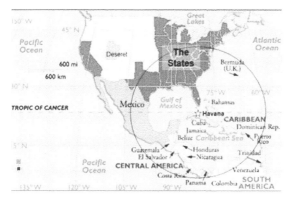

Map of the aspirational empire of the Knights of the Golden Circle, centered in Havana and 2,400 miles in diameter.

Seal of the secret society, Knights of the Golden Circle.

In 1858, the KGC became more politically influential when it merged with the extant Order of the Lone Star (OLS). After the abject failures of the Narciso Lopez expeditions against Cuba, American filibusters and Cuban exiles formed the OLS in New Orleans in 1851. Pierre Soule, a Parker French associate, was the founding president. The primary goal of the OLS was to bring Cuba into the Union as a slave-holding state. Absent a sale of the island by Spain, a filibuster operation would free Cuba from Spanish rule; annexation as a territory and then statehood would quickly follow. Manifest Destiny, the slave culture, and Congressional (especially senatorial) balance would all be fostered. OLS chapters were positioned across the South with thousands of members and popular, capable leaders, generating significant political credibility and clout. Its tentacles reached northward with chapters in the border states, as well as New York City. In New York, the OLS enjoyed the support from a cross section of New York power: shipping magnate George Law; journalists like John O'Sullivan and French associate George Wilkes; street gang leaders and fervent political agitators like Isaiah Rynders, Billy Mulligan, and Mike Walsh (all French colleagues); and Democratic power center, Tammany Hall, with William Marcy (Boss) Tweed. The combined mass of the KGC and OLS was positioned to protect and extend the slavery culture and pursue their expansionist agenda.[222]

The KGC had a hierarchical organization with three "degrees." The First Degree, the "Knights of the Iron Hand," was the largest part of the organization and represented its rank and file military muscle. The Second Degree, the "Knights of the True Faith," can be likened to a professional bureaucracy in administrative, financial, and logistics support. They recruited manpower, raised funds, and invested. The Third Degree, or "Knights of the Columbian Star," included the political and governing leadership; it was the most secretive. Many Southern political leaders were either members of the governing body or, at a minimum, very influential. This group included governors such as John Pettus of Mississippi and Beriah Magoffin of Kentucky, secessionist fire-eaters like William Yancey and Robert Rhett, Senator William Gwin of California, as well as a large group of congressmen led by Louis Wigfall from Texas. KGC adherents even reached into the highest levels

of the Buchanan administration; Vice President
Breckinridge, Secretary of the Treasury Howard Cobb,
and Secretary of War John Floyd were all suspected of
being KGC members.

Parker French probably knew many of the key
players within the KGC from past associations and
operations. George Bickley centered much of his
early KGC operation in Cincinnati, Louisville, and
Lexington. Kentuckian French, with connections
throughout the border and lower Northern states,
always seemed to have an ear to the ground.
French must have known Bickley through local
contacts, political cronies, or connections with other
filibusterers. French's Southern roots, elite family
connections, and filibuster history would show a
Southern "gentleman in good standing" and indicate
that he was supportive of the KGC philosophy, goals,
and objectives.

The previously documented partnership with Mike
Walsh in the "spirited and spicy" *Evening Sentinel*
deserves exploration in light of expansionist filibuster
operations and perhaps the KGC. The relationship
with French could appear to be one of strange
bedfellows, but there was a connection. Walsh had
been a long-standing advocate of Manifest Destiny. He
supported the annexation of Texas, the war against
Mexico, and annexation of Cuba as a slave state.
In support of filibuster operations against Spanish
occupation of Cuba, Walsh raised money, helped
recruit, and garnered political support. For example,
Walsh knew Senator Stephen Douglas, who supported
the recognition of the William Walker regime when
Parker French was seeking acceptance by Secretary
of State Marcy as Nicaraguan ambassador. Walsh
vehemently opposed abolitionism, thinking that
Northern interference with slavery was anti-
democratic and that slavery was the "mildest and

most rational" form of labor relationships between an employer and a worker.[223]

Press accounts of the French-Walsh newspaper enterprise did not scrutinize the partnership in connection with international intrigue. Walsh's activities in Mexico probably drew the rapt attention of French, if not his active involvement and support. A vicious civil war, the "War of Reform" was raging between conservative and liberal factions. A junta of conservative generals and clergy had seized power from the liberal President Comonfort, took over Mexico City, and declared Felix Zualoga president. After losing several battles with the conservatives, the liberal faction, under Benito Juarez, established their capital in the port city stronghold of Vera Cruz. There they could maintain contact with foreign support, collect custom taxes, gather arms, and rebuild their strength. The deposed liberal President Comonfort took up residence in New Orleans, where he was purportedly forming a coalition with Charles Henningsen and Samuel Lockridge; both were colleagues of French in the Nicaraguan operation. Lockridge, like French, had broken with William Walker and had become an early adherent of the Knights of the Golden Circle.[224,225]

While filibustering operations against Mexico were being contemplated in New Orleans, Walsh traveled to Mexico in March 1858 for an extended stay through June. Some believed he was there on a secret mission from the Buchanan administration to further the foreign policy agenda, which included Mexican concessions on territory, military access, and transit routes. Others presumed that he was there to determine the situation, with a mission to "spy out the nakedness of the land, and to report progress to the liberal anti-church and filibustering coalition at New Orleans." Feasibly he supported both agendas. That view is reinforced by a news report from Washington, D.C. that both Walsh and Henningsen were in the city on February 8, "on the way south." Returning by way of New Orleans to Washington, D.C. in early July, Walsh was very cagy in his interview with a *New York Herald* reporter: "Mike looks profoundly mysterious, but declares that he succeeded in effecting the object of his visit to Mexico; but what the object was the correspondent was unable to understand." Some newspapers just reported his visit to Mexico as "he went for the benefit of his health."[226,227,228]

In December 1858, about the same time as his newspaper partnership with Parker French, Walsh and Henningsen incorporated in New York the so-called Arizona, Mexican and Central American Emigration Association. The clandestine organization was headquartered in New York and was reported as having the support of "many persons of influence and wealth," including several prominent Georgians, Texans, and Louisianans. Recruiting offices opened in New York and several Southern cities, with reports of 2,000 members already having joined. Also, the leaders allegedly had an understanding with the Liberal party in Mexico and were acting in concert with it. In early 1859, Walsh went on another secret trip to Mexico, returning in mid-February. Speculation was rife on whether the trip was for the Buchanan administration or for the filibustering conspiracy led by Henningsen. Perhaps the trip was for both. Again, if there was money, power, and influence in the wind, Parker French was not too far away.[229,230]

On the night of March 16, 1859, Walsh visited Vice President Breckinridge, a known supporter of filibuster operations throughout the Americas. Conceivably, Walsh met the VP to discuss his findings from his trip to Mexico. On the way home after drinks with friends, Walsh was killed in mysterious circumstances. The next morning, he was found in a basement stairwell with his neck broken and robbed of valuables. Although there was an arrest of a suspect, no charges were ever proven.[231]

In June 1859, the KGC arrived in town and burst onto the newspaper scene. The KGC announced that they were forming two legions, each of 10,000 men. The first would be formed from indigenous revolutionists. The second fully American legion, to be headquartered in Baltimore, would consist of five regiments of infantry and one each of cavalry, mounted infantry, artillery, and a reserve guard. The target of the force was coded. The *New York Tribune* incorrectly interpreted the coded target as Cuba; it was actually Mexico. Recruiting focused on the poverty-stricken masses of the Northern cities and landless poor of the South and West with promises of land, pay, and glory: "We shall not ask you to a land of diseases and famine, but to a land where nature has emptied every treasure in the lap of the industrious; where there is health, wealth and every variety of natural beauty. To lands where there are openings for every man in his trade and where success will reward merit."

Of course, the officer cadre would consist of selected KGC members, known for their ideological fitness and loyalty to the cause.[232]

The *New York Tribune* dismissed the organization as a personal money-making operation for its leadership. Charles Bickley, nephew of KGC leader George Bickley, arrived in New York on June 14 and checked into the exclusive St. Nicholas Hotel. He immediately started an active public relations campaign to counter the negative press. Bickley wrote that it was definitely not a scheme to make money, as the *Tribune* reported, and it was not a filibuster operation. It had the "wisest and best men our country" and reflected "a spontaneous expression of public sentiment ... carrying out the Monroe doctrine." He also intimated that the operation had high levels of support, including President James Buchanan and Secretary of State Lewis Cass.[233],[234]

Charles Bickley had likely been tasked to take preparatory actions, seek financial and material support, and set up contacts and meetings. In late August, fresh from the organization's national convention, George Bickley and associates headed to Washington, D.C. and New York. The *New York Tribune* apparently had inside information. They reported on an alleged proposal by Bickley to "conquer Mexico, establish Negro Slavery there and either preserve the Union or break it in two, according to circumstances." In Washington the group checked into the National Hotel where they held secret meetings, presumably with officials of the Buchanan/Breckinridge administration and members of Congress. Moving to New York, they checked into the St. Nicholas Hotel, within an easy walk to the Parker French residence. The KGC leaders met with men who had interest in the operation. Attendees were not reported, but there had been plenty of past interest in similar operations in Mexico and Central America. Wealthy New York magnates, like Cornelius Vanderbilt, Charles Morgan, and George Law, would have represented commercial and shipping interests. They had all previously supported filibuster adventures. Journalists pumping Manifest Destiny and expansion into Mexico were prepared to support a public relations campaign. Tammany Hall, street gang, and political leaders would have been enlisted to support recruiting efforts amongst the teeming poor in the city. The Bickleys stayed in New York City for more than a month, negotiating with sponsors, accumulating money, buying war materiel, and recruiting. A correspondent asserted that over $4 million in cash would finance the operation and had been deposited by the end of September. With that much power concentrated and cash in play, French was bound to want part of the action.[235,236]

Living in New York since 1857, Parker French was in the center of commerce, power, influence, and information. He was well positioned to support the KGC. As a nephew by marriage of Duff Green, as well as connections through the Hardin family of Kentucky and the Edwards family of Illinois, French had wide access to the political elite of Southern power brokers and could lobby the Buchanan/Breckinridge administration. He had filibuster experience with the likes of Lockridge, Henningsen, Hornsby, and Wheat. Relationships with Pierre Soule and other expansionists gave him access to key supporters in New Orleans. He knew all the main players, especially the press and moneyed interests. He could influence the street leaders for recruiting. With such widespread and deep connections, he could tell the KGC that he would be an effective agent in New York City, Washington DC, and throughout the South. Even if KGC leaders were mindful of his past questionable exploits, the charismatic and smooth-talking French could charm and spin stories with the best.

In early March 1860, the Knights met in New Orleans. The *New Orleans Courier* reported that the KGC was preparing to assist Benito Juarez in the "full and peaceful occupation of the City of Mexico, and thus prove to the world that Americans will never refuse to other struggling people the aid so opportunely rendered us by the French in 1777." The KGC was compared to the likes of Lafayette, Kosciusko, and DeKalb. The paper named the leaders of the organization, stating that hundreds more were spread around the city in hotels and private homes. The order was said to have over 39,000 members across the Southern states with immense resources, ready to move on Mexico to intervene in the civil war.

Parker French was in New Orleans as well, possibly staying with a maternal cousin Samuel McChesney. McChesney had been a captain in Nicaragua under Walker, became a Walker recruiter in New Orleans, and later became a captain in the Confederate Army. There is no record of French's direct involvement in the KGC meeting or if his presence in the city was just an extraordinary coincidence. It is highly unlikely he would have missed it.[237]

There is, however, a time congruent record of an outlandish scam in the city that fed the starved national news appetite for the adventures of Parker French. He tried to defraud a large commission merchant company, Messrs. B. P. Ethell & Co. The company provided a market outlet for commodities from throughout the Mississippi river basin. French proposed a deal. He would deposit six boxes of opium for the merchants to market and sell on commission; Ethell would advance him $3,500 (2017 estimate, $98,000) and insure the opium for the full value. The proprietors declined the proposal, but they gave him a short-term loan of $600. When the loan period was over, French said he could not yet pay it back and requested a further advance on the opium. Curiosity and suspicions triggered, the merchants opened one of the boxes. Inside the box was a surprise: "Lo and behold! By some magical process, the opium was found to have changed to the cheapest kind of rock salt."

After an initial search for French, newspapers announced he was "scarce." The sheriff quickly tracked down the culprit in the St. Louis Hotel and arrested him. Unable to pay the $1,000 bail, French was jailed waiting legal proceedings.

The *Galveston News* correspondent in New Orleans picked up the story and recalled French's 1850 exploits, frauds, and forgeries in Texas. The correspondent embellished the story by reporting on French's association with General Collier Hornsby, who was in New Orleans and probably interested in the KGC's Mexico operation. Hornsby enjoyed Texas fame for his roles in the fight for Texas independence, the Mexican war, and operations against the Comanches. French knew Hornsby from California, and Hornsby was a fellow filibuster under William Walker in Nicaragua. The Galveston correspondent related that Hornsby bailed French out of jail. He also reported that French played cupid and marriage broker between Hornsby and a young widow from Georgia. Hornsby, the paper reported, was tall, dashing, and handsome; the widow was "fair and fascinating with the additional charm of $15,000." Newspapers throughout the country picked up the latest picaresque episode from the "delightful rogue."[238,239]

Over the next several months, the proposed KGC intervention in Mexico fizzled. The on-again, off-again operation had the press either reporting thousands of men moving to the Texas-Mexico border or frustrating inaction with thousands of men disbanding. Several factors could have contributed to the aborted operation either singularly or in combination: internal dissension within the KGC, which challenged the faulted leadership of Bickley; a lack of resources and financial support; and political opposition in both Washington and Austin. Two other events in August and September negatively impacted the commitment of leadership, the support of allies, and the morale of the rank and file. In August, the Mexican Juarez faction repudiated any ties to the KGC. Newspapers throughout the nation, and most importantly in New Orleans, printed the announcement that: "the so-called Knights of the Golden Circle have the approbation of the Liberal Government in their reported expedition to Mexico. It is true they had offered their services to President Juarez, but they were promptly and unreservedly declined." And, sure to qualm enthusiasm and stifle recruitment, William Walker died. After multiple tries to establish a Central American Empire, he was detained by the British Navy and turned over to the Honduran government. He was executed by firing squad on September 12, 1860.[240,241]

As the 1860 presidential election approached and the disunion crisis accelerated, the KGC transitioned in support of the secessionist cause. Their near-term focus would no longer be on the "Golden Circle," but on support of Southern secessionist governors. David Keehn asserted that "it should be evident that the Knights were a much more powerful force and played more of a role in precipitating the Civil War than historians have heretofore recognized."[242]

Mississippi Governor John Pettus, in a letter dated September 29, 1860 to Bickley, implored him to refrain from any foreign adventures until after the outcome of the presidential election. Indicating that he also represented the governors of South Carolina, Florida, and Louisiana, Pettus offered full support to the KGC regardless of the election outcome:

> "You have now nearly 70,000 of the first men in the South united. Do not carry off these men till you see whether you are needed at home. If Mr. Lincoln is not elected, you may rely on this State for an appropriation of five hundred thousand dollars. If he is elected, you must take the field for us. No odds, General, how much you may be abused, take the field for us, and trust to Mississippi to protect you--- Will

you obey me or not? If so, go to Texas, and organize that State as you have this, but suffer no move until Perry, Gist, Moore and myself write you ... wait and be circumspect. [243]

Bickley clearly accommodated the governors' requests. He stated, "If I learn Mr. Lincoln has been elected, no movement of the KGC will be attempted until it is determined by the Southern States whether they will submit or not." He also followed Pettus's guidance by going to Texas. He spent the next several months helping the Texas KGC organize, recruit, and acquire resources. Bickley's speeches emphasized that the KGC "would become the rallying army for the Southern Disunionist."[244]

Parker French would go to Texas as well. He would also turn up in several border and Northern states as the Civil War raged during 1861. He would later be arrested as a suspected operative of the Knights of the Golden Circle and as an agent of the Confederacy.

13

SECESSION AND CIVIL WAR: SUBVERSIVE AND SWINDLER

Parker French again disappeared from newspaper reports for about twenty months, but his exploits and activities were later documented and well-reported. The only contemporaneous newspaper entries were post office advertisements listing unclaimed letters, primarily in New Orleans, New York, and San Francisco. If friends and family were trying to find him, creditors were equally likely to seek him out.

His presence and activities around the country continued to suggest his membership in, or association with, some state element of the now decentralized Knights of the Golden Circle (KGC). He would also be implicated in secessionist agitation, arrested as an agent of the Confederacy, and jailed as a political prisoner. At his core, Parker French was still a barracuda, a con man. He was a political chameleon with no committed loyalties who backed the movements and organizations advantageous to him. And, if necessary or beneficial he had no trouble with betraying allies or abandoning causes. In everything, he was in it for himself.

In November 1861, French burst onto the newspaper scene again. Readers had a chance to catch up with his activities.

Hartford Daily Current: "'A Southern Confidence Man.' Parker H. French, the swindler, who was Billy Walker's Minister to the United States, and who is now in Fort Warren on a charge of treason, exhibited great ingenuity in his schemes."

Weekly Oregonian: "Parker H. French, a missionary of the Knights of the Golden Circle was arrested ... some weeks since, and sent to Fort Warren."

Sacramento Daily Union: "Our Detectives have lately bagged a gay and festive individual named Parker H. French who is accused of treasonable practices ... and ... jugged at Fort Warren."

By August 1860, French moved his family—wife Lucretia, daughter Matilda (ten), son Murray (six) and daughter Nancy (two)—into the home of Lucretia's sister, Ellen Edwards Metcalfe. Perhaps he wanted flexibility and freedom or create family stability. He may have done it at his wife's insistence. Whatever the reason, French's family now lived in the town of Waverly in Morgan County, Illinois, about fifty miles north of Alton. French's extended Hardin family also had links to the county. Morgan County, especially the county seat of Jacksonville just twenty miles away from Waverly, had a heavy population of Kentuckian and other Southern immigrants. They would provide a ready source for the Knights of the Golden Circle and would become a hotbed of secessionist sympathizers.[245,246]

As seceding states ratified the Confederate Constitution and named Jefferson Davis provisional president, the KGC became one of the first and most powerful allies of the newly created Confederate States of America. By then, Texas had become the greatest source of KGC strength. The state was home for at least thirty-two KGC Castles in twenty-seven counties, including the cities of Houston, Austin, San Antonio, Galveston, Marshall, Canton, and Castroville. Evidence suggests that San Antonio may have served as the organization's national headquarters for a time. KGC forces were on the march before the siege of Fort Sumter in April 1861 and even before the Texas secession referendum on February 23, 1861. On February 15, Texas volunteer forces compelled the surrender of the federal arsenal at San Antonio, which was under the command of Southern sympathizer, Brevet Major General David E. Twiggs. The units were largely manned by KGC members, commanded by French acquaintance and KGC stalwart Ben McCulloch. Following this coup, KGC-led volunteer units throughout the state forced the capitulation of all federal posts.[247,248]

Parker French was not inattentive to current affairs nor be absent from money, power, influence and self-serving ventures. Perhaps throughout the fall and winter of 1860, but certainly by March 1861, he was in the area of Houston, Texas. On March 18, 1861 he became an investor in the Texas and New Orleans Railroad Company. He bought sixty bonds for $500 each. Given his financial troubles the previous March—when he couldn't post bail in New Orleans for the opium scam—one wonders where he acquired $30,000 (2017 estimate, $790,000). Could the KGC have authorized the investment and provided the funds with French operating as a member of the organizations Second Degree and the Knights of the True Faith? Such a railroad investment would have been within the purview of the Second Degree and consistent with Confederate strategy, commercial needs, logistics requirements, and KGC intent. In the early days of the war, the railroad was heavily used as a Confederate supply line with several hundred soldiers assigned to protect it. The Confederate government wanted the railroad completed through eastern Texas and Louisiana to New Orleans as soon as possible; construction was a high priority in the early months of the war. The efforts ceased when New Orleans was captured by Union forces in the spring of 1862.[249,250]

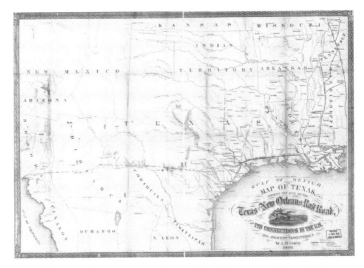

Map of Texas, showing the line of the Texas and New Orleans Railroad, 1860. Library of Congress.

The Texan terminus of the railroad was in Houston. Remarkably, French had family connections in the city and the surrounding Harris County; his maternal grandfather Martin L. Hardin (1780-1848) immigrated to Harris County in 1837. After French's grandmother died, Martin married Frances (Fanny) Hubbard Lynch (1790-1861). She was the widow of Nathaniel Lynch (ca. 1790-1837), an early immigrant to Texas. Nathaniel had received a grant from the Mexican government for a league of land over 4,400 acres. The settlement of Lynchburg grew up on a ferry and sawmill at the confluence of the San Jacinto River and Buffalo Bayou. In 1847, the son of

Nathaniel and Fanny Lynch, John J. Lynch, married Lydia Wickliffe Hardin, who was Martin's daughter. John, as step-son of Martin, had just married his step-sister; he was both step-uncle and uncle by marriage to Parker French. In 1861, the family still lived in Harris County and the city of Houston.[251]

Soon, French left Texas for South Carolina, where momentous events were occurring in Charleston harbor. It is probable that he visited Montgomery, Alabama, to join many colleagues from the Nicaraguan expedition and Golden Circle, along with thousands of others trying to gain appointment to the government or military forces of the nascent Confederacy. His uncle by marriage, Duff Green, was a Confederate government advisor on financial, industrial, commercial and foreign policy matters. French undoubtedly could not countenance being removed from the scene of action and power. While in South Carolina, the Georgetown Vigilance Committee honored him as a "trustworthy Southern Rights man." He was given a certificate to memorialize the occasion.[252]

Sometime during this period, French conceived and planned a marvelously complex, cunning, and stunning undertaking. Over the next eight months, French would embark on a daring campaign of subversion, deception, fraud, and forgery in the border and Northern states. The intricate operation involved agitation, sedition, and intelligence-gathering in support of Southern secession, as well as an elaborate con game targeting guileless unionists and abolitionists. Any useful intelligence would be provided to the Confederate government, and any accrued funds could be easily diverted to a handy pocket.

To support his parallel efforts, French had to construct sets of fake identities, believable backgrounds, credentials, and supporting documentation. The cover stories would convince both his prospective allies and his targeted dupes that he was legitimate. He fashioned three fictitious characters with names and backgrounds he could easily remember. All were from Adair County, Kentucky, French's real boyhood home. To facilitate anonymous and secure communications, each alias had the initials C.M. All had an infectious charismatic personality while presenting modesty and intelligence. They could especially ingratiate themselves with the ladies.

Alias one was Carlyle (sometimes misreported as Carlisle) Murray. A loyal patriot from Adair County, Kentucky, who had been expelled from the South, he was distraught over the nation's tragedy. His only wish was to support his beloved Union. Regrettably, because he had been heroically wounded and lost his arm in the Mexican War, he was unable to actively serve in the army. But, he was a man of means willing to use his energy, time, and resources in support of the Union and other loyal elements in the South, especially in Kentucky and Tennessee. He was also a religious man who could be a guest lay preacher, capable of convincing parishioners to donate to the just and sacred Union cause. He procured letters of introduction and recommendations from renowned and influential unionists in Kentucky and Tennessee. He alleged that he had a secure means of moving funds, supplies, and arms to those states. The name Murray likely came from his good friend, and namesake of his son, Hugh Murray, who died in 1857. Hugh was a fellow student at Shurtleff College in Alton, Illinois and close friend in California when Murray was the chief justice of the California Supreme Court.

Alias two was Charles Maxey (sometimes misreported as Maxy). He was a bona fide Southern rights man, a friend of fire-eaters, and a secessionist through and through. Maxey was reportedly chartered by Jefferson Davis and the Knights of the Golden Circle to go into the North to organize lodges of the KGC, incite anti-war sentiments, seed sedition, and gather intelligence. Maxey was armed with key documents: letters of introduction from Jefferson Davis and other Southern leaders; the constitution and bylaws of the Knights of the Golden Circle; and a certificate of good standing from the Georgetown South Carolina Vigilance Committee. The surname Maxey came from Samuel Maxey who was a fellow student at Robertson's Academy in Columbia, Adair County, in 1836. Maxey had immigrated to Texas, where he was a county district attorney and delegate to the Texas Secessionist Convention. He subsequently fought for the Confederacy and achieved the rank of brigadier general. After the war he was a senator from Texas.

Alias three was Christopher Monroe. The name was perhaps only for contingency purposes since there is no record that it was used. The Monroe family in Adair County descended from the founding father James Monroe. Several Monroe boys went to Robertson's Academy.[253,254,255,256]

The press across the country and a government investigative document reported that "Charles Maxey" circulated through the border and Western states, sewing disunion and establishing KGC Castles. Meanwhile, "Carlyle Murray" bilked eager abolitionists and loyalists, persuading them to donate funds to the Union League and other loyal Southern organizations. Parker French could visit openly with family and friends, especially in Kentucky, Illinois, and Indiana, while advancing his agenda as either Charles Maxey or Carlyle Murray.

To prepare for his adventure, French compiled lists

of wealthy and influential men in different cities; he annotated the lists with relevant notes showing the men's political, religious, and ideological sentiments as well as their hobbies.[257]

He first stopped in Tennessee to gain the confidence of leading Unionists and secessionists. Carlyle Murray acquired letters of recommendations from Unionists Emerson Etheridge and Parson William Brownlow. Etheridge was a former United States representative who was closely aligned with Senator Andrew Johnson. Brownlow was a preacher and editor of the *Knoxville Whig,* a bitterly critical anti-secessionist paper. He was so effective in winning followers in eastern Tennessee that Brownlow was convicted of treason and sentenced to hang. Instead, fearing that he would become a martyr, the Tennessee governor had him released into Union lines. French later got good results from both letters. In addition, he likely would not have missed the opportunity to coordinate with the large population of KGC and Confederate devotees. There is no record of such meetings, but later actions suggest their probability.

In Kentucky, French leveraged his extensive connections amongst family and friends in support of either persona. He had boyhood connections from Columbia with Thomas Bramlette, who would become the Unionist governor in 1863. Fellow students from Robertson's Academy in Columbia were also now influential: Timeleon Cravens was a secessionist lawyer, elector for John Breckinridge, and ally of William Yancy; Samuel Suddarth was a loyal Unionist who would later meet with President Lincoln; secessionist Thomas Monroe was the sitting secretary of state (as a major in the Confederate Army, he would be killed in combat in October); Isaac Caldwell was a prominent attorney in Louisville and loyal member of the Unionist Home Guard. French could even reach Confederate sympathizer and Governor Beriah Magoffin through his maternal cousin and foster brother Charles Hardin, who married the governor's niece.

Kentucky, unfortunately, embodied the "House Divided" and the "Brother against Brother" character of the Civil War. Like many families, the Hardins were a microcosm of bitter intra-family differences. There were both pro-Union and pro-Confederate adherents, dedicated to opposing causes in a life or death struggle. Some tried to strike a precariously neutral balance. Parker French's maternal cousins fought as general officers for both sides. Union General Martin Davis Hardin of Illinois was a friend and a legal profession protégé of Abraham Lincoln. Confederate General Benjamin Hardin Helm was Lincoln's brother-in-law through marriage to Emilie Todd. Upon learning of Helm's death at Chickamauga, it is said that Lincoln felt like "David in the Bible when he learned of the death of Absalom."

Some Hardin women were just as fervent as the men. Cousin Elizabeth Pendleton Hardin gained notoriety as a virulent advocate of the Confederacy. "Lizzie" was arrested by Union forces for simply waving a handkerchief in support of Confederate raider John Morgan. Jailed with her sister in Louisville, the trouble she caused was soon deemed unworthy of the effort to keep them in jail. Influential family members demanded their release in a constant drumbeat. Lizzie ardently expressed her infinite devotion and love for the South and attacked "dirty Yankees" for waging destructive war on her country. The commander offered release if she and her sister would just take an oath of allegiance, and he was surprised by their outright refusal: "I was born a Southerner and if God will give me the strength I

intend to die a Southerner." She questioned the
Commander's ethics and challenged his legal right to
keep her and her sister confined. Always looking for
an opportunity to cause trouble, they tried to subvert
the young impressionable guards into joining the
Confederacy. One observer asked Lizzie if her mother
was also a Hardin, to which she replied yes. The
old family acquaintance told the Colonel: "Well you
might as well let them go, for if they have all that old
Hardin blood in them you will never *make* them do
anything." The exasperated officer finally gave them
parole but on the condition that they leave Kentucky
immediately. The sisters left the colonel with his
admonishment: "Pardon me, ladies. But I think for a
woman to meddle with politics is ridiculous and the
women of Kentucky have driven many young men to
their graves." On a train heading to Confederate lines,
a federal officer grew irritated with their unabashedly
loud Southern support and hatred of all things
Yankee. He proclaimed, "the women are a damn sight
worse than the men."[258]

French's next targets were the Southern tier of the
North—Illinois, Indiana, and Ohio. To what extent
he was successful in establishing KGC Castles is
unknown, but newspapers certainly gave Charles
Maxey speculative credit. All three of these "free
states" perched on the Ohio River, the dividing line
between freedom and slavery. Much of the most
southern portion of each state was populated by
Southerners, especially Kentuckians. Regardless
of the wide-ranging support for the Union, there
was a sizable population of secession sympathizers.
French's adopted home town of Alton, Illinois, and
the surrounding area of southern Illinois—known as
"Egypt"—were especially ripe for sedition. It would
be easy for Charles Maxey to find willing and even
enthusiastic KGC recruits. French would recognize
influential citizens, and some would be ardent allies.

Former Senator James Semple, *Alton Democrat* editor John Dobelbower, and former Alton Mayor Thomas Hope were all KGC members. Hope had bragged that he fired the fatal shot that killed Elijah Lovejoy in 1837.

There were reported to be as many as 10,000 KGC members throughout "Egypt," including soon-to-be Congressman William J. Allen and Judges Mulkey and Duff. Lodges were formed throughout Illinois, including one in Chicago in the spring of 1861. In southern Indiana, there was widespread KGC and secessionist support, especially in the hotbeds of Crawford and Orange Counties. In both Illinois and Indiana, French could easily have innocent-appearing visits with Unionist family and friends while his alter ego pursued his schemes. In Alton and environs, he could visit his immediate family or the widely distributed Edwards clan. In Crawford County, Indiana, he could stay with his sister, Juliet French Banks, and her husband, Henry Banks. The area had a substantial population of former Kentuckians and an active KGC element, which was quickly and effectively subdued by loyalists.[259,260,261,262,263]

After clipping charitable loyalists and furthering secessionist sentiments in the West, Carlyle Murray and Charles Maxey headed to their next targets in the northeast corridor. From Boston to Philadelphia, the personas would weave through both the Unionist and so-called Copperhead and Peace Democrat movements.

14

CIVIL WAR: CONNING BOSTON ELITES

Parker French arrived in Boston by early May 1861 and unobtrusively started to exercise his plans, both as secessionist "Charles Maxey" and loyalist "Carlyle Murray." He could now move rapidly by railroad between Boston and Philadelphia to execute his parallel operations along the northeast corridor.

> *"A notorious man Parker French has been in Boston since May living ... under the name of Carlyle Murray. ... He has letters from Andrew Johnson, Emerson Etheridge and others and pretends to be a Unionist and a Patriot. ... He has committed great crimes against persons and against property. He is a ruffian of the worst kind who should be hung, but who, I fear, cannot be at present."*[264]

"HAVE WE TRAITORS AMONG US? A secret order exists in Boston called the Knights of the Golden Circle for the purpose of aiding the rebels."[265]

Secessionist Charles Maxey ranged up and down the eastern corridor. Knights of the Golden Circle castles were reportedly formed from Boston to Philadelphia. Although there was no proof that they were directly linked to French, both newspapers and the government implicated Charles Maxey.

French had family and friend connections in both Philadelphia and Berks County, Pennsylvania, where castles had been organized. The family had lived in Berks County with his wife's sister, Matilda Strong, while French was on his California Gold Rush expedition. Also coincident with his arrival in May, newspapers reported much more troubling KGC activity. First there was an alarming revelation of a KGC plot by the "inner Temple" to burn the cities of New York, Boston, and Philadelphia. An anonymous source asserted that the conspiracy was known to Jefferson Davis and that there were hundreds of men across the three cities waiting for a signal to set the fires. In another story, Alabaman fire-eater William Yancey asserted that there were thousands of KGC members in New York, Philadelphia, Boston and other Northern cities. They were organized, trained, and equipped to do the bidding of the South.[266,267]

Initially, Unionist Carlyle Murray lived quietly in Boston while corresponding with his patriotic contacts in Kentucky, Tennessee, and the border states. He would ask in what way he could help. Gladdened by his apparent patriotism, they would expose their plans and secret details of their support structure and key people. As the Boston Post later reported, Maxey likely sent that key and injurious information to Confederate contacts, as letters from "CM" would suggest.

Murray also transited the northeast from Boston to Philadelphia, leveraging the religious fervor of churches, milking their flocks, and absconding with their funds. In Philadelphia, he obtained a certificate of church membership along with supporting introductions and recommendations. In other cities he gained entrée built on repetitive success with succeeding victims. Murray had the obvious appearance of a successful, wealthy man with the manner of a loyal, generous citizen; he reinforced that notion with liberal pledges and subscriptions to local charities and the Union cause. Most egregiously, he swindled donations, ostensibly to help wounded, sick, and disabled soldiers. However, "when the time came for the payment of his subscription he was elsewhere." He acquired an estimated $4,000 of filched funds (2017 estimate, $100,000).[268,269]

Boston contained more important and profitable marks in the rich and influential merchants. Through them, French executed two plots: target the Unionist philanthropic community, as well as Senator Andrew Johnson of Tennessee, and convince the United States Navy to buy steamships, which evidence suggests he planned to spirit south to the Confederacy.

Likely unrelated to French's appearance in Boston, but amazingly coincident, a secessionists' plot originated in Tennessee. Confederates took advantage of exuberant Northern miscues. Amos Lawrence, a leading Boston businessman and philanthropist, was taken in by an ingenious scheme, which embroiled other Boston politicians, Northern businessmen, and Tennessee Senator Andrew Johnson.

Painting of Amos Lawrence by Chester Harding, circa 1845. Held by the National Gallery of Art.

Amos Lawrence was a particularly juicy target for secessionists and devotees of slavery culture. He was rich, a leading and vocal foe of the extension of slavery, and a vigorous supporter of anti-slavery "Free-Staters" in the conflict for "Bleeding Kansas." He was honored with the town of Lawrence, Kansas, taking his name. As the path to disunion accelerated, Lawrence was a leader trying to conciliate with the South to save the Union. He feared that regional partisanship would tear apart the nation, and he denounced radicals on both sides of the slavery issue. In the 1860 presidential election, Lawrence supported the Constitutional Union Party and the ticket of John Bell of Tennessee and friend Edward Everett of Massachusetts. After Lincoln was elected and the South resorted to violence, especially the siege and surrender of Fort Sumter, he became a zealous supporter of the Union cause and the Lincoln administration.

In early May 1861, Lawrence wrote Senator Johnson with an offer to support his pro-Union efforts in Tennessee. The senator replied on May 15 with hearty thanks "for the high regard you seem to have for my patriotism and my devotion to my country." Johnson went on to ask for assurances from Lawrence and his colleagues of "material aid in the way of money, men and arms." With such aid he could mobilize a formidable Union element in East Tennessee to resist the "damnable treason." Lawrence responded quickly on May 18 with a statement that "If your note to me were printed in our newspapers, it would be good for ten thousand dollars in three days' time. But of course, I must only use it as a private letter." Enclosing a draft for $1,000, he advised on where to cash it and told him "If you cannot use the draft, return it and tell me what to send."

Johnson sent at least two more letters. On May 23, he asked for assurance that he would receive money, men, and guns before June 8, "If I could command ...

say $10,000, I have no doubt I could hold this State onto the Federal Union." On June 6, he wrote of his inability to use the draft for $1,000 saying "it would not do to attempt to have it cashed, as I would be suspected." He requested instead $5,000 or $10,000 to be sent by normal mail, and he requested the cash in New England currency in large bills. Johnson again emphasized that help needed to be prompt because he could purchase a lot of arms if he had the means.[270]

Awkwardly for both Amos Lawrence and Senator Andrew Johnson, the letters from "Johnson" were forgeries. The postmaster of Knoxville, a secessionist and supporter of Governor Isham Harris, had intercepted the first letter from Lawrence and concocted the scheme to defraud Lawrence, as well as embarrass and implicate Johnson. He kept Governor Harris informed of the correspondence and the progress of the fraud, since any cash would be used for the governor's purposes. The mention of the need for the funds by June 8 coincided with the date set by the legislature for the popular vote on secession. The letters were leaked by the governor's office, perhaps unintentionally, but more likely to implicate Johnson in treason to both Tennessee and the Confederacy. On June 11, the *Richmond Enquirer* published Lawrence's May 18 letter under the headline: "Andrew Johnson—Treason Discovered." A warrant for Johnson's arrest was issued about June 14.

Over the next several days, reports appeared in Boston newspapers of the filched Lawrence letters, the forged Johnson responses, and the treason warrant, as well as Johnson's denial that he ever sought aid from Lawrence or anyone else in the North. Lawrence was shocked and dismayed about the part he had played in the hoax. In a June 25 letter to Johnson, he outlined some of his efforts in support of the Union cause in Tennessee, enclosed the forged letters, and expressed his embarrassment: "I am somewhat mortified by the deception practiced & particularly so because it has caused inconvenience and risk to you."[271,272]

Amos Lawrence was soon targeted again, this time by Carlyle Murray. Murray may have been informed of the Tennessee plot as it was unfolding, but more than likely, he merely read the press accounts. In any case, the plotter saw an enticing target; perhaps he thought that Lawrence was a serial sucker whom he could swindle. Lawrence probably was a very good mark, since by now he was heavily committed to saving Tennessee, or at least the eastern part of the state, for the Union. Newspaper reports and a federal investigator later concluded that Murray approached Lawrence with what they assumed was a forged letter from Andrew Johnson. The letter, in fact, was not forged. It would have been out of character for the cunning and thoughtful planner Parker French to risk being caught with a forgery. It was easier to get the real thing.

On July 12, Carlyle Murray wrote the real Senator Andrew Johnson. He described himself as a "Kentuckian born near the Tennessee line, and like yourself an unconditional Union man. Disabled by wounds received in Mexico, that will prevent me from taking the field in person—I am yet anxious to do all I can for my bleeding Country." He then asked the senator to whom he could send contributions. Johnson replied on July 31 that the government was providing aid for the defense of Eastern Tennessee, but William Brownlow was desperate for help to save his struggling newspaper, the *Knoxville Whig*. Johnson suggested that any money be sent to him, and he would forward it to Brownlow. Murray and Johnson shared more letters, including an invitation from Murray to visit Boston. Johnson, in return, suggested Philadelphia or New York.[273]

In August, Carlyle Murray, using the letter from his new friend Andrew Johnson, presented himself to Amos Lawrence. Combined with letters from Emerson Etheredge and Parson Brownlow, it was probably easy for Murray to deceive an unsuspecting Lawrence. Seeing an opportunity to support a loyal citizen of Kentucky, especially a friend of Andrew Johnson, Lawrence acted quickly. In a letter to Andrew Johnson that transferred funds for Parson Brownlow, he mentioned that "Mr. Murray of Adair Co. KY is here and I shall tomorrow put him in the way of collecting more."

Lawrence then increased the number of possible victims by introducing Murray to a wide circle of friends and business associates. He wrote to them: "Mr. Murray is an active Unionist, a loyal supporter of the US Gov't and a friend of Andrew Johnson of Tenn. He visits Boston for the first time to submit to surgical treatment rendered necessary by a wound received at Buena Vista while in command of a company in McKee's regiment. He has come here to "repair" in order to be ready for the approaching conflict in his section; and, he has consented to do some work, while detained here, for the Union cause."

It was not the first or last time that French falsely claimed disabled veteran status, but it may have been one of the more financially effective occasions. There is no record how much money Murray pinched from the broader group.[274,275]

Murray had much bigger plans for Lawrence and his influence with the federal government. On September 9, he presented a plan to sell two Lawrence-owned "propeller" steamships to the Navy. Lawrence thought it a grand idea and offered to provide what he called "magnificent vessels" at no

profit to him. They would "carry terror to traitors."
Lawrence invited Murray back the next evening for
dinner and more discussions, and Murray stayed the
night. They agreed that Murray needed to immediately
go to Washington and visit the Department of the
Navy. Lawrence offered Murray a small commission
for his time and noted that there would be other
expenses. Since Murray devoted his service "to a
holy cause," Lawrence did not want to see Murray's
commission diminished. He cautioned Murray that
"you may find it necessary to pay out a part to sub
agents, government brokers and the tribe of beggars
who live on the crumbs they can beg or steal from the
government table."

Lawrence gave Murray $1,000, who said he would
take it only on the condition that he would give all the
excess money to Senator Johnson in support of the
Union cause in Tennessee. Murray left for Washington
on September 11 with the $1,000. He also carried
a letter of introduction and recommendation from
Congressman William Appleton (Lawrence's father-
in-law) addressed to Captain Gustavas Fox, assistant
secretary of the navy. In the letter, Appleton asked
Captain Fox to give timely attention to Murray's
business. Appleton extolled the patriotism of Murray,
assuring Fox that Murray was not seeking any office
or favors and just wanted to "serve the country
according to his ability without reward." He also
mentioned that Murray carried letters from Andrew
Johnson, Emerson Etheridge, and other gentlemen
who knew Murray and whose letters were of "more
importance than anything from me."[276]

Unknown to Lawrence, Murray had been scheming
for some time. He had visited or written shipyards in
Boston, New Hampshire, and Maine looking for likely
vessels. One witness became suspicious and later
gave a statement. When the witness asked Murray if

he needed a captain and a crew to transfer the vessel to the navy, Murray replied in the negative and said he had his own captain and crew. In fact, Murray said that he would probably go with the ship on the first sailing, presumably to make sure all was in order. Murray also asked about the availability and prices of various ship stores, particularly gunpowder and percussion caps, of which he discussed buying a large quantity. Later investigation also found memoranda in Parker French's papers showing plans and cost estimates for altering, arming, manning, supplying, and navigating propellers as warships. A simple, innocent interpretation would be that Murray was in fact just working a deal with the Union Navy. Another obvious conclusion would be that Parker French intended to take the vessels to the Confederacy. The investigator left open the possibility of other purposes, such as using the vessels as a raiding privateer in service to the rebels, as a slaver, or for piracy. In any case, the price was right; the ships would be paid for by the federal government.[277]

On September 13, just one day too late, Amos Lawrence learned the outrageous truth—he had been scammed. Bostonian Caleb Cushing, former attorney general under President Pierce, was well aware of Parker French's participation in the Nicaraguan filibuster, and he told Lawrence that Carlyle Murray was a fictitious character. The swindler was in fact Colonel Parker French who gained notoriety in Nicaragua and had also been "a robber on a great and small scale and perhaps a spy for the rebels." The earlier enthusiasm for the loyal unionist Murray, the good friend of Senator Johnson, Etheridge, and Brownlow, now turned to embarrassment and anger against the fraudulent secessionist Parker French. The notes of Lawrence in his diary describe his pain: "Murray turned out to be a rascal" and "No hope of getting back my $1,000 advanced to the rogue

Murray; the villainous Filibuster has escaped," and
"Murray—alias French ... the rogue."[278]

Hoping to have the impostor intercepted in
Philadelphia, Lawrence wrote his agent in the city
to watch out for him. He also persuaded the Boston
police chief to telegraph the Philadelphia Police,
instructing them to hold French/Murray on a charge
of swindling. After hearing that the Philadelphia police
had arrested and detained Murray, Lawrence wanted
the culprit returned to Boston and charged, but he
could not develop any solid proof of a crime. Lawrence
had actually proposed to Murray that he accept the
$1,000. Murray, who still refused to acknowledge
that he was Parker French, was released on a writ of
habeas corpus.

Carlyle Murray, probably to assuage Lawrence
and gain time to elude the law, wrote a long sad
letter claiming to be bedridden from illness; he would
visit Lawrence as soon as he recovered from his
sickbed. Murray vociferously denied he was Parker
French and stridently protested his innocence;
he would soon visit Lawrence and show it was
all a misunderstanding and a mistake. To solicit
sympathy, Murray gave a detailed, and mostly false,
chronicle of his background, which included his
family's abandonment and delusions that he did
not remember. Due to his mental illness he was
committed to an asylum—in France. To protect his
family from further pain, he had changed his name
and disappeared. Murray then attempted intimidation
and a veiled extortion in case there was a court
case. Murray would testify the $1,000 Lawrence
gave him, was only an advance on $5,000 needed to
grease the hands of public officials; Lawrence would
be implicated in bribery and graft. Carlyle Murray
promptly left Philadelphia and disappeared.

In a letter to Secretary of State William Seward,

Lawrence related the background of the fictitious Murray and the real French. He wrote the deception included "fraudulently obtained" letters from Andrew Johnson and Emerson Etheridge, letters which were actually legitimate. Most importantly, Lawrence provided information on the scheme about purchasing the steamers and "probably turning pirate at gov't expense." Concerned that French would go free, he advised, "If the gov't has any information in regard to this filibuster and robber and wish him to be detained, it can be done by directing the Marshal in Philadelphia to take charge of him."[279]

With his Carlyle Murray cover blown, the fugitive Parker French needed a place to hide in plain sight. He chose Branford, Connecticut. The quiet little town had a train station on the railroad from Boston to New York, and it offered convenient access to his next targets in Connecticut, especially New Haven. He could continue to operate with his secessionist persona, Charles Maxey, but his compromised alias of Carlyle Murray was now deceased and had to be immediately shelved.

15

CIVIL WAR: A REBEL COMES TO CONNECTICUT

With his Carlyle Murray persona compromised, Parker French's new alias "Mr. Jackson" arrived in Branford, Connecticut, around the last week in September 1861. Jackson was an unassuming, upright, and religious citizen who quickly gained the respect and friendship of all he met in the quiet conservative community. For about six weeks, French successfully eluded the law. His luck ran out on November 5, 1861, when he was arrested. Californian journalists, who knew French well, spread the news throughout the state.

"A CALIFORNIAN, PARKER H. FRENCH AND HIS TREASONABLE TRICKS. The arrest of the notorious Parker H. French, of flibuster fame, caused for the moment no little excitement in these regions. The boldness of his movements, in organizing lodges of the Knights of the Golden Circle right in the midst of the Puritan population of loyal Connecticut, is a matter of special wonder to our people. But Parker has always been a reckless scamp and is said to have resembled more nearly his former leader, William Walker, than any other one of the followers of the arch-flibuster." [280]

Upon arrival in Branford, Mr. Jackson checked into the Totoket Hotel owned by an elderly couple, William and Lydia Covert. Even then the Totoket was historic at over 100 years old, built in 1755 by an ancestor of President Rutherford B. Hayes. The landmark hotel burned in 1971, but some of its bones remain today in the Esposito Building on Main Street. With a large lobby and attached tavern, the hotel was a natural, comfortable setting for meeting prominent citizens, as well as for entertaining friends. It was also convenient to the Town Green, Town Hall, the Masonic Hall, and importantly, to the Congregational and Episcopal Churches. Soon, Mr. Jackson connected and endeared himself with the religious community. He gave lectures on temperance and religion, had a class in the Sabbath School, and courted "one of the prettiest girls in Connecticut." There is no record of any filched funds or compromised damsels.[281,282,283]

Totoket Hotel, Branford Connecticut. Courtesy of the Branford Historical Society and the James Blackstone Memorial Library.

While Mr. Jackson enjoyed an unobtrusive, cozy, and boringly normal life in the town of about 2,100 souls, Charles Maxey was active in other communities in Connecticut. In his book *Connecticut for the Union,* John Niven asserted that Parker French had been specifically sent to Connecticut as one of the Confederacy's top-secret agents. He was to organize castles of the Knights of the Golden Circle and subvert the dissident portion of the population. Maxey would do his work with substantial success, especially in New Haven and Fairfield counties. He would "spread secession sentiments to no small extent" and succeed "in estranging many persons from loyalty to the government."[284,285]

There were many reasons for Confederate leaders to think there might be a receptive and sympathetic audience that French could leverage. Despite a popular notion that Connecticut was a center of anti-slavery and abolitionist sentiment, there was a sizable active element of Peace Democrats, Copperheads, Southern sympathizers, and subversives. Frustrated when his message of emancipation had been opposed, abolitionist William Lloyd Garrison had labeled Connecticut "The Georgia of the North." Headed by influential former governor Thomas Seymour, the Peace Democrats had long favored conciliation with the South and advocated conceding to the region's demands. They supported the Dred Scott decision and opposed state personal liberty laws, which protected violators of the Fugitive Slave Act. Republican William Buckingham barely beat Seymour in the gubernatorial election of April 1860. He had substantial help from an electioneering visit by Lincoln. In the presidential election, Lincoln won Connecticut's electors, but over 20 percent of the electorate voted for the Southern Democrat John Breckinridge of Kentucky. By comparison, Breckinridge was not on the ballot in neighboring states New York and Rhode Island; in Massachusetts the Kentuckian garnered less than 4 percent of the votes.[286,287]

After war broke out in April 1861, and especially after the disastrous Battle of Bull Run in July, Peace Democrats came out in stridently vocal opposition. Demonstrations, peace meetings, flying of white peace flags, and even hoisting of Confederate flags ensued across the state. Counter actions by loyalists inevitably led to clashes, which degenerated into violence and shootings. A peace convention was planned in Stonington, which was a convenient 55-mile train ride from Branford, but loyalists shut it down. The *Richmond Examiner* reported on the convention as if it had actually occurred. Intended resolutions would have emphasized: the unconstitutional nature of the war; that the Southern states still had constitutional and legal rights in the territories (i.e., slavery); that the union could not be "preserved by the bayonet"; the war was brought on by greedy contractors; and agitators in the Northern states had educated a generation to hate the South.[288,289]

Peace Democrat mouthpieces, such as the *Hartford Times* and the *New Haven Register*, rationally editorialized against the war from Constitutional, moral, and cost perspectives, but they were somewhat restrained in their approach and language. The *Bridgeport Farmer and Advertiser,* however, was accused of rampant treason. The *Farmer* regularly reprinted articles from Southern newspapers and launched offensive, defamatory broadsides against Lincoln, his administration, and his prosecution of the war. On August 24, a mob attacked the paper, sacked and gutted the building, and destroyed all the equipment and supplies, including two large presses. Found in the destruction were bags of documents addressed to leading secessionists in the South and "curious letters exposing the treason of politicians in Hartford and elsewhere."[290]

The disloyal opposition, civil disorder, and active subversion did not go unnoticed in Washington. Secretary of State Seward cracked down and ordered the arrest of key subversives and agitators. Nathan Morse, editor of the *Farmer*, escaped arrest; he was chased from town to town until he crossed into Canada. Morse eventually made his way into the

Confederacy and appeared in Richmond, where he would tell his side of the story garnished with condemnation of the "outrageous mob." Some of the arrests netted incriminating papers and correspondence with the Confederate government. Documents were found that implicated Hartford politicians and others in the state. The situation was not ignored in Richmond, either; the state of affairs in Connecticut was fully reported in newspapers throughout the South. Confederate officials must have sensed the continuing opportunity for subversion and seen damage done by Seward's crackdown and detention of dissidents. The circumstances alone would have justified sending Parker French into Connecticut to support the dwindling and deflated sympathizers.[291]

There was also a specific mission for Parker French in Connecticut. Author John Niven posited that a New Haven man named Thomas Yeatman must have had something to do with French being in Connecticut. Yeatman was a native of Tennessee, Mexican War veteran, Yale graduate, wealthy New Haven lawyer, and member of the National Committee of the Constitutional Union Party. In April, Yeatman had written Jefferson Davis offering to recruit Southern sympathizers for the Confederacy: "I can without the slightest difficulty, raise and equip from New Haven two companies of 100 men each to serve under your command, every man a Democrat upon whom you can rely."

Confederate Secretary of War Leroy Pope Walker promptly responded that the Confederacy could not yet accept the offer, but Yeatman should remain prepared. There would have been little doubt of Yeatman's credentials. He was scion of a wealthy and influential Tennessee family, as well as the step-son of John Bell, presidential candidate of the

Constitutional Union Party. Bell would later defect to the Confederacy.

There is no record of any contact, but by the time French reached Connecticut, the federal crackdown had probably cooled the ardor of sympathizers, subversives, and agitators, including Yeatman. It is highly likely that French knew Thomas Yeatman. When French was a commission merchant and shipbuilder in St. Louis in 1849, Thomas Yeatman was the editor of the newspaper *Intelligencer*. Brother James Yeatman was a fellow commission merchant and cofounder of the Merchants Bank, a financial institution vital to the business of commission merchants. Exemplifying the "brother against brother" dynamic of the Civil War, the Yeatman brothers had split loyalties. Thomas remained an inveterate Confederate supporter for the duration of the war, and brother Henry was a Confederate colonel. On the other hand, James was an ardent Unionist and drew accolades as the president of the Western Sanitary Commission, which established hospitals and raised money to provide care to wounded soldiers. Yeatman's brother-in-law was Union Major General John Pope, whose forces were famously routed at the Second Battle of Bull Run.[292]

Why was Yeatman confident he could successfully recruit in New Haven? He knew that Yale had many students from the South who would join the Confederate cause, there were former students from the South who remained in, or returned to, New Haven, and the county was a hotbed of Southern sympathizers. In January, Southern Yale students broke into Alumni Hall, locked and barricaded the doors, and raised a secessionist banner on the flagpole. Over 500 students or alumni served in the Confederate forces, including at least seven general officers. Confederate government officials included

Yalie Judah P. Benjamin, labeled the "Brains of the Confederacy." He was attorney general, secretary of state, secretary of war, and Jefferson Davis' right-hand man.[293]

Connecticut was a good target, but why would French choose Branford as his center of operation? In addition to being a convenient stop on the railroad, Branford historian Jane Bouley proposed several reasons: the town was large enough for anonymity with a decent respect for privacy; the people were hardworking, salt-of-the-earth citizens who did not prioritize national issues; and there was little appetite for strident advocacy on social issues such as abolition.

There is the possibility of an interesting linkage between Henry B. Plant and French for which Bouley advised further research. Plant, a Branford native, was sent to Georgia by his employer, Adams Express, to expand operations in the Southern states. Adams Express can be compared to FedEx or UPS; they transported small packages, important documents, and valuables. By the start of the Civil War, Adams Express was an integral part of the Southern infrastructure and economy. But fearing a complete loss of Southern business, the Yankee company sold all Southern assets to Plant, who formed the Southern Express Company. On the board of directors was William Parish Chilton. Chilton had been born in French's hometown of Columbia, Kentucky. He was the law partner of fire-eater and KGC associate William Yancey, the uncle of Texas KGC leader George Chilton, and a member of the Confederate States Congress. Did Plant advise French on Branford as an opportune place of operation? And did he provide introductory letters?[294,295]

Since the start of the war, reports of KGC intent and activity had been filtering into the Lincoln

administration from throughout the nation, especially
from Texas, the border states, and the lower tier of
the Northern states (Illinois, Indiana, and Ohio). At
first the reports were not taken as serious threats,
but the latest information from Boston about
the KGC, Connecticut. and the entire northeast
corridor must have sharpened attention across the
administration, notably in the Department of State.

In October, French made a mistake that likely
led to his arrest. The shelved persona Carlyle
Murray wrote to Amos Lawrence while on a visit to
Philadelphia. He again proclaimed his innocence, said
he had recovered from illness, and Lawrence would
soon see him. Lawrence telegraphed the authorities
and alerted them to watch out for the impostor. On
October 24, the chief detective of the Philadelphia
Police Department, Benjamin Franklin, apprehended
and detained Murray. Franklin found suspicious
papers including the constitution and by-laws of the
Knights of the Golden Circle, which were cleverly
but transparently camouflaged as belonging to the
Knights of the Golden SQUARE, a fictitious and
supposedly loyal organization.

By telegraph, Franklin notified State Department
Agent Lafayette Baker that he had arrested a
"one-armed man" named Carlyle Murray; Baker
immediately headed for Philadelphia to interview
Murray and look at the suspicious documents. Baker
reported that he attached no importance to the
suspicious papers because so little was known about
the KGC at the time. Murray also insisted that he was
an "intimate friend of a merchant prince of Boston,"
which drew no apparent query even though Franklin
should have known about the previous accusation
of swindling from Amos Lawrence. Without a reason
to hold Murray, he was released. Carlyle Murray
promptly disappeared; a relieved Mr. Jackson,

however, went back to Branford.

Upon further reflection, Baker recognized the importance of the incriminating papers, especially the thinly disguised constitution and bylaws of the KGC. He also recognized the "one-armed" impostor Carlyle Murray as Parker French. Baker and French had known each other in California.

The detective must have informed Seward of his suspicions and subsequently received an order from Seward to "arrest P. H. F., alias Carlisle (sic) Murray, and convey him to Fort Warren, Boston, Massachusetts. Examine his person and baggage, and send all papers found in his possession to this Department." Baker had just received a difficult task that, as he later wrote, he thought hopeless.

But Baker caught a break. Intercepted letters headed south from Branford, Connecticut, soon put Baker back on the trail; they were marked with the initials CM. Not knowing French's assumed name in Branford, Baker came up with an ingenious plan. Recruiting Detective Franklin from Philadelphia, the pair arrived in Branford on November 5 with their own fictitious identities to remain anonymous and not alert French. They checked into the Totoket Hotel, became known to prominent citizens, did not reveal their mission, and waited for the situation to develop. The pair represented themselves as weapon manufacturers with government contracts seeking a facility; they even toured a vacant machine shop. The disclosure that visitors were trying to establish a business in support of the Union motivated the citizens and loosened lips. It did not even take a couple of hours to find French.

At the hotel with William and Lydia Covert, Baker and Franklin were "strangers to all and in pursuit of a stranger with no clue to his person or place of abode." They needed as much information as possible from what was probably a center of information in the town. After disclosing their manufacturing plans, they offered to establish the enterprise's headquarters in the hotel. That pleasant surprise and the prospective revenue led to very friendly and open discussions, followed by an invitation to a private dinner.

At the dinner table there was an extra place setting, obviously planned for another distinguished guest. Lydia Covert inquired of her husband if Mr. Jackson was coming down to dinner. Baker and Franklin astonished their hosts by rushing upstairs to search the hotel. In the only two-room suite in the hotel, Baker found the celebrated guest and asked, "How are you, French?" Probably feigning confusion, French rose, and not showing that he recognized Baker, remarked, "You have the advantage of me sir." Baker replied that indeed he did have the advantage since "I have a warrant for your arrest, and I don't think you have one for me."

French then recollected, or admitted, that he did recognize Baker from California. In his typically cool and charming manner, French offered brandy and remarked that he was always happy to see someone from California. He added, "Well, how are my friends McDougal and Tilford?" This was a friendly yet personal attempt at intimidation. As a vigilante in San Francisco, Baker was implicated in lynchings, including that of an accused murderer who was defended by distinguished lawyers and French associates James McDougal and Franklin Tilford. McDougal was well known to French as a former attorney general in Illinois and a sitting senator from California in 1861. Tilford was a Kentuckian from a prominent family. Saying he thought he had actually escaped the clutches of the law, French described the whole affair to Baker as a "good joke." He further lamented that the people of the town thought he was a good man since he was heavily involved in the religious life of the community; he had lectured on temperance, preached from the pulpit, and taught Sabbath school.

William and Lydia Covert entered the room and learned the true character and traitorous background of their beloved friend Mr. Jackson. The encounter and conversation were comedic and pathetic. William became distraught with involuntary tremors and an anguished expression. His seething wife, Lydia, spouted her anger and dismay: "Why, Mr. Jackson, how could you be so wicked? These gentlemen say you are a rebel spy. To think that a secessionist has even slept under our roof, I'll have to air the bed and purify the whole house." Then, looking at her hands and crying bitterly, she added, "And I have washed your clothes! May the Lord forgive you, for I can't."

By the time French's belongings were packed, the weekly bill was paid, and the party was ready to depart, word of the arrest had spread through the town. Citizens—including the Congregationalist minister Jacob Miller, postmaster Philo Hall, and blacksmith Henry Nichols—came running, wondering what was happening to their wonderful Mr. Jackson. French tried to soften the blow on his landlady by softly stating, "I will return and explain this whole thing to you." A mysterious Texan in the crowd objected, rallied for resistance to the arrest, and tried to recruit the townspeople to help in a rescue. Baker reported that "a display of a six-shooter immediately quieted his rebellious spirit." Fearing a rescue attempt might still be attempted, Baker and Franklin took their charge out of town on the next train. Perhaps affected by the whole affair, the blacksmith soon enlisted in Company B of the Twenty-Seventh Connecticut Volunteer Infantry.[296,297,298]

Baker reported the arrest to Secretary of State

Seward and pronounced French as "one of the most accomplished villains in America." The detective detailed his search of French and laid out the initial case against him. He reported finding the letters from Andrew Johnson, Emerson Etheridge, and Parson Brownlow, all evidence of the charitable scam purportedly supportive of Brownlow's newspaper, the *Knoxville Whig*. In relating the steamship scheme, Baker unfortunately and falsely implicated Amos Lawrence in that he had failed to promptly report the suspected fraud. The investigator apparently did not know of the almost immediate action Lawrence took in September to have "Murray" arrested. The most damning evidence among French's papers "was a manuscript purporting to be the constitution and by-laws of a secret order or association, known as the Knights of the Golden Square. This document is copied almost verbatim from the constitution and by-laws of the Knights of the Golden Circle ... the object of which was, the overthrow of the United States Government." Further noted was the ingenious wording of the "Golden Square," meant to suggest an organization loyal to the Union cause, allay any suspicions, and preclude use of the document as evidence. Baker was fully satisfied that French was undoubtedly a member of the traitorous Knights of the Golden Circle. The papers Baker sent to Seward have been lost to history.[299]

A short account of the arrest promptly started an avalanche of newspaper articles throughout the nation; the capture was described as the most significant since the start of the war: "Boston, November 5, 1861. Important Arrest: Parker French, Of Filibuster Notoriety, Arrested By Government Detective."[300]

Personas Carlyle Murray, Charles Maxey, Christopher Monroe, and Mr. Jackson were now dead and would not be heard of again. The accused traitor and Confederate agent Parker Hardin French was on his way to confinement in Fort Warren, an island fortress in Boston harbor specifically designated for political prisoners.

16

CIVIL WAR: JAILED IN FORT WARREN

After Baker and Franklin quickly left Branford, Parker French was taken by train to New Haven and then to Boston. Newspapers throughout the nation reported on the arrest of the traitorous scoundrel, as well as the transport to Boston and subsequent imprisonment at Fort Warren in Boston Harbor.

The arresting agent, L.C. Baker, reported to Secretary of State Seward and insisted that:

> *"There can be no doubt but that F. is one of the most accomplished villains in America, I am satisfied that F. is a member of the Knights of the Golden Circle; that he has copied their constitution and by-laws; that the papers found in his possession have been altered or worded differently from the original, so that, if he should at any time be suspected or arrested, these papers could not he used as evidence against him."*

Parker French was to find himself in friendly company:

"Prisoners are generally apt to be a little cross for the first day or two after their arrival but this wears off as they find that their companions are cheerful. Most of them find acquaintances among the prisoners. Parker H. French found several friends, and made himself at home from the beginning, evidently well pleased with being in such good society."[301,302]

On the train trip to Boston, French was very friendly and chatty with his captors; he was "voluble and jaunty in his talk." The prisoner regaled his escorts with his views of the war. He assured the arresting officers that it was completely useless for the North to make war on the South, which was sure to succeed in the end. French asserted that "the more the opposition the Secessionists had to encounter, the more would their passions be inflamed and consequently the more the punishment which they would mete out to their enemies." He also openly attempted to curry favor with the lawmen and provide information to mitigate the charges against him, saying, "I can do you more good than you can do me harm; I will give you information which will be worth millions to you on condition of my release." French went on to tell them about prominent men and companies in Boston who were collaborating with the Confederacy, engaging in black marketeering, and smuggling and sending goods south through the neutral British seaport in St. Johns, New Brunswick. That statement was reported in newspapers, likely causing further investigation and more stringent attention to St. Johns.[303,304,305]

Upon reaching Boston, French was immediately taken to Fort Warren for confinement. Located in Boston Harbor on Georges Island (then called Governor's Island), the pentagonal star fort commanded the entrance to the harbor and was essential to its defense. Any passing ship came within very short range of its guns. Colonel Justin Dimick had taken command just one week before. He had been tasked with two missions: improvement of the fort's defensive capability to defend the harbor, as well as confinement of war and political prisoners. The windswept island was an ideal place for imprisonment as it was virtually escape-proof: "a more desolate place could not be imagined anywhere this side of the

Arctic regions." French was quartered with the rest of the political prisoners and the Confederate officers in rooms intended for the garrison officers.

Aerial photo of Georges Island and Fort Warren, Boston Harbor.

French indeed found friends amongst the more than 100 political prisoners, including some from Kentucky. One was ex-governor Charles Morehead, well known to the Hardin family. A Southern sympathizer supportive of Kentucky's neutrality and critical of the Lincoln administration, he worked for a peaceful resolution, hoping to avert war. He was charged, probably falsely and without proof, with treason and promoting rebellion. Most of the other Kentuckians were low-level secessionists who had been arrested for disloyal and seditious conduct. They were reported as scouring the country to persecute Unionists and to enlist men into the pro-Confederate militia. Some of his reported "friends" were doubtless new ones, captured by his charisma and gift of gab.

The political prisoners were granted considerable personal liberty consistent with confinement and lived much better than the hundreds of prisoners of war.

They did have to give their word that they would not go upon the ramparts, converse with the sentinels, or make any attempt to communicate with the shore. Formed into "messes," they contracted with a local merchant to buy food and drink to prepare reportedly sumptuous meals. For their rooms, the captives were allowed to have what personal goods and luxuries they could buy, including alcohol; Colonel Dimick was the "bank" for safekeeping of their money. The detainees could write and receive letters subject to review and censorship, read newspapers, and receive money and gifts from the outside. Gambling was a popular pastime. They gathered on the parade ground, walked, played games, and smoked. They could talk amongst themselves, but they were prohibited from talking to the lower-ranking prisoners of war. The *Boston Daily Traveler* described the prison's scene; prisoners were "smoking and conversing like a party of do-nothings in front of a fashionable hotel." Colonel Dimick later received accolades from prisoners and Union soldiers alike for his leadership and humanitarian treatment. He was said to exhibit "every disposition to make us as comfortable as possible; this example necessarily influences the behavior of the subordinate officers and soldiers."[307,308]

On Sunday, November 24, two distinguished Confederate officials, James Mason and John Slidell, arrived at the prison. Their presence created a sensation amongst the prisoners, who clustered around the celebrities to greet them warmly and hear their stories. Their detention, known as the Trent Affair, was a serious diplomatic incident that could have precipitated war between the United States and the British Empire. The two Confederate diplomats had been dispatched to Europe to seek recognition, financial support, and military aid. They were passengers on board the British mail packet *HMS*

Trent, which was stopped and searched by the *USS San Jacinto* under the command of Captain Charles Wilkes. Wilkes removed the two envoys and delivered them to Fort Warren. Parker French probably knew both of the celebrities from his efforts as a Nicaraguan ambassador to lobby expansionists in Congress to support the Walker regime. At that time, both were sitting senators, Mason from Virginia and Slidell from Louisiana; they supported expansionism as well as the protection and extension of slavery. For the month of confinement, the two were reportedly pleasant, generous of their time, and were the center of attention amongst the prisoners. The British government, their honor insulted, demanded the diplomats be released and threatened war; hotheads in the United States celebrated the capture and demanded they be kept incarcerated; the Confederacy hoped for recognition by Great Britain or at least a rupture in US-British relations. To avoid worsening the diplomatic crises and to avert possible war, President Lincoln disavowed the capture and released the two envoys; they left Fort Warren on December 26.

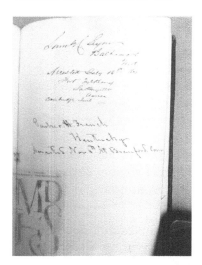

Parker H. French's signature from prisoners' record, Aug. 1861–Feb. 1862. Kept at Fort Warren, Mass. by the prisoners. Held by the Maryland Historical Society.

Previously on November 4, Secretary of State Seward informed Colonel Dimick that he had engaged lawyer Seth Hawley of New York to review the cases of political prisoners confined at Fort Warren. Public pressure had been mounting over the Lincoln administration's violations of personal liberty, specifically habeas corpus provisos. Seward asked the lawyer to make recommendations on whether each of the detainees could be safely released. Later in November, Hawley started a review of Parker French's case. French immediately tried to charm and convince Hawley of his innocence, appealing to Hawley in the most pathetic terms to give his case a careful and fair review. French admitted that there were "clouds upon his good name" and that "his reputation was so bad that unfavorable constructions were put upon all his acts." But, French declared, he was a loyal citizen and could never be charged with the crime of treason.

On November 30, Hawley wrote to Frederick Seward, who was William Seward's son and assistant secretary of state. Hawley asked Seward to provide any files associated with the case; he also left open the possibility that there was reason to transfer the case to local Boston authorities for their adjudication of local criminal cases. Frederick Seward immediately responded with the files and noted that the arresting officer, L.C. Baker, still insisted that French was an agent of the Confederacy. Unfortunately, the evidentiary files have been lost to history, but a summary provides some indication of the content. Hawley probably received preliminary charges with evidence of at least two crimes: efforts to fit out a privateer to serve the Confederacy "under pretense of arming a vessel for the public service" and "propagating a secret disloyal society called the Knights of the Golden Circle in Boston and other parts of New England."[309]

Starting on December 6, Hawley exchanged letters with Bostonian Amos Lawrence, trying to ascertain if there were any chargeable offenses related to the steamship caper. Secretary Seward wanted assurance that all the political prisoners were being detained on rock-solid grounds, so Hawley pressed Lawrence for compelling evidence of disloyalty or traitorous intent. While acknowledging that French was a "thoroughly bad man" who should be charged criminally, he doubted whether he yet had enough evidence supporting charges of treason or disloyalty. Hawley noted that he had the captured letters between Lawrence and Carlyle Murray. Interestingly, Hawley also mentioned captured letters addressed to the secessionist persona of Charles Maxey. Since the Maxey persona was never involved in the steamship swindle, one can only wonder about the lost history from those missing letters. Lawrence maintained his assessment that French intended to operate the steamships in support of the Confederacy, but he admitted he had no proof which would support such a charge of treason. Other evidence in Hawley's possession was perhaps more suspicious but not proof enough. A witness indicated that Carlyle Murray intended to take charge of the vessels himself with his own crews while also inquiring about the availability and pricing for large quantities of stores, including gunpowder and percussion caps. Memoranda in French's possession also showed plans and cost estimates for altering, arming, manning, supplying, and navigating propellers as warships. Frustrated that he still lacked direct proof of treason, Hawley told Lawrence that unless more information was provided, French would have to be released. He especially asked for any more evidence about any planned hostile naval effort; Lawrence replied that he had none, although he still had suspicions. Hawley's personal thoughts on French are also revealing: "he is a reprobate-a spiritualist-an opium eater, and very nearly if not quite insane ... he ought to be in a penitentiary or a madhouse."[310]

There may have been more information in the lost investigatory files, but the inquiry seemed to have fizzled. There are no historical artifacts about any examination of the ancillary circumstances surrounding the arrest: the subversion and agitation as an agent of the Confederacy and the Knights of the Golden Circle; the implication of a smuggling ring in St. Johns, New Brunswick; or the spying and sending of information to the South. Plenty of implicating newspaper articles could have aroused suspicion and precipitated a more encompassing investigation. Did Parker French give evidence on wider conspiracies and operations? Did he make good on his initial statement on the train, that if released, he could give information worth millions? Had he used his extensive family connections to seek release? Arresting agent L.C. Baker continued to insist that French was a dangerous proxy of the Confederacy. He commented on the need for detectives at the national level when "traitors in arms and in the disguise of loyal citizens are plotting with unscrupulous hate against the Government."[311]

Some have theorized that French was merely involved in a minor scam in Boston since there was no definitive proof of an effort to transfer ships to the Confederacy. It is true that French was not averse to pocketing small profits from a scam, but he was more interested in grand schemes with a big payout. Swindling Amos Lawrence out of a small commission for the ships would not have been worth the effort required to lay the groundwork evident in the investigation; French could have acquired that amount with less trouble and less risk. A magnificent ploy to move ships to the Confederacy and have the Union pay was just as likely. And, it was more in character for Parker French, more consistent with his past major exploits with substantial rewards.

Seth Hawley concluded his inquiry on February 13, 1862, wrote Assistant Secretary of State Frederic Seward, and perhaps just finally conceded that he had no proof. "Everything connected with his career is mysterious or feigned," Hawley wrote. He could find no evidence against French "which cannot be reconciled with his loyalty." Hawley further recommended release: "I do not think the conditions upon which he should be discharged are important. If he is a Union man ... conditions are not needed, but if he is a well disguised traitor conditions will be useless, as he has no moral qualities to command any degree of confidence in his promises."

The release was accomplished with a simple pair of telegraphs between the War Department and Colonel Dimick at Fort Warren. On March 17, Colonel Dimick reported that Parker French had been released; he had signed his parole-of-honor that he would render no aid or comfort to Confederacy.[312]

Parker Hardin French was no longer considered a "delightful rogue," he was now just a despised scoundrel. He had been arrested as a Confederate agent, marked as a traitor in the public consciousness and disdained throughout the nation. The next stop for Parker Hardin French was in the nation's capital. Remarkably and bizarrely, shortly after his release he was allowed to support Union Army forces. He operated first as a lawyer and then was authorized to sell goods to both corps and division headquarters. Both positions would have been perfect cover to continue as a Confederate agent.

17

CIVIL WAR: LAWYER AND PURVEYOR

Shortly after release from Fort Warren, Parker French arrived in Washington, D.C. Over the next three years, he supported Union Army units as both a lawyer and a purveyor, providing goods and services to corps and division headquarters. Tax and draft registration records from June 1863 show French was a lawyer with residency in Washington of a year; he falsely claimed he was in military service for two years in Mexico. How did this man with a nefarious background and suspected service to the Confederacy gain such positions of trust? Perhaps he was always under the watchful eyes of Union agents. One of his legal adversaries said:

> *"If I fail with General Hooker I shall try the Judge Advocate General with whom I can throw the whole case for illegality. The worst thing is that the Judge Advocate has allowed the whole proceeding to be in the hands of that damnable Parker French. I have no hesitation in saying that I believe him none too good to change both questions and answers to suit himself."*

And about being a purveyor: *"A dirty rotten snake, I hope he gets smashed out of business—but not until I'm gone from here."* [13,314]

Upon arrival in Washington, D.C., in March 1862, French took a room at 462 New York Avenue and acquired occasional work representing soldiers in courts-martial. The work must have been spotty and had little prospect of adequate compensation. It was also not beneath him to engage in common and illegal peddling on the streets. Shortly after he arrived, he was arrested for selling military-type goods without a license. A landlord related that, from all appearances, he was very poor and frequently "destitute of means wherewith to defray his ordinary expenses and was frequently in arrears for the rent of his room ... he was very much in want of proper clothing ... without means to purchase the same." At other times, French appeared to have come into a small amount of funds; rent would be paid, and his appearance would improve.[315],[316]

Aquia Harbor, 1862. As a lawyer, Parker French supported the 2nd Division of XII Corps.

In the spring of 1863, French's prospects improved considerably; he started developing a relationship with the Division Headquarters of Second Division of the XII Corps, encamped some fifty miles south of Washington at Aquia Creek. The Commanding General John White Geary was not a regular army officer. The editor of the book publishing his letters, William Blair, declared that Geary was "first and foremost a politician." At the start of the Civil War, he raised the Twenty-Eighth Pennsylvania Regiment and was its colonel. Geary had won acclaim as a militia officer during the Mexican War, had been a colonel commanding the Second Pennsylvania Regiment, and was the military governor of the Mexico City. Political patronage from his service followed. A post office appointment by President Polk sent him to San Francisco, where he became the city's first mayor from 1850 to 1852. Geary and French would not have known each other in California because the timeframes did not overlap, but they had a common frame of reference upon which to build a friendship. Geary knew French's good friend Hugh C. Murray, who was sequentially a San Francisco city official, an associate justice of the Superior Court in San Francisco, and a justice on the California Supreme Court. The pair could certainly entertain themselves discussing the exciting and wild brand of politics practiced in the nascent state of California. They could also share discussion about their ancestral linkage to Westmoreland County, Pennsylvania. Geary's father, Richard (1779–1834), and French's maternal grandfather, Martin L. Hardin (1780–1848), were both born in the county.[317]

At the time, General Geary was dealing with a significant problem with a subordinate artillery unit, "Hampton's Battery," commanded by Robert B. Hampton. Parker French would become intimately involved. Since the previous August, when the Second Battle of Bull's Run took place, unit officers in two opposing groups had been spatting with each other when they were not engaged with the enemy. They were accusing and counter-charging. Geary said, "with a vehemence of malignity which I regarded and am satisfied was the offspring of a degrading brawl." The allegations were disturbing: cowardice, drunkenness, disobedience of orders, conduct unbecoming of an officer, mutinous conduct, neglect of duty, and absence without leave. Lieutenant Nathaniel Irish brought the situation to a head in November 1862; he preferred charges against his Commanding Officer Captain Robert Hampton for cowardice and drunkenness. General Geary immediately sent the charges to his chief of artillery hoping that, upon reflection, the artillery officers would realize their actions were "valueless and unworthy of men." He further reprimanded the officers in no uncertain terms. He said he was deeply mortified that his subordinates would demean themselves and said that "were their minds more given to the destiny of their country than to their private likes and dislikes, these bickerings would have no existence nor any cause for the same."

After the charges were rebuffed by Geary, politics reared its ugly head. Lieutenant Irish bypassed the entire chain of command and sent his charges against Hampton to the Secretary of War Edwin Stanton. In rapid succession, Stanton asked for information on the case, Geary forwarded the entirety of the charges, General in Chief Halleck recommended that the case be left to the discretion of Geary, and the case wound itself back through channels to the Second Division. There was no direction to proceed with the courts-martial, but Geary used his discretion to convene them. In the meantime, Captain Hampton countercharged Lieutenant Irish with multiple serious offenses.

Both protagonists were politically connected. Captain Robert Hampton had been in California for the entirety of the 1850s. He was active in San Francisco grassroots politics, with the support of both the powerful firemen association and the vigilantes, while Geary was mayor. Hugh C. Murray was a city officer and on the bench. Active in the state's Whig Party central committee, Hampton also probably knew Parker French from the rough and tumble politics of Sacramento. Back in Pennsylvania when the war broke out, he raised "Hamptons Battery"; Governor Andrew Curtin commissioned him as its commander.

Nathaniel Irish was connected as well. Brother Elias Hicks Irish was a legal protégé of Edwin Stanton, the secretary of war, and a former member of the Pennsylvania legislature. Lieutenant Nathan Irish often wrote his brother Elias of the conflicts in the battery and the progress of the legal battle. Elias sent a summary of the case to Secretary Stanton, defending his brother and alleging that "the official record had been copied with the greatest carelessness (if carelessness it was) ... several changes had taken place ... part of the evidence and proceedings entirely omitted." Politics, with the possibility of unethical command influence, was clashing with military command, discipline, and prerogative.

The courts-martial for Lieutenant Irish and Captain Hampton were conducted sequentially, starting on March 5, 1863, and ending on April 1. Nathaniel Irish went first. At that time, a judge advocate presented the cases, seeking the truth, protecting the interests of the army, and moving the case along. The officer who preferred the charges acted as the prosecutor—Hampton against Irish and vice versa; each defendant engaged his own defense counsel. Parker French was defense counsel for Captain Hampton, and he was a legal advisor to Hampton in his role as prosecutor against Irish. French proved to be remarkably effective in questioning witnesses and answering challenges from Irish, especially in his closing argument. During each court-martial,

Lieutenant Irish protested the process, claiming illegal rulings, chicanery, and injustice. He wrote his family and alleged falsified records and perjury, as well as manufactured and suppressed evidence. He saved a good part of his bitterness for the "notorious" Parker French, who, Irish stated, was allowed illegal and unprecedented practices and tactics. On April 1, Captain Hampton was cleared of all charges of cowardice and drunkenness and found not guilty; he was also praised by the judge advocate for his "disposition and conduct ... shown to be that of a high toned, honorable gentleman." Lieutenant Irish, on the other hand, was found guilty of mutinous and un-officer-like conduct, neglect of duty, and absence without leave. The judge advocate general pilloried Irish for his "spirit of malevolence and malignance" and said that Irish should "blush for his own unmanliness." Lieutenant Irish was sentenced to dismissal from the service with forfeiture of all pay and emoluments since December 31, 1862.

The saga of Lieutenant Irish continued. He was under arrest while his case was reviewed. At the Battle of Chancellorsville on May 3, 1863, he was temporarily released from arrest to fight in the battle. He was present when Captain Hampton was killed, hit by a Confederate cannonball above the knee.

The Irish family continued to lobby Secretary Stanton to reverse the court-martial findings and return Nathaniel to duty. Even though the chain of command reviewed and approved the findings and the dismissal, Secretary Stanton eventually reinstated Lieutenant Irish. The whole court-martial record was available to Stanton. Did he notice the name of Parker H. French, whom he had authorized to be released from Fort Warren in early 1862?[318]

After the Battle of Chancellorsville, Parker French likely lost any worthwhile contact with Geary's division for several weeks. During the operational movements associated with the Gettysburg Campaign, civilians were severely restricted from transport with the Army of the Potomac. After the Battle of Gettysburg, Geary's Second Division, as part of the XII Corps, moved back into Virginia and formed a line along the Rappahannock River. Geary's headquarters was established by early August 1863 at Ellis Ford, about seventy miles southwest of Washington, D.C., and just a couple of miles upstream from the confluence of the Rappahannock and Rapidan Rivers. The Rappahannock offered tremendous strategic importance as a natural barrier; control of the river became a centerpiece of eastern operations and multiple pitched battles bloodied its banks. Parker French would get back in the game and support Geary.

While the Army of the Potomac was settling into position, the fortunes of Parker French were on the rise. The Army of the Potomac's commander, General George Meade, tried to get a handle on the large number of civilian sutlers and purveyors selling to and trading with the army. As a predecessor to the Post Exchanges of today, these traders played an important role in supporting soldiers. Some, though, were crooks—perhaps a majority, if the many anecdotes are true. They often charged outrageous prices, especially after payday. Throughout the army, appointment of purveyors and sutlers was fraught with ethical issues, including tacit partnerships and collusion between commanders and the profitable businesses. This was especially a problem among state militia officers who were politicians at heart and who did not intend to stay in the army as a career. It was common custom in the militias that the commander personally appointed the purveyor/sutler or had him selected by a chosen group of officers. In an attempt at control, Meade authorized one sutler per regiment and one purveyor for each

division and corps headquarters. French convinced
General Geary of the Second Division to appoint him
to the position. He was granted exclusive rights to
sell commercial goods and provisions to the division
headquarters, to the officers and men individually.
and to the officers' mess. Maybe French's defense of
Captain Hampton and prosecution of Lieutenant Irish
had impressed and pleased Geary. Geary may have
stepped over the ethical line and violated Meade's
intent and direction; French later claimed that he had
received a loan from Geary and paid him back within a
couple of months.[319,320]

The many sutlers, typically one per regiment,
were authorized to sell a restricted list of supplies
to enlisted men; generally, no hard alcohol was
allowed. As a purveyor, French had tremendous
advantages working with the headquarters, where
he enjoyed the access and social status of an officer
without authority or responsibility. He sold goods
to a discerning and well-heeled clientele; with the
exclusive rights, he could not only supply common
goods but could also provide choice items like hard
alcohol. The typical list of available items challenged
the inventory of a good size market; modern
customers would recognize some of the brands,
especially in liquor and beer: Yuengling, Guinness,
Anheuser-Busch, Jim Beam, and Haig.

As a purveyor, Parker French also had a huge
advantage in transport; he could ship "officers' stores"
on army transportation, including via rail. Sutlers
servicing common soldiers were generally prohibited
from use of rail and had to provide their own wagons
for road movement. The difference was striking. A
sutler had to transport his supplies by wagon some
seventy miles to the vicinity of the Rappahannock
under the gauntlet of Confederate guerilla forces led
by John Mosby, the feared "Grey Ghost." The capture

of any supplies provided sustenance to the rebels, but they also could be the basis for potential indemnity claims; spy rings and collusion between sutlers and guerillas were also a concern. The army acted. No longer would individual sutler wagons be allowed. On Monday of each week, a train of sutler wagons, protected by a cavalry regiment, left Washington for Warrenton Junction, about twenty miles behind the Rappahannock. The escorted convoy returned to Washington on Thursday. Meanwhile French, as a purveyor, could move demanded supplies on a daily basis to the XII Corps and Geary's division using the Orange and Alexandria Railroad. Bealeton Station, near the current crossroads of routes 17 and 28, was just about ten miles from the division.[321]

Parker French did not have the initial capability to provide the service. On August 12, 1863, he partnered with an established sutler named John Paul Jones (of no relationship to the Revolutionary naval hero). They contracted to share the expenses and profits equally. Jones agreed to advance all the goods and articles and furnish all the equipment, such as tents and scales. French would pay for the horses and wagons as needed. After each sale of goods there was to be a full accounting; Jones would be paid for the goods, any necessary expenses would be split, and the profits shared. The books were to be "open to, and in possession of, both parties jointly." The contract allowed for termination if Jones made a deal with another sutler to take over the business; upon termination French was supposed to provide a full accounting. Jones was a busy man supplying other units and probably went about his business trusting French. He would soon learn that his confidence and trust were misplaced.

On August 29, the partnership was dissolved under the termination provision. Jones had sold his business and now sought a full accounting. For several weeks, French delayed, dissembled, and gave excuses. In October, Jones took legal action, and a subpoena for French's appearance was issued by the Supreme Court of the District of Columbia. The subpoena was returned by the marshal to the clerk's office with a note, "not found." French had disappeared, along with the books.

A subsequent estimate by Jones and his clerk disclosed a cunning pattern by French. He had paid Jones periodically from the revenues of the business, probably just enough to satisfy Jones that all was well. In his deposition to the court, Jones said that he had received $2,350 (2017 estimate, $44,000): a pretty lucrative business in less than three weeks. A deposition by the partnership's clerk, Thomas McCabe, exposed much larger revenue as well as fraud and embezzlement. He stated that French conducted a lively business, obviously pocketing large sums of money. French would return from the day's transactions, drop off the smaller change, and leave with the proceeds and the books. McCabe estimated that French got away with over $6,000, which was due Jones (2017 estimate, $112,000). French also absconded with the tents and equipment, including a fine horse and tack.[322]

John Paul Jones was not particularly ethical himself. In August 1864, he and his brother William were convicted by a special court martial for "unlawfully obtaining and appropriating government Property." They were each sentenced to pay a fine of $2,500 (2017 estimate: $35,000) and one-year imprisonment, or until the fine was paid.[323]

There was a good reason that French could not be found in October. He was in Tennessee, having participated in one of the greatest strategic movements in military history: the largest troop movement by rail to that time. Following the bloody two-day Battle of Chickamauga, the decisively defeated Union forces, under General Rosecrans, retreated to Chattanooga. By September 22, they were concentrated in the city. Confederate forces seized dominating terrain surrounding the town, besieged the vulnerable force, and cut off rail and river traffic.

Recognizing the critical situation and the threat to their entire western strategy, Lincoln and Secretary of War Stanton reacted quickly. They met the evening of September 23 with key staff and the superintendent of military transportation. The XI and XII Corps, which included Geary's Second Division, were pulled out of line on the Rappahannock. By September 25, they were loading trains at Bealeton Station and Manassas Junction. Five days and over 1,100 miles later, the first trains unloaded at Bridgeport, Alabama, about forty miles southwest of Chattanooga. By the middle of October, the entire force of 20,000 troops and artillery, with 3,000 horses and mules, was in position to break the siege under the command of General Hooker.[324]

Chattanooga, 1863. Sketch map by G. H. Blakeslee showing fortifications, Union and Confederate picket lines, rifle pits, rebel camps, roads, railroads, and streams. Library of Congress.

Parker French, with the filched money, equipment, and the fine horse from Jones, established his first purveyor's store at Bridgeport, Alabama. After the siege of Chattanooga was lifted, he established another store at Lookout Mountain to support Geary's division. In December 1863, French was appointed as purveyor for General Hooker's XX Corps, as well as Geary's division. He was given another lucrative charter; he gained the rights to dispose of all the cattle hides for the corps, which likely slaughtered over seventy-two cattle per day.[325],[326]

Having broken the siege and wintered in and around the city, Hooker's corps and Geary's division attacked south in the spring of 1864. They were engaged in the campaign to capture Atlanta, to be followed by the March to the Sea. French remained with his stores in the Chattanooga area through May 1865 with no known authorization; perhaps inertia, complacency, and confusion in the rear area served him well.

In early April, Duff Green, uncle by marriage and mentor of Parker French, visited President Lincoln in Virginia on a Navy ship. After Green refused to shake hands with a greeting Lincoln, he called the president a tyrant and murderer and berated him for reveling in the defeat of the Confederacy. An angered Lincoln responded by calling Green an unprincipled traitor, political tramp, and hyena. "Miserable imposter, vile intruder!" Lincoln heatedly barked, "Go, before I forget myself and the high position I hold!" Whatever Green thought he was going to accomplish is a mystery, but he quickly exited the ship. The time when Parker French could leverage family connections to visit the halls of power was past.

From his almost two-year stint as a purveyor, he later claimed profits of more than $45,000 (2017 estimate, $650,000). But then calamity struck when a fire broke out at his Lookout Mountain store, destroying $25,000 worth of goods along with his books. French may have fallen victim to the all too common attitude of soldiers toward sutlers and purveyors—they despised the merchants for the typically shoddy merchandise and unreasonable prices. Then again, he could have been responsible for the arson. With the war ended, French first consolidated his operations in Bridgeport and then joined his family in Louisville.[327]

Through the summer of 1865, Parker French lived with his family in Louisville on Sixth Street between Chestnut and Broadway. He was on the tax roles as a peddler, likely selling goods to units and soldiers in the city. Business must have been very lucrative. Louisville was designated as the headquarters for the Armies of the West and as a mustering-out center for troops. Soldiers crowded the city as they waited to be sent home; in June alone, some 70,000 troops passed through Louisville. By August, the Armies of the West under General Sherman had disbanded.[328]

In the fall of 1865, French and his family headed back to St. Louis, where he would begin a new life, mostly out of the limelight.

18

SMALL TIME SCAMS – BITE-SIZE CHUNKS

For the next thirteen years, Parker Hardin French made his way without a lot of fanfare. Besides St. Louis, he appeared in Sacramento, New York, and Washington, D.C. Apparently legitimate attempts at business would either fail or be peppered with attempted deceits, spawning contentious lawsuits, property foreclosures, and sheriffs' sales. French garnered local notoriety, but now there were few stories worth national attention. There were no enamored editors to report on every activity of the "delightful rogue." There were no foreign adventures, no grand exploits, no outrageous scams, and no trans-continental expeditions. But French was still a barracuda; he was still Parker Hardin French. He just scaled back his schemes to more bite-size chunks. Acquaintances reported him engaging in some streetwise cons and falling into drunken dissipation. He married again, this time to a clergyman's daughter with whom he had a namesake son. In the last years of his life, the family had an apparently comfortable life in a prestigious neighborhood.

Among some editors who remembered French's misadventures, there was still a spark of interest:

"The Federal City is duller now than for many years but occasionally we meet with men of note, who come here on business. Those who

*come here, it should be said, always come on
business, not for pleasure. At least, no person
ever visited Washington City a second time
for amusement. Amongst the visitors lately
was Colonel Parker H. French, a native of
your State, whose romantic career is somewhat
familiar to the people of the West and South.
When I last met French, he was ambassador
to this country from Nicaragua, sent hither by
the filibuster Walker. He is now a resident of St.
Louis.* "[329]

In the fall of 1865, Parker French and his family
returned to St. Louis, where daughter Ellie Lucretia
was born on October 21, 1866. Reprising his role as
merchant, French invested $10,000 for a third share
in a partnership with long-time St. Louis merchants
Francis and George Buchanan. They ran a wholesale
grocery and boat store under the name of George
Buchanan and Company. By June 1866, French
apparently felt comfortable enough to buy a city lot
from George Buchanan for over $2,800.

Remarking that he was "still a soldier of fortune,"
the *Adair County News* reported a visit to his uncle
Parker Hardin and a trip to nearby Burkesville in
Cumberland County, Kentucky. There he likely
invested in business opportunities in the ongoing
oil boom; shallow gushers were coming in, and one
oil well was estimated to be flowing as high as 3,000
barrels per day.

Back in St. Louis, a successful court suit garnered
a settlement, and he received proceeds from a sheriff's
sale. All seemed to be going well with the French
family and the Buchanan partnership.[330,331,332]

In parallel efforts, however, the story was not so
rosy. French became half owner in the steamboat
Little Rock to transport passengers and supplies

up the Missouri River to Fort Benton, which was
the gateway to the gold fields of southern Montana.
Captain John S. Doyle and David Hill were one-
quarter owners. French managed the funds, paid
the vendors and crew, dispersed the profits and kept
the books. Under the command of Captain Doyle,
the steamboat left St. Louis on May 16, 1867 for the
2,300-mile trip up the Missouri.

Fort Benton
Montana with
steamboat.
Courtesy of
Overholser
Historical
Research
Center, Fort
Benton,
Montana.

The ship carried ten crew and forty-nine
passengers, including eleven women and twelve
children, and 125 tons of cargo were in the hold or
lashed to the deck. On board was Mrs. Elizabeth Fisk,
who sent letters home with detailed information. At
first, she extolled Captain Doyle for his gentlemanly
demeanor, crew discipline, his navigational
understanding of the river, and the fine food.

Showing some discontent, letters soon remarked on
the slowness of the boat as faster vessels passed. The
boat's relatively slow speed was aggravated by a burst
boiler, which required a delay of four days to repair.

Morale on the boat plummeted and was reflected
in Mrs. Fisk's letters. Passengers started complaining
about the captain and the slow pace, speculating that
the officers and men were being paid by time. They
also complained that all the preparations for the trip
were "of the cheapest kind," food was spoiling from

lack of care, and there were not enough men. The steamer finally reached Fort Benton on July 14, and the disgruntled passengers disembarked.[333]

When Captain Doyle and David Hill returned to St. Louis, they discovered that they had been duped by French. The partners filed suit on September 3, requiring an accounting from French and a freezing of the assets. They alleged that French had about $36,000 (2017 estimate, $568,000) of revenue. He had not paid some $26,000 in expenses, including captain and crew pay, repair expenses, boat stores, and supplies. An estimated $10,000 was left to split amongst the owners. French was also charged with refusal to adjust the accounts, pay the debts, or dispense any of the funds. Telling the court that French had no visible links to St. Louis, they feared that French would abscond with all $36,000; he would "make way with all the funds and money ... to avoid paying the plaintiffs and the debts." The legal action was noted in the *Daily Missouri Democrat* and picked up in newspapers throughout the country as an interesting tidbit:

"Parker H. French—It has been a long time since we heard anything of Parker H. French, the man who, in 1849 advertised that a certain ship would sail from this port on a certain day. French acquired a good deal of notoriety, and was regarded by many at that time as a man of wonderful talents. He was captured a short time after his ship enterprise by the authorities at Durango, Mexico, and we believe, sentenced to be shot, but worked his way out of the difficulty and went to California. Yesterday the County Court granted an injunction against Parker H. French and others ... to restrain them from disposing of certain funds of the boat."[333]

The parties submitted to arbitration, and Doyle and Hill soon had full ownership of the vessel, with all debts satisfied. On December 23, while on the

White River in Arkansas, the *Little Rock* hit a snag, burned and sank. There were no lives lost, but the steamboat and cargo were a total loss. Captain Doyle was praised for his calmness, efficiency, and bravery in saving passengers and their baggage.[334,335]

Other bad deals and unpaid debts resulted in at least eight other court cases between February and October 1867. French's property was seized, trustee and sheriffs' sales were held, and he was compelled to sell his share of George Buchanan and Company for $2,000. With debts piling up and out of money, French filed for bankruptcy with liabilities of $88,345 (2017 estimate, $1.47 million). In a long rambling statement with little relevance to the actual bankruptcy, he falsified his loss of the train in Mexico and alleged "cruelty and indignity" by the governor of Durango. He did not mention his foray into Nicaragua nor his arrest and confinement as a suspected Confederate agent. He did falsely claim veteran status as a member of General Geary's staff, even though there was no official relationship. Civil suits against French continued to be filed in St. Louis as late as 1874.

His finances in shambles, French left his family in St. Louis and moved around the country seeking opportunities and connections. In California, he operated as a lawyer, primarily in probate cases.

Acquaintances saw him in New York City in July 1868 at the Democratic Party Convention. It is instructive in understanding the tenor of the times that the motto of the Democratic Party in 1868 was "This is a White Man's Country, Let White Men Rule." French was at the convention among friends of Frank Blair, who was a fellow Kentuckian, St. Louis lawyer, former congressman and future senator. French knew him in St. Louis as early as 1850. Blair would be nominated for vice president alongside presidential nominee Horatio Seymour of New York. They eventually lost to Republican Ulysses Grant. By early August, French was likely buttonholing congressmen and bureaucrats in Washington.[337]

About this time, French reportedly scammed actor and stage manager Hezekiah Bateman. The father and manager of noted actresses Kate and Ellen, Bateman was an affable figure in New York society and friends with many of Parker French's acquaintances, including journalist George Wilkes, a political ally and associate in both California and Nicaragua. According to the story, French convinced Bateman to partner with him on a speculation; the mark invested several thousand dollars. The con was simple: a friend had discovered a process to mix expensive ginseng with other roots and plants; they could certainly double their money in a short time. Boxes of the mixture arrived and were found to contain "mud more than anything else." Perhaps the gunk was the remains of rotten roots and vegetables. The unfortunate pigeon was out his several thousand dollars; he had agreed to the proposal and took the loss without going to the police. For George Wilkes and French's other New York associates, the conning of the popular Bateman was the last straw, and friendships with French were ended.[338]

In late November, French went to Washington, D.C., to press claims against Mexico and the Mexican Claims Commission for "seizure of his property and for personal detention."

While he was gone, on December 1, 1869, Lucretia died of "inflammation of the brain," probably either meningitis or encephalitis. Lucretia, perhaps not trusting French with her money, left the four children under the care of her executor and brother-in-law, Webb Quigley, husband of Lucretia's sister Isabella. Lucretia left $9,600 (2017 estimate, $166,000) in interest-bearing notes and cash for the exclusive support of her children. Parker French was not mentioned in the will or probate files. In the 1870 census, Hugh (sixteen) was living with the Quigleys in Alton. Twenty-year-old Matilda had taken charge of Nancy (twelve) and Ellie (four), and they were all living in Alton with a widow Hollingsworth.[339]

By 1870, French was a real estate agent in New York and apparently lived there for the rest of his life, doing business in real estate and as a lawyer. Periodically the press would have a historical article on his various exploits, but there was no longer an allure for the "delightful rogue." There must have been some embarrassment in 1872 as Michael Baldridge, French's secretary in 1850, toured the country giving lectures as *"one of the victims"* of the "Parker H. French Expedition" from more than two decades before. Newspapers highlighted the lectures as *"…a strange story…a remarkable narrative told in a style singularly graphic and picturesque."*[340,341]

In May 1872, Parker French finally had success in court. He won a fraud case against the trustees of the defunct Texas and New Orleans Railroad. In March 1861, he had bought sixty bonds for $500 each. Recognizing the legal standing of his bonds, the court awarded him $53,760 (2017 estimate, $1.04 million), which included interest.

There was unwelcome news as well. His pending claim against the Mexican government was dismissed. He had fraudulently asserted damages of $426,399 (2017 estimate, $8.25 million) for "depredations on ranch on Rio Grande by Mexican and American robbers and false imprisonment." French's statement was a typical butchering of the truth with fanciful claims: the "American robbers at El Paso" were instigated and assisted by Mexican officials; those officials were complicit in, and benefited from, the illegal sale of his property; Mexican officials withheld protection as he was being attacked, resulting in the loss of his arm; the governor of Durango violated his contract; French was attacked and wounded; and he was thrown into prison where he and his men were "treated with great cruelty and indignity and robbed of all the property they had."

In a very inconvenient twist of history, Caleb Cushing was the counsel for the Mexican government and was key in the dismissal of the claim. Already Cushing had twice tormented Parker French and frustrated his efforts. In 1855–1856, he was the attorney general for the United States when French was refused recognition as ambassador from Nicaragua. In 1861, Cushing informed Bostonian Amos Lawrence that the Union loyalist Carlyle Murray was, in fact, the notorious Parker French.[342]

On July 1, 1875, French married Reba B. Claggett, the daughter of a New England Congregationalist clergyman. The marriage was performed by Reverend Isaac Riley, pastor of Thirty-Fourth Street Reformed Church. The witnesses were lawyer Daniel D. Dudley (1833–1909) and his wife Elizabeth (Rule) Dudley (1844–1919). The Claggett and Dudley families were neighbors, close friends, and church associates in New Hampshire. These relationships suggest that French may have met his wife through his real estate work; Elizabeth Dudley's father was prominent real estate broker William G. Rule, who was possibly French's boss. On August 31, 1876, the marriage was blessed with a son Parker Hardin French, Jr. The family had a comfortable life in a prestigious New York City neighborhood near the center of money, power, and high society. They lived at 46 West Twenty-Fourth Street, less than a block from the intersection of Broadway and Fifth Avenue. The section of Broadway from Twenty-Third Street to Twenty-Fifth was the home of exclusive hotels like the Fifth Avenue Hotel, which was a hangout for Republicans, the Albemarle, and the Hoffman House, a favorite rendezvous of Democrats. The Fifth Avenue Hotel was also a choice hangout for fat cats like Boss Tweed, Jay Gould, Jim Fisk, and Commodore Vanderbilt. Famous people of culture would also visit, such men as Mark Twain, Edwin Booth, William Cullen Bryant, and Stanford White.[343,344]

Unfortunately, Parker Hardin French was in his last days, he was succumbing to the effects of a dangerous life and hard living. Perhaps, as Ned McGowan wrote in the summary of French's life, alcohol was a contributing factor: "French appeared to be a perfect wreck of his former self, was drinking hard and taking a modicum of chloroform in each drink of whiskey."

19

DEATHBED AND FUNERAL

Based on previous reports that French sometimes appeared sickly, it is likely that he suffered from long-standing rheumatism, recurring bouts of malaria, and probable alcoholism. Both rheumatism and malaria were noted as medical conditions on his death certificate. For his last year, Parker French was attended by Doctor George Miller Beard, a prominent physician who later gained worldwide acclaim. Beard would be renowned for his seminal research and writings associated with psychology and neurological disorders. He also gained a measure of fame after President Garfield was assassinated. Doctor Beard sought leniency for the assassin Charles J. Guiteau, a continuation of his unpopular stance against the death penalty for persons with mental illness.

Early in the morning of June 18, 1878, Parker French became extremely ill with very painful "congestion and sepsis of the lungs and stomach." Dr. Beard was called to the house and attended him until death at 5:00 a.m. on June 19.[345]

The *New York Herald*, in a simple entry with no remembrance, family comments or notice of arrangements: "Died French—June 19, Colonel P.H. French." While newspapers recorded his feline-like propensity for multiple lives on numerous occasions, this time the colonel was, in fact, dead.[346]

The obituary posted in the *Alton Telegraph* was simple:

"The remains of Col. Parker Hardin French arrived yesterday morning attended by his wife and infant son for burial in our cemetery. The colonel died in New York City, where he was residing, after a very brief illness. Col French was a native of Kentucky and in the 53d year of his age, he leaves a wife and infant son and four children by a former wife."

There were no comments about his life history or record of his accomplishments.

After a 950-mile train trip from New York City, the remains of Colonel French arrived in Alton, Illinois, on Monday morning June 24, 1878. His body was accompanied by his wife of less than three years and their toddler of twenty-two months, Parker Hardin French Jr.

Later in the afternoon, funeral attendees gathered at the home of Doctor William Quigley, French's brother-in-law from marriage to his first wife. Overflowing the expansive home on Twelfth Street, a large group of residents, friends, and acquaintances from Alton, Madison County, and St. Louis arrived throughout the afternoon. His first wife's powerful and influential extended family of brothers, sisters, uncles, and cousins also attended the gathering. Attendees reflected the population from a town on the boundary between north and south: former abolitionists as well as supporters of slavery; Union men and secessionists; soldiers from both Union and Confederate armies; and old Whigs, Republicans, and Democrats. Likely for the first time, French's new wife met his children from his first marriage. Traveling from Huntsville Alabama were his three daughters: Matilda Strong French Mayhew (age twenty-eight), Nancy "Nannie" Reed (twenty), and Ellie Lucretia (twelve). Matilda's husband, James Howard Mayhew, accompanied the sisters. From St. Louis came French's son, Hugh Murray French (twenty-four).

The pallbearers were pillars of the community, an eclectic and powerful group of bankers, businessmen, publishers, veterans, and politicians. They were all influential citizens who rightly could be called city fathers. In an earlier life, some could have been sworn enemies.

Henry Southard Baker was a lawyer, judge, and politician. A vigorous opponent of slavery, he was an early convert to the Republican Party; Baker was one of four local citizens who sat on the speakers' platform at the Douglas-Lincoln Debate held in Alton on October 15, 1858.

Colonel (CSA) John Quincy (Jack) Burbridge was a prewar business man and banker in Louisiana City, Missouri. He fought for the Confederacy as commander of both infantry and cavalry regiments in Missouri and Arkansas. After the war he moved to Alton and owned flour mills. French likely knew him as a business associate.

Dennis S. Hoagland was a businessman who owned clothing stores, banks, and insurance companies.

Charles A. Murray was a former county sheriff, lawyer, and businessman. He was the older brother of Hugh C. Murray, who became chief justice of the California Supreme Court and had been a close friend of French in California. Both Charles and Hugh likely met him at Shurtleff College. Hugh was also the namesake for French's son Hugh Murray French. Although Hugh was an inveterate white supremacist, there is no record of the position of Charles regarding race relations. French used the surname Murray as an alias when he was arrested during the Civil War.

Edward P. Wade was a businessman, four-time mayor of Alton, president of the Alton National Bank, local historian, and committed abolitionist.

He was also president of a local commission to erect a monument to the murdered abolitionist Elijah Lovejoy.

William Theodore Norton was a local politician and editor of the *Alton Telegraph*, the largest newspaper in Southern Illinois and influential mouthpiece of both the Whig and Republican Parties.[347]

In the early evening, the assembled group formed a procession that made its way for about a mile down Union Street to the Alton Cemetery. There, the graveside service was conducted by Reverend Dr. Armstrong, pastor of the Presbyterian Church, assisted by Reverend T.G. Field of the Baptist Church. The hymns and scriptures were selected by Mrs. French as favorites of her husband. They were Cowper's hymn, "There is a fountain filled with blood," and Mrs. MacKay's hymn, "Asleep in Jesus." The fifty-first Psalm was read with comments for the assembled to cast their burden on the Lord.

In his funeral sermon, Reverend Armstrong cited three sources of comfort in trial: first, bright views of God; second, a vital faith in an unseen world; and third, the word of God. Just before 7:40 p.m., as the sun was setting, "his remains were lowered to their last earthly resting place in a beautiful spot in our cemetery."

As Colonel Parker Hardin French was being laid to rest, the assemblage sang the hymn "Some are Fallen Asleep":

"Asleep in Jesus! O for me

May such a blissful refuge be!

Securely shall my ashes lie,

Waiting the summons from on high"[348]

Everything about the day would seem to cement Parker French's legacy as an admired and stalwart citizen, as well as a committed and loving father. Two influential members of the clergy, along with the trappings of the religious ritual itself, reinforced notions of a religious man of character. His wife's choice of hymns and prayers connoted an acknowledgment of his sins and the notions of forgiveness, redemption, renewal, mercy and salvation. The attendees, as well as the very positive newspaper article, indicate a man who could demand deferential respect from a wide array of friends and acquaintances, as well as undaunted love from his family.

There must have been some in attendance who wondered about the irony, who might have questioned the suitability of the religious occasion. French's adventurous, scandalous, always manipulative, and mostly disreputable life contradicted the entire ceremonious day. Why did so many reputable men, who must have known of French's notorious life, seem to honor him by their participation in the funeral? Were they devoted friends, captured by French's magnetic disarming personality? Were they at the funeral to support the powerful family and children of French's first wife?

Did his new wife seek some measure of respectability, a recovery of a shattered reputation, a renewal of a relationship with his estranged children? Or was the ceremony an indicator of a late and true religious conversion of French, engineered by his devout and pious wife?

The adult children, as youngsters, had endured the span of their father's absences; perhaps Matilda, the oldest, was aware of her father's disrepute. The youngest, Ellie Lucretia, would never remember either of her parents. Later they would have learned of his notoriety and public disgrace, the scorn of newspapers, and the heartache and embarrassment of their mother. They would learn of the torment their mother had experienced as she read the well-documented news of his dishonorable exploits and had to brave the rollercoaster emotions of multiple false accounts of his death. How did they accept the finality, express and repress their emotions? How did they grieve, if they grieved at all? Or were they just there to perform their family obligations? There was perhaps some comfort for the children as they saw the extended family and friends, town notables, and respected clergy, all come together to mourn the passing of their father.

At the gravesite there is no grand memorial, no engraved headstone—not even a simple marker.

"Death is more universal than life; everyone dies but not everyone lives."

Alan Sachs.

Parker Hardin French certainly lived—fully.

Gravesite of PHF. Photo by Lori Stover for "Findagrave." Alton Illinois Cemetery, Block 17, Lot 4k.

EPILOGUE

Siblings, Wives, and Descendants

SIBLINGS: Parker Hardin French had three known sisters, no known brothers, and one half-sister.

Juliet (Julia) Catherine (1822-1905). M: Henry Bartlett Banks (1809-1868); Henry was a farmer. Sons: James W. (1843-unknown); Edward J. (1849-unknown); Henry B. (1852-1932); David French (1854- unknown); Nathaniel P, (1857-unknown); Alexander French (1861-1948).

Mary Jane (1830-1913). M: John Hancock Crutcher (1820-1899); John was a farmer. Daughters: Katherine (Kate) (1854-1926); Emma (1857-unknown); Callie (1862-1947); Lizzie F. (1862-1956).

Arzelia (or Argelia) (1832-1924). M: John R. Sullivan (1831-1920). Son: Charles F. (1855-1920). Daughter: Lute (1858-1932).

Half-Sister **Fannie French** (1847-1917), Daughter of Hiram Duncan French and Frances Ann Henderson.

WIVES AND CHILDREN:

Lucretia Clay Edwards (1830-1869) Married, April 10, 1849; Daughter of Cyrus Edwards (1793-1877) and Nancy Harriet Reed (Reid) (1803-1834). Lucretia was likely a wonderful mother who raised her children by herself a great deal of the time. From all appearances her children had successful lives, marriages, and families.

Matilda Strong (1850-1921). M: James Howard Mayhew (1850-1917). Matilda probably met her husband when he worked as a civil engineer on Mississippi river projects near St. Louis and Alton.

Hugh Murray (1854-1912). M: Anna Odelle Sale (1860-1886); M: Susan Lewis (1860-1948). President of a St. Louis Paper Company. Hugh died September 22, 1912 at Hot Springs Resort in Virginia. Both his obituary and Virginia Death Records recorded his parents as Parker French and Lucretia Edwards. Sons: Hugh Sale (1885-1886); Dudley (1887-1976); Charles Sale (1893-unknown).

Nancy (Nanny) Reed (1858-unknown). M: Reverend Percy Gordon (1862-1923). Son: George Anderson Gordon (1885-1959).

Ellie Lucretia (1866-unknown). M: Cyrus Baker Kitchen (1870-1906). Cyrus was a New York Stockbroker. Sons: Cyrus Baker (1893-1972); Hugh M. (1895-1963); Harold G. (1900-unknown); Gerald (1906-1990). Daughter: Helen T. (1898-1980).

Rebecca (Reba) Claggett (1842-1930). Married, July 1, 1875; Daughter of William Claggett (1796-1870) and Sarah Kimball Morrill (1805-1875).

Parker Hardin (possibly Harding) French Jr (1876-1937). M: Lillian May Jennings (1888-1951). Sons: David (1915-unknown); Son who is still living (private).

On November 26, 1892, the United States Army Pension Office received a widow's pension request, case number 350986, from Mrs. Parker H. French (Reba Claggett). Charles E. Hopgood of the Veterans Rights Union was her agent. The case was immediately returned to Hopgood since he did not have a power of attorney filed. No further action was noted. Mrs. French claimed two service

periods, stating that Parker Hardin French was in
the Kentucky Regiment in the Mexican-American
War, where he purportedly lost an arm; he was a
member of General Geary's staff in the Civil War; and
a member of either the New York or Pennsylvania
regiment. These were probably the result of
apocryphal stories which French told his wife.
There is no record of him ever being with Kentucky
regiments that were raised to fight in the Mexican-
American War. According to Civil War records, he was
never a member of General Geary's staff. General
Geary was the commander of Second Division of the
XII Corps in both Virginia and Tennessee campaigns;
Geary's division was incorporated into the XX
Corps in the spring of 1864 and operated as part
of the corps through the rest of the war, including
the Atlanta campaign, the March to the Sea, and
the Carolina campaign to end the war. French
was a purveyor to Geary's staff in both Virginia
and Tennessee. He also operated occasionally as a
lawyer in courts-martial as a defense counsel and a
consultant to prosecutors. While he was not an officer
on the roster, he likely did enjoy social recognition
and privilege, but he had no official status.

ABOUT THE AUTHOR

Emmet Joseph (Joe) Goodbody Jr. is a retired United States Army Colonel and corporate leader with a bachelor's degree from University of Nebraska (Omaha) and a master's in logistics management from Florida Institute of Technology. Joe and his wife Carol have been married for fifty years with two sons and four grandchildren. His great-grandfather was a victim of Parker Hardin French as a passenger on the fraudster's California-bound gold rush expedition. The adventure faltered in mismanagement and collapsed in deception, fraud, and forgery.

ENDNOTES

1. M. Baldridge, A Reminiscence of the Parker H. French Expedition through Texas & Mexico to California in the Spring of 1850 (Los Angeles: Privately Printed, 1959)
2. M. Baldridge, A Reminiscence of the Parker H. French Expedition through Texas & Mexico to California in the Spring of 1850 (Los Angeles: Privately Printed, 1959)
3. New York Times "Col. Parker H. French, December 15, 1855
4. Death Certificate of Parker Hardin French, recorded in the Health Department of the City of New York, which lists his parents as Hiram Duncan French and Margaret C. Hardin; Return of a Marriage between Parker H. French and Reba B. Claggett, lists same parents. It was recorded in the Bureau of Records of Vital Statistics, Health Department of the City of New York on July 1, 1875. The Register of the Kentucky State Historical Society, Volume 2 (Kentucky State Historical Society, 1904) shows parents of Arzelia as Hiram D. French and Margaret Hardin. Margaret Hardin French died October 24, 1832 per obituary held by the Kentucky Gateway Museum Center. Marriage Bond between Hiram and Frances, dated December 7, 1835, held in Bracken County, Kentucky.
5. Adair County News: "Many Years Ago" December 5, 1900; "Interesting Reminiscences" April 16 1902; "The Hardin Family" Feb 24 1904; "Sketches of Adair County" Mar 20, 1918
6. "Many Years Ago," Adair County News, December 5, 1900
7. http://www.historic-shipping.co.uk/monwigram/Blenh%2013.html. Accessed June 7 2016
8. Edward McGowan, The Strange Eventful History of Parker H. French. Reproduced and Edited by Kenneth M. Johnson (Los Angeles: Dawson, 1958).
9. http://www.historic-shipping.co.uk/monwigram/Blenh%2013.html Accessed June 7 2016
10. William L. Clowes, The Royal Navy, A History From The Earliest Times To Present (London: S. Low & Marston, 1903)
11. http://www.pbenyon.plus.com/18-1900/B/00596.html
12. George Wythe Baylor, Into the Far Wild Country (El Paso: Texas Western Press, 1996)
13. "Many Years Ago" Adair County News, December 5, 1900
14. "Parker H. French," Louisville Courier, April 10, 1851
15. Elizabeth Pendleton Hardin, The Private War of Lizzie Hardin: a Kentucky Confederate girl's diary of the Civil War in Kentucky, Virginia Tennessee, Alabama and Georgia, edited by G. Glenn Clift (Frankfort: The Kentucky Historical Society, 1963)
16. "Lecture of A.D. Madeira," Daily State Journal, January 8, 1858. Madeira gave a "beautiful rhetorical picture of Parker H. French who was an old schoolmate." It was "graphic and interesting in the highest degree." Addison Madeira graduated from Alton's Shurtleff College in 1844.
17. Edward McGowan, The Strange Eventful History of Parker H. French, reproduced and edited by Kenneth M. Johnson (Los Angeles: Dawson, 1958).
18. W.T. Norton, Centennial History OF Madison County, Illinois and Its People 1812 to 1912, (Chicago: Lewis, 1912).
19. Paul Finkelman, Slavery and the Founders: Race and Liberty in the Age of Jefferson Armonk, (NY: M.E. Sharp 1996).
20. Journal of the House of Representatives of the Tenth General Assembly of the State of Illinois, 1836. Page 243.
21. Richard Lawrence Miller, Lincoln and his World: Prairie Politician (Mechanicsburg, Stackpole Books, 2016)
22. W.T. Norton, Centennial History of Madison County, Illinois and Its People 1812 to 1912 (Chicago: Lewis, 1912)
23. "Jubilee Memorial of Shurtleff College," Alton Daily Telegraph, 1877. French is not listed as a graduate, but friends such as the Murrays were noted. Reverend Addison Madeira, in an 1856 lecture, mentioned Parker French as a classmate.
24. Edward McGowan, The Strange Eventful History of Parker H. French, reproduced and edited by Kenneth M. Johnson (Los Angeles: Dawson, 1958)
25. Probate Court Files of Cyrus Edwards who died in 1877, held by the records/archives section Madison County Courthouse, Edwardsville, Illinois. The file establishes that Matilda, Isabella, Lucretia, and Ellen were daughters of Cyrus and provides names of Parker French's children with Lucretia. The file also shows bills paid to Monticello Academy for each girl.
26. Michael Burlingame, Abraham Lincoln: A Life (Baltimore: Johns Hopkins University Press, 2008)

27. Journal of the Illinois State Historical Society, Volume Nine, Nos. 1-4 April 1916-
     January 1917. Establishes that General Duff Green was the husband of Lucretia
     Maria Edwards the sister of Cyrus Edwards and Aunt of Lucretia Clay Edwards
     French, wife of Parker Hardin French

28. W. Stephen Belko, The invincible Duff Green: Whig of the West (Columbia: University
     of Missouri Press, 2006)

29. Marilyn J. Coleman, Lawrence H. Ganong, Impact Of The Southern Culture And
     Slavery On Development Of Young Men (Thousand Oaks: SAGE Publications, Sep 2,
     2014)

30. Lori Glover, Southern Sons: Becoming Men in the New Nation (Baltimore: Johns
     Hopkins University Press 1967)

31. "Parker H. French Still Alive," San Francisco Bulletin, January 3, 1859, letter from
     St. Louis, Dec 9, 1858

32. Jeffrey S. Adler, Yankee Merchants And The Making Of The Urban West: The Rise
     And Fall Of Antebellum St. Louis (Cambridge: Cambridge University Press, 1991)

33. "California Gold Mines," New Hampshire Gazette, December 26, 1848

34. John Thomas Scharf, History of Saint Louis City and County, from the earliest
     periods to the present day: including biographical sketches of representative men
     (Volume v.2)

35. Notecards held by the Missouri History Museum, St. Louis

36. "Blocks, Tackle and Rigging," Daily Missouri Republican, March 31, 1849

37. Picture of Matilda, courtesy of the Missouri History Museum, St. Louis

38. "For California," Daily Illinois State Journal, March 13, 1849

39. Notecards held by the Missouri History Museum, St. Louis

40. Marriage Register, Volume 1, 1813-1850, page 3, held by Haynor Library, Alton,
     Illinois. Edited by Jane Shelley and Elise Wasser.

41. "Illinois Marriages to 1850," Jordan Dodd, Ancestry.com, 1997

42. "Hotel Arrivals," Daily Missouri Republican, April 11, 1849

43. "The Ship Matilda Launched," Daily Missouri Republican, May 4, 1861

44. "For Sale," Boston Atlas, September 30, 1853

45. M. Baldridge, A Reminiscence of the Parker H. French Expedition through Texas &
     Mexico to California in the Spring of 1850 (Los Angeles: Privately Printed, 1959)

46. "Great Northern," Rockford Free Press, January 12, 1850

47. "French's Overland Passenger Train," Waukegan Gazette, February 21, 1851

48. John J. Halsey, LL.D., History of Lake County Illinois (Chicago: Harmegnies &
     Howell, 1912). Details sixteen men as well.

49. Andrew Steele, Diary of a Journey to California. Unpublished typescript held by the
     Abraham Lincoln Presidential Library, Springfield, Illinois. Steele names the fifteen
     Lake County men who were with the expedition.

50. M. Baldridge, A Reminiscence of the Parker H. French Expedition through Texas
     & Mexico to California in the Spring of 1850 (Los Angeles: Privately Printed, 1959);
     William Miles, Journal of the Sufferings and Hardships of Capt. Parker H. French's
     OVERLAND EXPEDITION TO CALIFORNIA (Chambersburg: Valley Spirit, 1851).
     Family oral history suggests that the brothers departed a couple of weeks apart and
     left New York on separate ships. How Richard received the news is speculative, but
     the telegraph was first operational from Chicago to Little Fort (Waukegan) in March
     1849.

51. "Departure of the Ohio," New York Spectator, April 29, 1850

52. "Arrival of the Steamship Ohio," Times Picayune, May 8, 1850

53. William Miles, Journal of the Sufferings and Hardships of Capt. Parker H. French's
     OVERLAND EXPEDITION TO CALIFORNIA (Chambersburg: Valley Spirit, 1851)

54. M. Baldridge, A Reminiscence of the Parker H. French Expedition through Texas &
     Mexico to California in the Spring of 1850 (Los Angeles: Privately Printed, 1959)

55. C.H. Lockwood, My Trip to California in 1850 (Daytona: Halifax Printing, 1910)

56. Tom Chaffin, Fatal Glory: Narciso Lopez And The First Clandestine U.S. War Against
     Cuba (Baton Rouge: Louisiana State University Press, 1996)

57. M. Baldridge, A Reminiscence of the Parker H. French Expedition through Texas
     & Mexico to California in the Spring of 1850 (Los Angeles: Privately Printed, 1959);
     Andrew Steele, Diary of a Journey to California, unpublished typescript held by the
     Abraham Lincoln Presidential Library, Springfield, Illinois.

58. C.H. Lockwood, My Trip to California in 1850 (Daytona: Halifax Printing, 1910)

59. Alejandro Bolanos-Geyer, William Walker: The Gray-eyed Man of Destiny (Lake Saint

Louis, 1989). The author also asserted that both William Walker and Parker French were there. Other sources indicate that Walker moved to California in 1849; French left town on the Palmetto on May 31.

60. "Parker French," North American, August 20, 1850

61. Louis A Perez, Cuba and the United States: Ties of Singular Intimacy (University of Georgia Press, 2011)

62. C.H. Lockwood, My Trip to California in 1850 (Daytona: Halifax Printing, 1910)

63. The narrative of the expedition between Lavaca and El Paso is a compilation of several references: William Miles Journal of the Sufferings and Hardships of Capt. Parker H. French's OVERLAND EXPEDITION TO CALIFORNIA (Chambersburg: Valley Spirit, 1851); Andrew Steele, Diary of a Journey to California, unpublished typescript held by the Abraham Lincoln Presidential Library, Springfield, Illinois; C.H. Lockwood, My Trip to California in 1850 (Daytona: Halifax Printing, 1910)

64. M. Baldridge, A Reminiscence of the Parker H. French Expedition through Texas & Mexico to California in the Spring of 1850, (Los Angeles: Privately Printed, 1959)

65. "Parker H. French," Times Picayune, from a report of the Victoria Advocate, September 21, 1850

66. William Miles, Journal of the Sufferings and Hardships of Capt. Parker H. French's OVERLAND EXPEDITION TO CALIFORNIA, (Chambersburg: Valley Spirit, 1851); Andrew Steele, Diary of a Journey to California, unpublished typescript held by the Abraham Lincoln Presidential Library, Springfield, Illinois

67. Andrew Steele, Diary of a Journey to California, unpublished typescript held by the Abraham Lincoln Presidential Library, Springfield, Illinois

68. John Russell Bartlett, Personal Narrative of Explorations & Incidents in Texas, New Mexico, California, Sonora, and Chihuahua, Connected with the United States and Mexican Boundary Commission, During the Years 1850, '51, '52, and '53 (New York; D. Appleton, 1854)

69. This story of the expedition across Texas to El Paso is a compilation of four journals and a newspaper article: M. Baldridge, A Reminiscence of the Parker H. French Expedition through Texas & Mexico to California in the Spring of 1850 (Los Angeles: Privately Printed, 1959): Andrew Steele, Diary of a Journey to California, unpublished typescript held by the Abraham Lincoln Presidential Library, Springfield, Illinois; William Miles, Journal of the Sufferings and Hardships of Capt. Parker H. French's OVERLAND EXPEDITION TO CALIFORNIA (Chambersburg: Valley Spirit, 1851); C.H. Lockwood, My Trip to California in 1850 (Daytona: Halifax Printing, 1910); "Parker H. French," Albany Evening Journal, April 26, 1851, reprinted from a report of a New York Herald correspondent in Mazatlán.

70. Rex W. Strickland, Six who came to El Paso: Pioneers of the 1840's, (El Paso: Texas Western Press, 1963)

71. Ben Pingenot, "The Great Wagon Train Expedition of 1850," The Southwestern Historical Quarterly, Volume 98, July 1994 - April, 1995 (Texas State Historical Association). Ron Tyler, editor, Journal/Magazine/Newsletter, 1995.

72. "Parker H. French," Times Picayune, from a report of the Victoria Advocate, September 21, 1850

73. M. Baldridge, A Reminiscence of the Parker H. French Expedition through Texas & Mexico to California in the Spring of 1850 (Los Angeles: Privately Printed, 1959)

74. "Parker H. French," Times Picayune, from a report of the Victoria Advocate, September 21, 1850

75. Report of the Senate Committee on Military Affairs, No. 455, January 30, 1855

76. Handbook of Texas Online, Thomas W. Cutter, "Lewis, Nathaniel C.," accessed November 24, 2017, http://www.tshaonline.org/handbook/online/articles/fle47

77. Handbook of Texas Online, G. E. Baker, "Groesbeeck, John D.," accessed November 24, 2017, http://www.tshaonline.org/handbook/online/articles/fgr73

78. M. Baldridge, A Reminiscence of the Parker H. French Expedition through Texas & Mexico to California in the Spring of 1850 (Los Angeles: Privately Printed, 1959)

79. George Wythe Baylor, editor, with an introduction by Jerry D. Thompson, Into the Far Wild Country (El Paso: Texas western Press, 1996)

80. Report of the Senate Committee on Military Affairs, No. 455, January 30, 1855

81. Ben Pingenot, "The Great Wagon Train Expedition of 1850," The Southwestern Historical Quarterly, Volume 98, July 1994 - April 1995 (Texas State Historical Association). Ron Tyler, editor, Journal/Magazine/Newsletter, 1995.

82. Randolph Barnes Marcy, Captain, U.S.A. The Prairie Traveler: A Hand-Book for Overland Expeditions (Wash. DC: War Department, 1859). Marcy provided detailed

locations of watering holes and stopping places along with the miles between them.

83. "Letter from Parker French," Commercial Advertiser, August 19, 1850
84. George Wythe Baylor, ed., "Into the Far Wild Country," (introduction by Jerry D. Thompson) (El Paso: Texas Western Press, 1996)
85. "From Texas," Times Picayune, September 6, 1850
86. Rex Strickland, Six who came to El Paso (El Paso: Texas Western College Press, 1963)
87. "Parker H. French," Albany Evening Journal, April 26, 1851. Reprinted from a report of a New York Herald correspondent in Mazatlán.
88. M. Baldridge, A Reminiscence of the Parker H. French Expedition through Texas & Mexico to California in the Spring of 1850 (Los Angeles: Privately Printed, 1959)
89. C.H. Lockwood, My Trip to California in 1850 (Daytona: Halifax Printing, 1910)
90. Thomas Smith, The US Army and the Texas Frontier Economy: 1845 – 1900 (Texas A&M University Press, 1999)
91. "From Texas," Commercial Advertiser, November 14, 1850
92. M. Baldridge, A Reminiscence of the Parker H. French Expedition through Texas & Mexico to California in the Spring of 1850 (Los Angeles: Privately Printed, 1959); George Wythe Baylor, ed., with an introduction by Jerry D. Thompson, Into the Far Wild Country (El Paso: Texas western Press, 1996); C.H. Lockwood, My Trip to California in 1850 (Daytona: Halifax Printing, 1910)
93. Ben Pingenot, "The Great Wagon Train Expedition of 1850," The Southwestern Historical Quarterly, Volume 98, July 1994 - April, 1995 (Texas State Historical Association). Ron Tyler, editor, Journal/Magazine/Newsletter, 1995
94. All the narratives of the final distribution of property offer confusing, contradictory stories. This is a compilation of the three versions using the Lockwood story as the model. Lockwood's clear and organized version may indicate that he was a member of the committee responsible for the auction. C.H. Lockwood, My Trip to California in 1850 (Daytona: Halifax Printing, 1910); M. Baldridge, A Reminiscence of the Parker H. French Expedition through Texas & Mexico to California in the Spring of 1850 (Los Angeles: Privately Printed, 1959); William Miles, Journal of the Sufferings and Hardships of Capt. Parker H. French's OVERLAND EXPEDITION TO CALIFORNIA (Chambersburg: Valley Spirit, 1851)
95. "A MODERN MAZZARONI," Boston Herald, April 26, 1851
96. William Miles, Journal of the Sufferings and Hardships of Capt. Parker H. French's OVERLAND EXPEDITION TO CALIFORNIA (Chambersburg: Valley Spirit, 1851); M. Baldridge, A Reminiscence of the Parker H. French Expedition through Texas & Mexico to California in the Spring of 1850 (Los Angeles: Privately Printed, 1959
97. Charles Cardinell "Adventures of the Plains," California Historical Society Quarterly, July, 1922, Vol. 1, No. 1; George Wythe Baylor Into the Far Wild Country, (El Paso: Texas Western Press, 1996); John Holmes, The Adventures of John Holmes of Canaan on the Overland Expedition to California with Capt. Parker H. French in 1850 (The Cadmus Book Shop, New York: 1916); The Buffalo Daily Republic, "Interesting Narrative," December 4, 1851 (narrative by John Holmes in the Skowhegan Press).
98. Dan Cooper, "The Gunfight at Corralitos," History Magazine, April 2010, Vol. 11 Issue 4; Charles Cardinell, "Adventures of the Plains," California Historical Society Quarterly, July, 1922, Vol. 1, No. 1; George Wythe Baylor Into the Far Wild Country (El Paso: Texas Western Press, 1996)
99. Mrs. F. F. Victor, "On the Mexican Border," Overland Monthly and Out West Magazine, Volume 6, Issue 5, May 1871
100. George Wythe Baylor Into the Far Wild Country (El Paso: Texas Western Press, 1996)
101. Andrew Steele, "Diary of a Journey to California," unpublished typescript held by the Abraham Lincoln Presidential Library, Springfield, Illinois
102. George Wythe Baylor, Into the Far Wild Country (El Paso: Texas Western Press, 1996); M. Baldridge, A Reminiscence of the Parker H. French Expedition through Texas & Mexico to California in the Spring of 1850 (Los Angeles: Privately Printed, 1959); New Orleans Crescent, "Parker H. French not Dead," April 29, 1851 (reprint of a New York Herald article with a letter from a Herald correspondent, February 26, 1851)
103. "Parker H. French," The Washington Union, April 17, 1851 (reprint of a New York Herald article with a letter from a correspondent dated February 14)
104. "Parker H. French," Albany Evening Journal, April 26, 1851 (reprinted from a report of a New York Herald correspondent in Mazatlán); C.H. Lockwood, My Trip to California in 1850 (Daytona: Halifax Printing, 1910); George Wythe Baylor, Into the Far Wild Country (El Paso: Texas Western Press, 1996)

105. "Parker H. French, "Alexandria Gazette, April 15, 1851 (reprinted from a report by the Louisville Courier).

106. "Parker H. French," New York Spectator, April 24, 1851 (reprinted from a report by the New York Herald; "Parker H. French," New London Democrat, May 5, 1851

107. "Capt. Parker H. French," Trenton State Gazette, February 2, 1852

108. George Wythe Baylor, Into the Far Wild Country (El Paso: Texas Western Press, 1996

109. "Parker H. French not Dead," Albany Evening Journal, April 26, 1851 (reprint of a New York Herald article with a letter from a Herald correspondent, February 26, 1851)

110. "Parker H. French Turned up Again," San Francisco Herald, August 28, 1852. The Herald reprinted a report from the Durango, "El Registro Official," which published the long letter from Parker French to the governor; "Notorious Parker H. French," Little Falls Democrat, October 7, 1852; George Wythe Baylor, Into the Far Wild Country, (El Paso: Texas Western Press, 1996); Edward McGowan, The Strange Eventful History of Parker H. French, reproduced and edited by Kenneth M. Johnson (Los Angeles: Dawson, 1958).

111. Edward McGowan, The Strange Eventful History of Parker H. French, reproduced and edited by Kenneth M. Johnson (Los Angeles: Dawson, 1958)

112. "Captain Parker H. French," New Orleans Crescent, Dec 4, 1851 (originally a Houston Telegraph report from a "Gentleman who recently returned through Mexico."

113. Bankruptcy records for Parker French held at National Archives, Kansas City, Missouri, July 7, 1869.

114. M. Baldridge, A Reminiscence of the Parker H. French Expedition through Texas & Mexico to California in the Spring of 1850, (Los Angeles: Privately Printed, 1959); Edward McGowan, The Strange Eventful History of Parker H. French," reproduced and edited by Kenneth M. Johnson (Los Angeles: Dawson, 1958)

115. "Crabbe's Filibusteros," Arizona Sentinel, December 22, 1877

116. William O. Scroggs, Filibusters And Financiers: The Story Of William Walker And His Associates (New York: The Macmillan Company, 1916)

117. "American Brig Hallowell," Times Picayune, October 28, 1852. The story notes Captain Gesenius as commanding. Multiple contemporaneous records confirm. Captain Noyes was the recorded owner and has been cited by some as commanding the vessel.

118. "Parker H. French," Richmond Daily Dispatch, October 16, 1852

119. Chester Wright Blaisdell, a letter written aboard the North America on August 18, 1852. Held by the Franklin County Historical and Museum Society of Malone, NY.

120. "Arrival of Hallowell in San Luis Obispo," Daily Alta California, Nov 16, 1852

121. Myron Angel, History of San Luis Obispo County, California (Oakland: Thompson and West, 1883)

122. Horace Bell, Reminiscences of a Ranger: Early Times in Southern California (University of Oklahoma Press, Norman, 1999). Bell probably got the visit to Los Angeles right; very little of the rest of his sketch on French was correct. Bell lived in Los Angeles at the time, lending credence to his account of the visit.

123. Extract of Probate Cases in San Luis Obispo, http://www.slocgs.org/pdf-files/SLO-Probate-Radcliffe.pdf

124. Myron Angel, History of San Luis Obispo County, California (Oakland: Thompson and West, 1883)

125. Annie L. Stringfellow Morrison, John H. Haydon, History of San Luis Obispo County and Environs (San Luis Obispo: Historic Record Company, 1917)

126. Edward McGowan, The Strange Eventful History of Parker H. French, reproduced and edited by Kenneth M. Johnson (Los Angeles: Dawson, 1958); Horace Bell, Reminiscences of a Ranger: Early Times in Southern California, University of Oklahoma Press, Norman: 1999

127. Joseph A. Carotenuti, "Parker H. French," Journal Plus, October 2012; https://issuu.com/journalplus/docs/10-2012_journal_plus_web/32

128. "William G. Dana against Parker H French; Samuel Pollard against Parker French," Los Angeles Star, January 14, 1854

129. "From Los Angeles," Sacramento Daily Union, December 13, 1853

130. Legal Notice, Bill for Divorce Lucretia C. French vs Parker H. French, Alton Telegraph, May 17, 1853

131. Albert Nelson Marquis, The Book of St. Louisans (St Louis: St Louis Republic, 1912). Gives birthdate of Hugh Murray French and notes his father/mother as Parker

Hardin French and Lucretia Clay Edwards French.

132. Journal of the Fifth Session of the Legislature of the State of California (Sacramento: B.B. Redding, State Printer, 1854)

133. Jeremiah Lynch, A Senator of the Fifties: David C. Broderick of California (San Francisco: A.M. Robertson), 1911

134. Arthur Quinn, The Rivals: William Gwin, David Broderick and the Birth of California (Lincoln: University of Nebraska Press, 1997)

135. Herbert Asbury, The Barbary Coast (New York, 1933)

136. "Address of the Majority of the Democratic Member of both Branches of the Legislature," Sacramento Daily Union, February 16, 1854

137. Kenneth M. Johnson, "A Little Bit More on Parker H. French," Southern California Quarterly, Vol 49, no. 3 (September 1967)

138. "Printing Contract," Sacramento Daily Union, May 9, 1855

139. Edgar Whittlesey Camp, "Hugh C. Murray: California's Youngest Chief Justice," California Historical Society Quarterly, Vol. 20, No. 4 (Dec., 1941)

140. "Parker H. French," Daily Alta California, January 19, 1855

141. "Parker H. French," Daily Alta California, March 17, 1855

142. The story of Nicaragua and Walker's rise rely on multiple resources: W. Walker, The War in Nicaragua (Mobile, AL: Goetzel, 1860), reprint, Tucson: University of Arizona Press, 1985; T. J Stiles, The First Tycoon: The Epic Life of Cornelius Vanderbilt (New York: Alfred A. Knopf, 2009); W.O. Scroggs, Filibusters and Financiers, the History of William Walker and His Associates (New York: Macmillan, 1916); F. Rosengarten, Freebooters Must Die, (Wayne: Haverford House, 1976); R. E. May, Manifest Destiny's Underworld: Filibustering in Antebellum America (Chapel Hill: University of North Carolina Press, 2002); A Bolanos-Geyer, William Walker: The Grey-Eyed Man of Destiny (St. Charles, MS: 1992, privately printed, 1992); W. P. Allen, William Walker, Filibuster (New York: Harper & Brothers, 1932); Charles W. Doubleday, Reminiscences of the "filibuster" war in Nicaragua (New York: G.P. Putnam's Sons, 1886); S. Dando-Collins, Tycoon's War (Cambridge: DeCapo Press, 2008); W. Scroggs, William Walker and the Steamship Corporation in Nicaragua, The American Historical Review Vol. 10, No. 4 (Jul., 1905), pp. 792-811; R. E. May, Slavery, Race and Conquest in the Tropics (New York: Cambridge University Press, 2013)

143. "The Expedition to Central America," Daily Alta California, June 30, 1855

144. "The Career of William Walker: By one who knows," Washington Star, two-part series, October 13/15, 1857

145. "Central American Colonization Society," Sacramento Union, July 4, 1855

146. "Parker H. French," Marysville Daily Herald, September 11, 1855

147. "Letter from Central America," State Tribune, August 13, 1855 (published September 19, 1855, after French returned from Nicaragua)

148. "Nicaraguan Affairs," Democratic State Journal, September 18, 1855

149. "Departure of the Walker Expeditionists," Daily Alta, October 6, 1855

150. "Parker H. French," Daily Alta, October 5, 1855

151. "Mississippi Rifles," San Francisco Bulletin, January 14, 1856

152. "Parker H. French," San Francisco Bulletin, November 7, 1855

153. Worcester Palladium "From El Nicaraguense" November 14 1855

154. San Francisco Bulletin Thursday, "From Nicaragua," November 22, 1855

155. San Francisco Bulletin: "The Present Conditions and Prospects of Nicaragua – No. 1" January 6 1857.

156. "Extraordinary Examination of General William Walker, the Filibuster," New York Herald, Feb 19, 1859

157. "The Present Conditions and Prospects of Nicaragua," San Francisco Bulletin: January 6 1857.

158. "Grand Scheme to Annex Cuba and San Domingo," New York Tribune, December 26, 1855

159. "Parker H. French," Boston Courier, December 13, 1855

160. "Spicy Conversation," Sacramento Daily Union, January 21, 1856

161. "Letter from Senator Cass" Washington Daily Union May 27, 1856

162. "Movements in Regard to the Nicaragua Question" Weekly Messenger May 7, 1856

163. Robert E. May "Slavery, Race and Conquest in the Tropics (New York: Cambridge University Press, 2013)

164. "Col French Again Denied," New York Tribune, February 9, 1856

165. "Central America, diplomatic relations," New York Evangelist, February 21, 1856

166. "Col. Parker H. French," New York Times December 15, 1855
167. "Col. Parker H. French," Times Picayune, March 2, 1856
168. "A Nicaraguan Hero Speculating in Stocks," San Francisco Bulletin, July 7, 1857
169. "Col. Parker H. French," Daily Alta. April 13, 1856
170. "Parker H, French," Daily Ohio Statesman, August 26, 1857
171. John Franklin and Loren Schweninger, In Search of the Promised Land: A Slave Family in the Old South (New York: Oxford University Press, 2006), 123
172. Ibid., 123
173. "Parker French Dismissed," Los Angeles Star, June 21, 1856
174. "Arrival of Steamship Granada-Passenger List," Times-Picayune, April 29, 1856
175. John Franklin and Loren Schweninger, In Search of the Promised Land: A Slave Family in the Old South (New York: Oxford University Press, 2006), 124
176. "Hotel Arrivals," Times-Picayune, April 29, 1856
177. "Nicaragua," Frank Leslie's Illustrated History, May 17, 1856
178. "Nicaraguan Question," New Orleans Crescent, April 29, 1856
179. "Nicaragua Affairs," New York Herald, May 17, 1856
180. "Letter from Col. Parker H. French," New York Herald, May 20, 1856
181. Andres Bear, A Transactional Analysis of Representations of the US Filibusters in Nicaragua, 1855-1857 (New York: Palgrave Macmillan, 2016)
182. "Affairs in Nicaragua Special Correspondence of the N.O. Picayune," New York Herald, July 4, 1856
183. "Affairs in Nicaragua: From El Nicaraguense of April 30," Daily National Intelligencer, June 4, 1856
184. "Arrest of Col. Parker H. French," New York Herald, May 22, 1856
185. "Colonel Parker H. French in Court Again," New York Herald, May 29, 1856
186. "The Crowd at Cincinnati," Baltimore Sun, June 4, 1856
187. "Enthusiastic Meeting—Speeches of Hon. Pierre Soule and Parker French," Times-Picayune, April 29, 1856
188. Official Proceedings of the National Democratic Convention Held in Cincinnati, June 2-6, 1856 (Cincinnati Enquirer Company Steam Printing Establishment, 1856)
189. "Lecture of Parker H. French," New York Herald, June 9, 1856
190. "Parker French," New Orleans Crescent, June 20, 1856
191. "Parker H. French Still Alive," San Francisco Bulletin, January 3, 1859
192. John Franklin and Loren Schweninger, In Search of the Promised Land: A Slave Family in the Old South (New York: Oxford University Press, 2006), 134
193. "Distinguished Arrival," Weekly Minnesotian, August 16, 1856
194. Minnesota, Territorial and State Censuses, 1849-1905
195. Rock River Democrat (Rockford, Illinois), August 19, 1856
196. Benton County Historical Society, http://mnbentonhistory.org/history/watab.html
197. Benton County Historical Society, http://mnbentonhistory.org/history/benton.html
198. John Franklin and Loren Schweninger, In Search of the Promised Land: A Slave Family in the Old South, (New York: Oxford University Press, 2006), 135
199. Christopher Andrews, Minnesota and Dacotah: Collection of Letters, 62
200. Collections of the Minnesota Historical Society, Volume X, Part 1, St. Paul, Minnesota
201. John Franklin and Loren Schweninger, In Search of the Promised Land: A Slave Family in the Old South (New York: Oxford University Press, 2006), 138
202. "From the San Francisco Town Talk, a sketch of Mississippi by Parker H. French," Weekly Arkansas Gazette, May 30, 1857
203. "Another Newspaper and a Notable," San Francisco Bulletin, April 24, 1857
204. "The Americans and John O'Meara," Sacramento Daily Union, September 5, 1859
205. , "Rose Murders Lucas," Mariposa Gazette, January 2, 1857
206. "Important Trial in Mariposa," Daily Globe, June 27, 1857
207. Rene De La Pedraja, A Historical Dictionary of the U.S. Merchant Marine and Shipping Industry: Since the Introduction of Steam (Westport: Greenwood Press, 1994), 4
208. "A Nicaraguan Hero Speculating in Stocks," San Francisco Bulletin, July 7, 1857
209. "Untitled," New York Herald, August 9, 1917
210. "Parker H. French," Sacramento Daily Union, July 16, 1857
211. "The Redoubtable Parker H. French," San Joaquin Republican, July 11, 1857
212. Trow's New York City Directory, 1859

213. "Central America: The Transit-Route Negotiations," New York Tribune, December 29, 1857
214. "Walker's Career in Nicaragua," Washington Evening Star, October 13 and 15, 1857
215. "Prospectus," The Evening Sentinel, Vol 1, No 9, December 14, 1858
216. Peter Adams, The Bowery Boys: Street Corner Radicals and the Politics of Rebellion (Westport: Praeger, 2005)
217. "The Evening Sentinel," New York Herald, December 2, 1858
218. "New Paper," Brooklyn Evening Star, December 2, 1858
219. "Mike Walsh and Parker H. French Fizzling," San Francisco Bulletin, January 31, 1859
220. David C Keehn, Knights of the Golden Circle (Baton Rouge: Louisiana State University Press, 2013). Most of the information about the KGC is derived and adapted from Keehn. Other citations are for unique information from that source.
221. "Knights of the Golden Circle," New Orleans Courier, March 6, 1860
222. David C Keehn, Knights of the Golden Circle (Baton Rouge: Louisiana State University Press, 2013); Robert E. May, Manifest Destiny's Underworld: Filibustering in Antebellum America. (Chapel Hill: University of North Carolina Press, 2002), 258
223. Robert E. May, Manifest Destiny's Underworld: Filibustering in Antebellum America (Chapel Hill: University of North Carolina Press, 2002), 258
224. "Mexico and Our Relations with Mexico-Manifest Destiny," New York Herald, March 30, 1858
225. Aragorn Storm Miller, Handbook of Texas Online, "Lockridge, Samuel A." (Accessed November 05, 2017, http://www.tshaonline.org/handbook/online/articles/flo83.
226. "Mike Walsh" Washington Evening Star February 8, 1858
227. "Mexico and our relations with Mexico-Manifest Destiny," New York Herald, March 30, 1858
228. "The Hon. Mike Walsh," Daily Confederation, July 12, 1858, from a report of the New York Herald
229. "Washington Rumors and Speculations," The States, December 21, 1858
230. "Emigration to Mexico," Richmond Whig, February 11, 1859
231. "Hon. Mike Walsh Killed," New York Tribune, March 18, 1859
232. "More Manifest Destiny," Milwaukee Sentinel, June 17, 1859
233. "K.G.C.," New York Tribune, June 13, 1859
234. "The Knights of the Golden Circle," New York Tribune, June 15, 1859
235. "Untitled," New York Tribune, August 18, 1859
236. "Knights of the Golden Circle," Weekly Wisconsin Patriot, October 1, 1859
237. 1860 United States Federal Census. Samuel was living with his father and mother, John and Jane nee Hardin McChesney. Jane was French's maternal aunt. Robert E. May "Slavery, Race and Conquest in the Tropics" (New York: Cambridge University Press, 2013) identified McChesney as a Walker recruiter. Clement Anselm Evans "Confederate Military History: a library of Confederate States history, Volume 10" (Atlanta: Confederate Publishing Company, 1899)
238. "A Salty Trick," New Orleans Daily Crescent, March 10, 1860
239. "Parker H. French," The San Antonio Ledger and Texan, March 24, 1860
240. David C Keehn, Knights of the Golden Circle (Baton Rouge: Louisiana State University Press, 2013)
241. "The Reported Expedition to Mexico," The San Antonio Ledger and Texan, August 4, 1860
242. David C Keehn, Knights of the Golden Circle (Baton Rouge: Louisiana State University Press, 2013)
243. "The Filibuster's War—What They Designed," The Gallipolis Journal, August 29, 1861
244. David C Keehn, Knights of the Golden Circle (Baton Rouge: Louisiana State University Press, 2013)
245. United States Federal Census, 1860
246. Don Harrison Doyle, The Social Order of a Frontier Community, Jacksonville, Illinois 1825-70 (Urbana: University of Illinois Press, 1978)
247. David C Keehn, Knights of the Golden Circle (Baton Rouge: Louisiana State University Press, 2013)
248. Linda S. Hudson, "The Knights of the Golden Circle in Texas, 1858-1861" (chapter four of The Seventh Star of the Confederacy), edited by Kenneth W. Howell (Denton: University of North Texas Press, 2009)

249. Calvin C. Campbell and Parker H. French vs. The Texas and New Orleans Railroad Company and Others: On Bill in Equity (1871). Campbell and French won the judgment; French's share was $53,760 for costs plus incurred interest, over $1 million in 2017.

250. Howard C. Williams, "Texas and New Orleans Railroad," Handbook of Texas Online, accessed July 17, 2017, http://www.tshaonline.org/handbook/online/articles/eqt06

251. Texas Marriage Collection, 1814-1909

252. "Col. Parker H. French," New York Herald, December 11, 1861. The Herald reported that French had been in South Carolina in the early spring.

253. "Many Years Ago," December 5, 1900; "Interesting Reminiscences," April 16, 1902; "The Hardin Family," February 24, 1904; and "Sketches of Adair County," March 20, 1918. All from Adair County News.

254. "A Southern Confidence Man," Hartford Daily News, December 28, 1861

255. La Fayette Curry Baker, History of the United States Secret Service (Philadelphia: L.C. Baker, 1867)

256. J. Niven, Connecticut for the Union: The Role of the State in the Civil War (New Haven: Yale University Press, 1965)

257. "Col. Parker H. French," New York Herald, December 11, 1861. The Herald reported that French had been in South Carolina in the early spring, visited the border and Western states to establish KGC Castles and then arrived in Boston in May.

258. Elizabeth Pendleton Hardin, The Private War of Lizzie Hardin: a Kentucky Confederate girl's diary of the Civil War in Kentucky, Virginia Tennessee, Alabama and Georgia, edited by G. Glenn Clift (Frankfort: The Kentucky Historical Society, 1963)

259. "Col. Parker H. French," New York Herald, December 11, 1861. The Herald reported that French had been establishing KGC Castles in the west.

260. John J. Dunphy, Abolitionism and the Civil War in Southwestern Illinois (Charleston: History Press, 2011)

261. Arthur Charles Cole, Centennial History of Illinois: The Era of the Civil War (Chicago: McClurg and Co., 1922)

262. Hazen H. Pleasant, A History of Crawford County, Indiana (Greenfield: Mitchell, 1926)

263. W.H.H Terrell, Indiana in the War of the Rebellion (Indianapolis: Douglas and Bonner, 1869)

264. Amos A. Lawrence, Papers Ms. N-1559, Letterbook 1857-1861, Box 38 Vol 6 (Massachusetts Historical Society)

265. "Have we traitors among us?" Boston Herald, April 12, 1861

266. "Alleged Plot to Burn Northern Cities," New York Herald, May 5, 1861

267. "Yancey Heard From," Chicago Tribune, reprinted by the New York Post, May 24, 1861

268. "A Southern Confidence Man," Hartford Daily News, December 28, 1861

269. La Fayette Curry Baker, History of the United States Secret Service (Philadelphia: L.C. Baker, 1867)

270. Amos A. Lawrence, Papers Ms. N-1559, Letterbook 1857-1861, Box 38 Vol 6 (Massachusetts Historical Society)

271. Barry A. Couch, "The Merchant and the Senator: An Attempt to Save East Tennessee for the Union," East Tennessee Historical Society Publications, 46 (1974): 53-75.

272. "Andrew Johnson," Boston Evening Transcript, June 22, 1861

273. The Papers of Andrew Johnson, Volume 4, 1860-1861, edited by Leroy P. Graf and Ralph W. Haskins (Knoxville: University of Tennessee Press, 1976)

274. "Amos A. Lawrence Papers Ms. N-1559, Letterbook 1857-1861, Box 38 Vol 6," (Massachusetts Historical Society)

275. The Papers of Andrew Johnson, Volume 4, 1860-1861, edited by Leroy P. Graf and Ralph W. Haskins (Knoxville: University of Tennessee Press, 1976)

276. "Amos A. Lawrence Papers Ms. N-1559, William Appleton Letter, Box 12," (Massachusetts Historical Society)

277. "Amos A. Lawrence Papers Ms. N-1559, Hawley files, Dec 11, 1861, Box 13," (Massachusetts Historical Society)

278. "Amos A. Lawrence Papers Ms. N-1559, William Appleton Letter, Box 12," (Massachusetts Historical Society)

279. "Amos A. Lawrence Papers Ms. N-1559, Letterbook 1857-1861, Box 38 Vol 6," (Massachusetts Historical Society)

280. "Parker H. French," San Francisco Bulletin, December 6, 1861
281. Baker, L.C., History of the United States Secret Service (Philadelphia: L.C. Baker, 1867)
282. Interview with Jane Bouley, town historian for Branford Connecticut, August 4, 2017
283. Baker, L.C., History of the United States Secret Service (Philadelphia: L.C. Baker, 1867
284. John Niven, Connecticut for the Union (New Haven and London: Yale University Press, 1965)
285. "Important Arrest in Connecticut," Massachusetts Spy November 13, 1861
286. Joanna D. Cowden, "The Politics of Dissent: Civil War Democrats in Connecticut," The New England Quarterly Vol. 56, No. 4 (Dec., 1983), pp. 538-554
287. Matthew Warshauer, Connecticut in the American Civil War (Middletown: Wesleyan University Press, 2011)
288. John Niven, Connecticut for the Union (New Haven and London: Yale University Press, 1965)
289. "The Latest Northern News," Richmond Examiner, August 17, 1861
290. "Destruction of the Bridgeport Farmer Office," New Haven Palladium, August 26, 1861
291. John Niven, Connecticut for the Union (New Haven and London: Yale University Press, 1965)
292. "War of the Rebellion: A Compilation of the Official Records of the Union and Confederate Armies," Sec 4, 1:216
293. Nathaniel Cheairs Hughes, Yale's Confederates: A Biographical Dictionary (Knoxville: University of Tennessee Press, 2008)
294. Interview with Jane Bouley, town historian for Branford, Connecticut, August 4, 2017
295. Dudley S. Johnson, "The Southern Express Company: A Georgia Corporation," The Georgia Historical Quarterly, Vol. 56, No. 2 (Summer, 1972), pp. 224-242
296. Baker, L.C., History of the United States Secret Service (Philadelphia: L.C. Baker, 1867)
297. "Important Arrest in Connecticut," Massachusetts Spy, November 13, 1861
298. Interview with Jane Bouley, Historian of Branford, Connecticut
299. Baker, L.C., History of the United States Secret Service (Philadelphia: L.C. Baker, 1867)
300. "Important Arrest," New York Herald, November 6, 1861
301. L.C. Baker, History of the United States Secret Service (Philadelphia: L.C. Baker, 1867)
302. "The Prisoners at Fort Warren," Cincinnati Daily Press, December 7, 1861, reprinted from Boston Traveler
303. "Parker H. French and His Treasonable Tricks," San Francisco Chronicle, December 6, 1861
304. M. Baldridge, edited by John B. Goodman III, A Reminiscence of the Parker H. French Expedition through Texas & Mexico to California in the Spring of 1850 (Los Angeles: Privately Printed, 1959), page 21
305. "Arrest of Parker H. French," Boston Post, December 4, 1861
306. Frank Key Howard, Fourteen Months in American Bastilles (Baltimore: Kelly, Hedian & Piet, 1863)
307. "Prisoners at Fort Warren," The Huntington Democrat, December 5, 1861. Condensed from Boston Daily Traveler.
308. Lawrence Sangston, Bastilles of the North (Baltimore: Kelly, Hedian & Piet, 1863)
309. "SUSPECTED AND DISLOYAL PERSONS," War of the Rebellion, Serial 115, page 127
310. "Amos A. Lawrence Papers," Ms. N-1559, Hawley files, Dec 11, 1861, Box 13 (Massachusetts Historical Society)
311. L.C. Baker, History of the United States Secret Service (Philadelphia: L.C. Baker, 1867)
312. "SUSPECTED AND DISLOYAL PERSONS," War of the Rebellion, Serial 115, page 127
313. Harton Singer Semple, Jr., The Irish Boys (Self-published, 2013)
314. https://www.nps.gov/fosc/learn/education/sutler5.htm, accessed January 6, 2018. Quote is not specifically about Parker French, but it is instructive of the general attitude about sutlers and purveyors.
315. "Arrested for Peddling," Evening Star, March 12, 1862
316. John Paul Jones vs. Parker H. French, Supreme Court, District of Columbia, Lawsuit

in Equity #83, deposition of Benjamin Eggleston

317. William Alan Blair, ed., A Politician Goes to War: The Civil War Letters of John White Geary (University Park: Pennsylvania State University Press, 1995)
318. Harton Singer Semple, Jr., The Irish Boys (Self-published, 2013)
319. "The Army Lawyer: Pamphlet 27-50-283," June 1996, Headquarters, Department of the Army
320. "Petition for Bankruptcy of Parker H. French," 30 December 1868, District Court of the United States for the Eastern District of Missouri
321. Francis A. Lord, Civil War Sutlers and Their Wares (Cranberry,: Thomas Yoseloff, 1969)
322. John Paul Jones vs. Parker H. French, Supreme Court District of Columbia, Lawsuit in Equity #83; filing by John Paul Jones and Deposition of Thomas McCabe.
323. Supreme Court, District of Columbia, Lawsuit in Equity #83, John Paul Jones vs Parker H. French; filing by John Paul Jones and Deposition of Thomas McCabe. "Sutlers Arrested," New York Times, August 17, 1864
324. "The Siege of Chattanooga," http://www.hctgs.org/Military/siege_of_chattanooga.htm, accessed January 5, 2018
325. National Archives Record Group 393, Part 2 #5487, XX Army Corps, Volume 14i
326. Rodney C. Lackey "Notes on Civil War Logistics: Facts & Stories" http://www. transportation.army.mil/History/PDF/Peninsula%20Campaign/Rodney%20 Lackey%20Article_1.pdf Accessed January 5, 2018
327. "Petition for Bankruptcy of Parker H. French," December 30, 1868 (District Court of the United States for the Eastern District of Missouri)
328. City Directory for Louisville, KY, 1865-1866
329. "Parker H. French," Louisville Daily Courier, August 7, 1868
330. "Petition for Bankruptcy of Parker H. French," December 30, 1868, District Court of the United States for the Eastern District of Missouri
331. "Oil and Gas History of Kentucky: 1860 to 1900"; https://www.uky.edu/KGS/ emsweb/history/1860to1900.htm accessed January 8, 2018
332. "Sketches of Adair County," Adair County News, Mar 20, 1918
333. * Elizabeth Chester Fisk, edited by Rex C. Myers, Lizzie: The Letters of Elizabeth Chester Fisk, 1864-1893 (Missoula, Mountain Press Publishing Company, 1989)
334. "Parker H. French," Daily Missouri Democrat, September 4, 1867
335. John S. Doyle and David H. Hill vs Parker H. French and others, St. Louis Circuit Court October term, 1867 #6624
336. "Little Rock Sank and Burned," Cincinnati Daily Gazette, December 26, 1867
337. Petition for Bankruptcy of Parker H. French," December 30, 1868. District Court of the United States for the Eastern District of Missouri.
338. "Parker H. French," Louisville Daily Courier, August 7, 1868
339. Edward McGowan, The Strange Eventful History of Parker H. French, reproduced and edited by Kenneth M. Johnson (Los Angeles: Dawson, 1958)
340. St. Louis City Death Records, 1850-1902; "Parker H. French," San Luis Obispo Daily Telegram, Dec 3, 1869; Probate Files of Lucretia Clay Edwards French, held by the Clerk of the Circuit Court, Madison County, Illinois
341. Records of the United States and Mexican Claims Commissions, 1815-1947, Claim #587, National Archives Records Group 76.7
342. Return of Marriage, Records of Vital Statistics, Health Department of the City of New York; Certificate of Marriage, State of New York #3858.
343. http://daytoninmanhattan.blogspot.com/2013/05/the-lost-hoffman-house-hotel-broadway.html (accessed February 18, 2017)
344. Death Certificate of Parker Hardin French, recorded in the Health Department of the City of New York
345. "Died," New York Herald, June 20, 1878
346. History of Madison County Illinois, W.R. Brink & Co., 1882
347. "Funeral of Col. French," Alton Telegraph, June 27, 1878